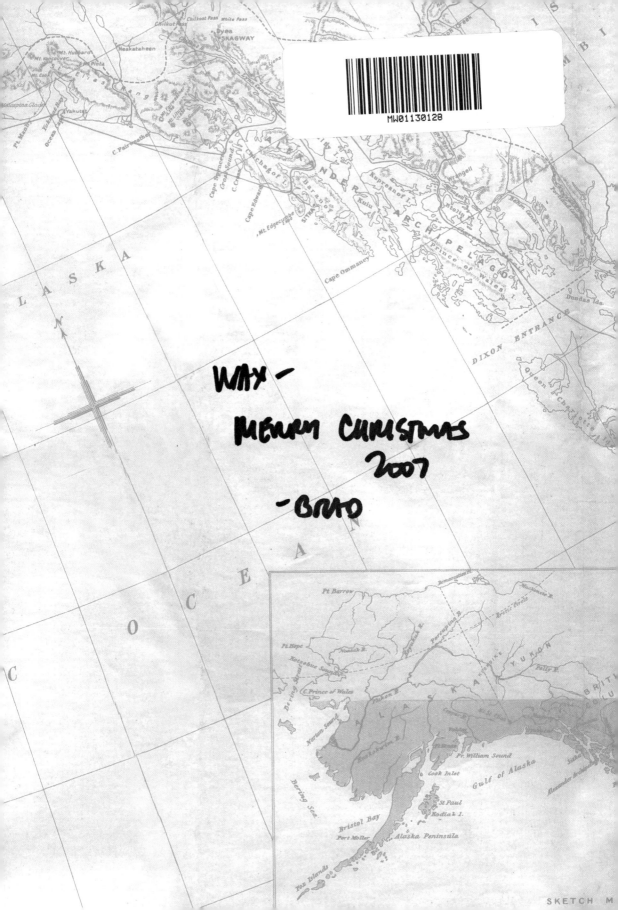

WAX -

MERRY CHRISTMAS
2007

- BRAD

BIG GAME SHOOTING IN ALASKA

THE AUTHOR'S RECORD BEAR (*URSUS DALLI GYAS*).

For Measurements, etc., see p. 114.

BIG GAME SHOOTING
IN ALASKA

BY

CAPTAIN C. R. E. RADCLYFFE

(RESERVE OF OFFICERS, LATE 1ST LIFE GUARDS)

AUTHOR OF 'NORWEGIAN ANGLING,' 'SMALL GAME SHOOTING IN HUNGARY,'
'MODERN FALCONRY,' ETC., ETC.

Safari Press

Radclyffe, C.R.E.

Safari Press Inc.

2008, Long Beach, California

ISBN 1-57157-298-8

Library of Congress Catalog Card Number: 06001833

10 9 8 7 6 5 4 3 2 1

Readers wishing to receive the Safari Press catalog, featuring many fine books on big-game hunting, wingshooting, and sporting firearms, should write to Safari Press Inc., P.O. Box 3095, Long Beach, CA 90803, USA. Tel: (714) 894-9080 or visit our Web site at www.safaripress.com

DEDICATION

AS A TOKEN OF APPRECIATION OF HIS QUALITIES AS A SPORTSMAN

IN RECOGNITION OF THE KEEN INTEREST WHICH HE HAS TAKEN

IN THE SHOOTING OF BIG GAME, AND IN ADMIRATION OF

HIS ABILITIES WITH THE RIFLE AND THE PEN

THIS BOOK IS DEDICATED TO

THEODORE ROOSEVELT
PRESIDENT OF THE U.S. OF AMERICA

WITH THE RESPECTFUL COMPLIMENTS OF THE AUTHOR

PREFACE

In submitting this small work to the criticisms of brother sportsmen, or others of the reading public into whose hands it may fall, it is the earnest desire of the author that the following facts may be borne in mind during its perusal: Firstly, that it is not the outcome of a wild desire on the part of the writer to rush into print and air his own views on certain matters, or to lay down, after spending only one season in Alaska, any hard and fast rules as to the habits of certain kinds of game, and the best mode of killing them. Such a mistake is only too common on the part of many young sportsmen, and even of others of more mature years in search of small notoriety. Men of far greater experience on the same subjects hesitate to express any opinion, or to place on record in print any of their own ideas, for fear of appearing ridiculous in the eyes of a very few who may know more about these matters than the writers themselves.

Secondly, I am fully aware of my inability to do adequate descriptive justice to the scenery and to many incidents here narrated, since a remark of Tennyson, when speaking of Browning's works, is appropriate to my case, in that I "lack the glory of words." All that can be claimed as a merit in the book is that most of it was written almost at the actual time of occurrence of each event described, and that it purports to be a true record of facts by an eye-witness as he saw them. I may take this opportunity of apologising to my readers if the style of writing seems to be somewhat egotistical, but it is hard to avoid the use of the first person singular when writing of one's own personal exploits. Moreover, it is almost impossible to describe clearly and accurately the experiences of one's friends and companions when one was not actually a spectator of the events. It would have given me no small pleasure could I have induced my friend and companion, Mr. R. F. Glyn, to contribute something to this work, giving some of his own experiences during our trip; but I have been utterly unable to overcome his modest fears that his capabilities as a writer are not equal to the task.

There must always be a certain amount of dull reading in accounts of shooting-trips when recorded, as they usually are, somewhat in the form of extracts from a diary. To the writer himself these may be sufficiently interesting in after days, but they are seldom equally so to those who did not actually participate in the incidents described.

Alaska is to-day one of the few remaining countries where there are yet many thousands of miles untrodden by the foot of man, and, in consequence, it still has that great charm of the unknown which ever entices the roving British sportsman.

It was only the urgent requests of a number of my

own friends that I should bring out this work which finally induced me so to do. Had any more competent writer, or sportsman of wider experience, previously undertaken a similar task, it is probable that this book would never have seen daylight. At the time of commencing the volume, it had no rival in the field to overshadow it, and therefore I felt that, poor as it might be, it would not suffer by comparison, as I believed it likely to be the one first published in England which dealt with sport in Alaska. Since the date of commencement my friend Colonel Claude Cane has, however, brought out an excellent book entitled *Summer and Fall in Western Alaska.* But having gone so far, I decided to risk the publication of this book in the hope that there is still room for another descriptive work on a country so vast as Alaska.

Suffice it, then, that I hope the information given may be found useful to others contemplating a visit to that fine country, and if such prove to be the case, one good object at least will have been accomplished.

C. R. E. RADCLYFFE.

HYDE, WAREHAM, 1904.

CONTENTS

CHAPTER I

CHAPTER II

CHAPTER III

CHAPTER IV

CHAPTER V

CHAPTER VI

CHAPTER VII

xiii

LIST OF ILLUSTRATIONS

With few exceptions taken by Author

CHAPTER I

ALASKA : ITS HISTORY, INDUSTRIES, POPULATION, ETC.

THE ideas about Alaska prevailing in the mind of the average Englishman of to-day are very vague ; and although the country has been partly explored for many years by small wandering parties of prospectors, it is surprising how little even Americans in the Eastern States know about the valuable territory owned by them in the far North-West. The majority of persons are uncertain as to the exact position of Alaska on the map, while others look upon it as merely a wild uninhabitable little tract far up in the north-west corner of the American continent, and chiefly celebrated for the great gold-reefs first exploited along the valley of the Yukon in 1895. As a matter of fact this so-called small territory comprises an area of little less than 600,000 square miles ; and when it is remembered that hitherto only very small portions of it have been visited by naturalists, we are able to form some idea of the field that lies open for scientific research, when men of the right class are found with sufficient energy to explore the country properly. It is a country teeming with mineral wealth, mammal and bird life, grand forests and other vegetable products, and numerous remains of extinct creatures, dear to the heart of the palæontologist.

The list of explorers who have visited the country from time to time includes Russians, Englishmen, Americans, and Spaniards, but it is far too long to be quoted in any detail. A Russian traveller, Peter Popoff, appears to have been the first to bring reports to his native land concerning the wondrous new country across the ocean, his voyage having been made about the year 1711. In 1728, and again in 1741, Russian expeditions were sent out under Bering. They collected some valuable and authentic information about Alaska, but Bering himself did not survive his second voyage. He died after the shipwreck of his party on one of the Aleutian Islands.

In 1776 the celebrated James Cook sailed from England, and after coasting along the shores of British Columbia, reached Icy Cape on the coast of Alaska. He, like Bering, did not live to bring back in person the reports and charts of his voyage, which finally reached England, but died by a tragic fate on one of the islands of the Hawaian group. Another important British expedition, which left England in 1827, was led by Beechey, who succeeded in reaching Point Barrow, the most northern cape of Alaska ; and during the same year Franklin made a voyage to the Arctic regions along the extreme northern coast of Alaska.

From its first discovery until the end of the eighteenth century the coast of Alaska was overrun by parties of Russians, who looted or traded furs from the natives. At the end of this period, that is to say about 1800, the Russian-American Company was started by an imperial order, and under its auspices the general state of affairs in the country somewhat improved. It does not appear, however, that, previous to the sale of Alaska to the Americans in 1867, the natives can have enjoyed a particularly good time. Unarmed as they were, they were no match for the Russians, who annexed their furs and women at their pleasure, although on one occasion the natives did inflict a terrible defeat, with much slaughter, on the Russians near Sitka.

The four principal industries of Alaska are mining, salmon-canning, fur-trading, and sea-fishing ; and the different classes of people encountered on a trip through the country are chiefly occupied in these pursuits. Unless a visit be paid to some of the great mining centres, such as the Yukon or Nome, it is true that no great number of successful miners will be met with; but there are undoubtedly many other spots, as rich as those already worked, remaining to be discovered and opened up in the near future. There is, however, a class of men encountered all along the Alaskan coast which is distinct in its peculiar way from all others. I refer to the so-called prospectors, who are to be found at all local stopping-places of the coasting steamers, in the vicinity of most up-country stores, and occasionally in isolated little camps of their own. They form a free-and-easy, "happy-go-lucky," and proverbially hospitable class of men. Many of them come from far-distant countries, and doubtless have a history on the other side of the water; but little is thought of that in a land where no questions are asked, and where all men are equal and are hailed as strangers well met. Hope springs eternal in the prospector's breast, and it is wonderful to see how each of them in turn is elated by the discovery of traces of good quartz, or signs of oil, and at once stakes thousands of acres in claims, and adjourns to the nearest store to affirm positively to all comers that he has got the whole world at last. Nevertheless, the fact remains that, on arrival at any of the coast settlements, a visit to the store will present the spectacle of a number of men lounging idly about, sitting on the counters, usually whittling bits of wood with their knives to kill time, and probably discussing the rights or wrongs of the American people with the assistance of a few newspapers some four or five weeks old. Most of them are chewing gum, or some villainous form of plug-tobacco, and from time to time make marvellously accurate long-range shots at the spittoon, too often situated in dangerous proximity to the feet of some other member of the party. The newcomer's first impression will very likely be that he has encountered some of the local unemployed; but no greater error could be made, as these men are really the type of the Alaskan prospector, and a few chance questions on the possibilities of the district in the mining line will probably at once bring to light various specimens of quartz, etc., hidden away in the depths of each man's trouser-pockets. This exhibition is accompanied by a little advice given gratis as to the most infallible method of getting rich quickly. Some of these men may have already made comfortable little fortunes, and lost them again, in some of the great gold rushes ranging between California and Nome; but, no matter what their age or present position, there always looms in front of them the fascinating picture of a big strike to be made some day. Alas, for the majority of them this is always to-morrow, and never to-day!

Passing on to the salmon fisheries, whole pages might be directed to the description of this wonderful industry. It is no exaggeration to say that the number of fish in certain rivers defies description; and the wildest stories ever told on the subject scarcely exceed the actual facts. Indeed, this is almost the only point on which I have never heard an Alaskan exaggerate, and the Alaskans are people who take a good deal of beating at drawing the long-bow. It must,

SENDING OFF A SEASON'S CATCH OF SALMON.

Steam tug loading with cases, Kussiloff Cannery.

however, suffice to say that as many as 100,000 salmon
have been taken in a single haul of the seine nets at
Karluk, which is the greatest place for this kind of fishing
in Alaska. A powerful "combine," known as the Alaska
Packers' Association, controls some of the best rivers in the
country, and the way in which the fishing, canning, and
packing are carried out in its canneries is well worth
seeing. Every appliance known to man in the way of
machinery for this purpose is used : and the fish are hardly
touched by hand from the moment of leaving the water
until they are sent down-country packed in tin cans. So
rapid indeed is the process that only a few minutes elapse
from the time the fish arrive on a steam-tug alongside the
cannery wharf, until they issue in tins from the other end of
long lines of machinery, which are often working night and
day during the big run of fish. All forms of nets are used
for catching the salmon ;—from traps to seine and gill nets.
Boats and men are kept working at high pressure while the
fish are running thick. Nevertheless, there are countless
millions of fish which escape and run up the rivers to spawn
and die, since they never return to the sea again after spawning. If evidence of this be required, a walk along the shores
of a lake, or the river-banks in autumn, will soon convince the
unbeliever, who will not be long in forming an opinion,
since the sight of dead salmon, and the awful smell arising
therefrom will soon drive him as far as possible from the
spot. The canneries only work for a short time during June,
July, and the early part of August. Each spring expeditions
leave San Francisco early in April; big sailing vessels
conveying a staff of men, and materials for making the tin
cans and packing cases. The men employed are chiefly
Chinese and Italians, over whom are placed able super-

intendents.   In one cannery at Kussiloff, Cook's Inlet, where
we remained some time in August, and which is not by any
means considered a large one, the catch and pack of salmon
during nine weeks in 1903 was over 45,000 cases.   Each
case contains 48 cans of 1 lb. each, and as it takes an average
of 13 or 14 of the Alaska red salmon to fill each case, this
will give an idea of the number of fish captured.   Upwards
of 630,000 salmon must have been killed to make up this
pack.   When packed, the best parts of the fish weighed

<small>FLEET OF NATIVE BIDARKIES STARTING TO HUNT SEA-OTTER,
SALDOVIA, JULY 1903.</small>

964 tons, and as much again in weight may be reckoned for
the rejected offal.

The fur-trade is chiefly carried on by the natives,
and although the valuable fur-bearing animals are rapidly
becoming scarce, it still constitutes a big industry.   The
days of the sea-otter are numbered; and this valuable
fur will soon be a thing of the past in Alaska.   Poison and
traps have indeed wrought havoc with many of the species
of animals along the coast.   On certain of the islands fox-
ranches have been established; the owners of which are
chiefly white men, who turn down a number of foxes and

let them breed. During the winter months these are fed
by their keepers with cooked meal, dried fish, and seal-
meat. When a good stock has been raised, a certain
number are annually killed for their skins; this being
done between the end of November and the beginning of
January, when the fur is at its best. Fur-seals are now confined to the Pribiloff Islands, in Bering Sea, which are hired
from the Government at an enormous rent by the North
American Commercial Company for the purpose of catching
seals.

The description of the natives inhabiting the coast of
Alaska is too large an undertaking to be dealt with, even
briefly, in a work of this kind. The number of small tribes
(if they may be so called), differing slightly from one another,
is bewildering. We find distinct racial types, ranging from
the Indians around Sitka and in the south, to Aleuts along
the Alaska Peninsula, and westward again, to tribes of
Esquimaux along the Bering Sea shores. There are indeed
so many forms and varieties of language that often the
natives of one place cannot understand the language of those
in another settlement at no great distance from their own.
In such cases they generally have recourse to the Russian
tongue, which is more or less universally spoken by all.
Taken as a whole, the natives on the coast may be classed
as fishermen rather than hunters. Fish of all kinds are in
profusion, and form their staple form of food. Hence it is
really a hard matter to obtain good native hunters, as
compared with those of other wild regions.

The influence of the Russian Church still predominates
amongst the natives throughout the country; and most of
the big settlements can boast a local priest, who in many
cases is the controlling factor amongst the inhabitants.

As Russian is still taught in the schools and at such places as Kenai, where the natives are also taught English during two or three months, their ideas must be somewhat mixed.   An old resident of the latter place, who is an American, told me that the priests still teach the natives that they owe allegiance to the Tsar of Russia; and he also stated that not long ago an intelligent half-breed came to consult him concerning the possibilities of a war between Russia and the United States, and asked under which flag he as a loyal subject ought to fight.

A curious instance of the superstitious dread in which the priests are held, and also of the ease with which a man can live in this country, came to my notice near Unga Island.   A native of that island who had committed some petty misdeed fell under the displeasure of the local priest, and, fearing some dreadful calamity, disappeared from the village.   Nothing was heard of the man for months, until he was finally discovered living on the shore of an island many miles from any human being.   Here he had built himself a small barabara, or native dug-out hut, with the sides and roof made of driftwood logs, and a bed of dry grass inside. His sole clothing was an old shirt, and his only implement part of an old hunting-knife.   Thus he had lived for eighteen months, his food being berries, fish, etc., which he collected along the shore; and when taken home to his people he looked fat and well.   Small wonder, then, that these men are lazy by nature and independent to such a degree that they will only accompany visitors on hunting-trips as a matter of favour, and then only—at least in the neighbour-hood of Unga Island—at the exorbitant pay of two and a half dollars per day, which wages they can easily earn, if so inclined, by working in the mine on the island.   With the exception of the natives on Kodiak and Afognak Islands, the dwellers along the shores of Cook's Inlet were by natural instinct the best hunters encountered during my expedition. Here, however, the same spirit of independence as else-where is evinced, and their feeling of equality with white men is freely displayed in their manner and conversation. They expect to live on the same luxuries, and to furnish their houses in a manner similar to those of their employers. The introduction of new diseases, and the sale of bad spirits, etc., have largely diminished the native population of Alaska in recent years. A few seasons ago an epidemic of measles killed them off like flies, and during 1903 almost every native along the Alaska Peninsula and Cook's Inlet was attacked by mumps.

Sea-fishing is still an extensive business along the Alaskan coast, and employs men of all nationalities from Europe and America. They are a hardy class of men, particularly along the Bering Sea shores, where they are exposed for weeks at a time to all kinds of bad weather while cod-fishing in their small open sailing dories. Although generally within reach of some vessel carrying supplies of food, etc., only men of the toughest possible type can stand, for any length of time, the daily exposure to wet and cold which their profession necessitates. It is by no means uncommon for a small fleet of dories to sail 100 or 200 miles to the nearest local store. Here their jovial crews, bearing unmistakable signs of their calling in their weather-beaten faces, at once raid the store, soon to emerge from it laden with all kinds of small luxuries, and often with the necks of suspicious-looking bottles, suggestive of spirits, protruding from their pockets. The exact place whence the latter have been obtained is generally discreetly left as a matter of conjecture, since the vendor is probably infringing the laws of his country in selling them.

Judging from conversations on the subject with my own friends in England, the prevailing idea at home seems to be that the hardships which one should be prepared to endure, as regards climatic conditions in Alaska, are closely allied to those experienced by members of a party in search of the North Pole. If it is possible to form a sound opinion after spending only some seven months in the country, and without any knowledge of the Polar regions, I do not hesitate to pronounce the idea a gross fallacy. The season of 1903 was noteworthy owing to the extreme lateness and severity of the spring, which was stated by many of the old pioneers to be a record in this respect, so far as their memory served them. Even then, although the conditions were not those of actual comfort, life in a small cotton tent was not unbearable even as early as the end of April. Many days in May left much to be desired from the point of view of a man living in camp on the Alaska Peninsula, but others were just about as good as could be wished. During June, and from then onwards to the end of September, the weather was a great revelation to our party, bad weather being an unknown quantity. The summer closely resembled a very fine summer season in Norway, with the exception that I have not seen in that country such long spells of days without rain or wind as those in the Kenai Peninsula. On many days during August and September, when climbing mountains after sheep, or toiling over fallen timber in the moose-country round Cook's Inlet, the heat of the sun and the absence of wind were so marked that our only desire was for less of the former and more of the latter. Briefly then, if England could be favoured every year with such a summer as we experienced in Alaska, there would be less groaning amongst our friends and neighbours over their spoilt garden-parties or ruined crops of hay and harvest. It is not, however, to be inferred from this that I should advocate living in tents all the year round in Alaska,—a performance which has undoubtedly often been accomplished, but which I for one would rather leave to others during the four or five months of winter.

CHAPTER II

THE first question a sportsman is likely to ask on deciding to visit Alaska is, " Where shall I go? " and the second, " Where can I get guides or natives? " The answer to the first question must be a long and complicated one, and depends on several circumstances, the two chief considerations being, first, what kind of game is required, and secondly, how long a period, and what part of the year, can be given up to the trip.

If bears be the game desired, then it is a *sine qua non* that the early spring must see the hunter on his ground, and he should leave Seattle not later than by the first boat in April, or by the last boat in March. The first good place at which to stop for bears, if the sportsman does not wish to make a long journey, would be Kayak. Striking inland from that place, the brown bear known as *Ursus dalli* is reported to be numerous in the neighbourhood of Mount St. Elias. The so-called Glacier Bear (*Ursus emmonsi*) is also found in the same district; but up to the present time no sportsman has properly worked this country. It might be very well worth exploring. Judging by the number of skins sent out from Kayak by the natives, there would seem to be no lack of bears in the district in question. Passing

13

farther north, we reach Montague Island, where bears are reported to be so abundant that prospectors are afraid to land. I should not, however, advise any sportsman to try this spot, as the only men I could find who had actually remained any time on the island declared that bears were few and far between. A trip overland from Valdez into the Copper River country might produce good sport. From this district is reported a bear known locally as the "bald-faced bear," which is said to be particularly savage, and to lie up near the trails for men. Several authentic instances are on record of men being attacked and killed in this district without any previous molestation on their part of the bear. My own experience, however, goes to prove that the average Alaskan brown bear does not play this game half well enough, and that this is what makes the big ones so hard to procure. Towards the head-waters of the Copper River wild sheep are plentiful, but to what species or variety they belong I am unable to state definitely, never having seen one in the flesh. Here also tales of the fabled Alaskan ibex are rife; and prospectors from that district have spent hours describing these animals to me in the hope that I should credit their existence.

Going still farther to the north-west, the Cook's Inlet district is reached. Here one may land at Saldovia, and put in the season in search of brown and black bears, as well as sheep and moose. For bears, the bays and rivers on the west side of the Inlet are best, the most likely spots being Chinitna Bay, Snug Harbour, Krison River, and Polly Creek. The last three places have been well described by Colonel Cane in his book on Alaska; and the first bay has been visited by two or three sportsmen at different seasons, who have generally done well with brown and black bears. This district, indeed, is peculiarly well adapted for bear-hunting, since there is a large tract of mud-flats near the shore intersected by numerous creeks. Bears may be found in April and May eating the grass on the hill-sides, and in June fishing for salmon in the creeks on the flats. In a few weeks' hunting in Chinitna Bay in 1901, Messrs. Kidder and Blake killed nine brown and four black bears. During summer there is little difficulty in crossing Cook's Inlet, and then leisurely making one's way into the sheep and moose country on the Kenai Peninsula. In fact, this is the easiest trip in Alaska, and can be done in comparative comfort. Two American ladies have already accompanied their husbands on shooting trips in Cook's Inlet, and neither experienced any great hardship.

Probably one of the finest trips in this part of the territory would be up the Sushitna River, at the head of Cook's Inlet. The mouth of the river can be reached by a steamer which runs up and down the Inlet, while natives and canoes can be obtained at the Sushitna settlement. According to trustworthy information I have been at some pains to collect, it seems probable that an expedition up the left, or western, branch of the Sushitna, called the Skwentna River, would result in a good bag of bears, wild sheep, moose, and caribou, all of which are to be found abundantly. Moose in that part are not so numerous, nor are they likely to carry quite such fine heads as those on the Kenai Peninsula, but the caribou heads from this country, of which I have seen many, are remarkably good. Moreover, the sheep on the mountains in this district have far better horns than those on the Kenai Peninsula. So far none but natives have hunted in these mountains, but the horns brought out by them prove either that the sheep are a different variety, or that their horns are far superior to those of the ordinary *Ovis dalli* of the Kenai mountains.   On this trip it would be necessary to tow boats up the west branch of the Sushitna River, a distance of some 60 or 80 miles, and so to reach the ground lying on the divide between the head-waters of that river and the Kuskoquim.   From information supplied by an American gentleman who visited this country a few seasons ago, at the head of an expedition sent out by the Geographical Survey Department of Washington, I have every reason to believe that the neighbourhood is particularly good for big game, especially on the western side of the divide between these two rivers.   This is a trip well suited to a sportsman desirous of getting off the beaten track; and if no one else attempt it in the near future, it is the intention of the present writer some day to pay this country a visit.

If, however, distance be no objection, and the largest bears are wanted, the sportsman should harden his heart and set out at once for Kodiak, or Unga Island.   The bears on the islands of Kodiak, Afognak, and Uganuk belong to the form known to American naturalists as *Ursus middendorffi*, and appear to be the largest brown bears in the world. They are, however, no longer very numerous on these islands, and a whole spring spent there might only result in the capture of one or two.   In spite of what has been said by others, I am inclined to think that there is really only a slight difference between the size of these bears and that attained by *U. dalli gyas* found along the Alaska Peninsula.

The best mode of procedure is to hire a small vessel from Kodiak or Unga and coast along to the most noted bays on the Pacific side of the Peninsula; the bears, according to men who profess to know the country well, being more numerous as you travel farther west.   Between Kodiak and Unga lie three bays, called respectively Aniakchak Bay, Three Star. Point, and Stephanoff Bay (otherwise Stepovak Bay).   At either of these, but particularly at the two latter, during May and June, a sportsman should have no trouble in picking up the maximum of four bears now allowed by law.   There are also several good bays on the Peninsula to the west of Unga, and on Unimak Island, where the bears are still numerous.

There are likewise many good places on the Bering Sea side of the Peninsula, but unless the sportsman has the time to send a small vessel of some kind round to this coast he is likely to have a "tough job" if he attempts this trip. I made the trip myself provided only with a canoe and a small boat, but the Bering Sea, at its best, is no place for very small craft.   If, however, a long journey, such as this, be undertaken, it would be well worth pushing on as far as some of the rivers which flow into Bristol Bay.   Here the big game shooting would once more be far off the beaten track, and caribou could easily be obtained, as this region lies outside the area in which they may not be killed on the Alaska Peninsula.   I am not certain whether moose are to be found in any country accessible from Bristol Bay, nor am I clear on the point of how far the timber line extends in that direction; but, judging from the map, it ought to be possible to find moose near the head-waters of the Nushagak River.   This is, however, entirely conjectural on my part, since I have no personal knowledge of the country, neither have I ever met a man who has visited the district.

In conclusion, I may append a list of the known guides and hunters, and also give the names of certain influential

c

persons to whom sportsmen should apply in the various districts.

SALDOVIA

J. W. Herbert.—A local storekeeper and hunter, who will supply and outfit sportsmen with stores, natives, etc.

J. Kilpatrick.—Generally works in conjunction with Herbert, and is an experienced hunter. Has been out with Mr. Dal de Weese, Mr. A. J. Stone, and others.

H. Olsen.—In 1903 accompanied Mr. P. Niedieck, who spoke well of him.

E. Edelman.—The owner of a small sloop generally available to take sportsmen along the shores of Cook's Inlet. He accompanied Col. Cane in 1902.

J. Cleghorn.—Storekeeper and postmaster. He has considerable knowledge of the Sushitna River country, having lived there some years, and would be prepared to outfit and accompany an expedition going up the Sushitna, if notified some time in advance.

KUSSILOFF

Andrew Berg and Emile Berg.—These two brothers are noted hunters, the former being undoubtedly the best moose-hunter on the Kenai Peninsula. He has accompanied Mr. Dal de Weese, Mr. A. S. Reed, and others.

KENAI

W. Hunter.—A very good man, with many years' experience, and always highly spoken of by sportsmen who have employed him.

Lennox.—Accompanied W. Hunter with Lord Elphinstone, and Mr. Vander Byl in 1903.

Philip Wilson.—A half-breed, thoroughly trustworthy, who accompanied Mr. David Hanbury in 1903.

Vein.—A Frenchman, who has done a certain amount of hunting, and was out with an English sportsman in 1902.

Mr. G. Mearns.—Manager of a large store at Kenai, postmaster and notary public. He will outfit and help sportsmen in every way, especially as regards procuring boats and natives when going up from Kenai or Kussiloff.

Mr. H. Wetherbee.—Manager of the Alaska Packers' Cannery at Kussiloff. He and Mearns work in conjunction, and application to either is equally good.

Kodiak

Mr. Goss.—Manager of the Alaska Commercial Company, Kodiak. The man to apply to for help in obtaining natives, or small vessels for hunting in that district.

Nicolai Picoon.—A good native Aleut hunter, who was with our party in 1903.

Unga Island

Peter Larsen.—Owner of a small sloop and a hunter. With Mr. A. S. Reed and also Mr. A. J. Stone in 1903.

Sand Point

Messrs. Groswald and Scott.—Storekeepers. Will outfit and help sportsmen going to the Alaska Peninsula.

As regards the wages paid to the head guides, these range from 5 to 10 dollars per diem, but when the last-named sum is given, the guide generally supplies a boat and a native as well. Such a man will be found more than useful on a first expedition in the country, since he knows exactly what to take and what to leave behind. He can also be trusted to collect a staff of natives who can be relied on, whereas a stranger may be imposed upon by some of the worthless lazy natives so numerous in the neighbourhood of Cook's Inlet.

The pay of natives in the district just mentioned ranges from 1 dollar 25 cents to $1\frac{1}{2}$ dollars per diem; but in the neighbourhood of Unga the natives will ask as much as $2\frac{1}{2}$ dollars per day, as they can earn this by working in the mines. Such pay seems excessive to the average Englishman, when he considers the wages of his own countrymen at home, but in Alaska, as the miners say, " It is not what you want but what you get," and if a man does not care to do all his own packing, he has to pay practically what the natives like to ask.

SUPPLIES AND OUTFIT

To any one who has read Colonel Cane's well-known book on the country, such remarks as I can make on camp equipment will appear superfluous, since the author has dealt exhaustively with the whole subject, and named practically every article required for a trip in Alaska. In the matter of tents our party followed the example of that author; and we had all that was required made in Chinatown, Victoria, B.C. For a sportsman's own use, I should suggest a tent, without walls, made in a V-shape, of cotton drill, 8 feet by 6 feet in width, and 6 feet high at the ridge-pole. Colonel Cane, however, used tents exactly one foot smaller in each dimension than the above, but the extra foot in size adds very little to the weight, and very considerably to personal comfort. Such tents weigh only about 7 lbs. each, and will accommodate two or even three natives; two or three of them may be taken. In addition to their lightness, they have the advantage of being very easy to pitch. Even on the desolate Barren Lands of the Alaska Peninsula will be found here and there a patch of alders high enough to furnish a ridge-pole 8 feet long, and four sticks, which when lashed together at the tops will afford the necessary support. Another advantage of these tents is that they do not catch the wind to anything like the same extent as the square ones with walls. Although they are so light and thin, yet, owing to their shape and the steepness of the roof, they will shoot off any quantity of rain.

A larger tent of different shape may be taken into the timber country, and can be used with advantage as a cache-tent for stores and skins, or employed as a dwelling, when remaining any length of time in a permanent camp. For

NATIVE PACKING A BEAR SKIN INTO CAMP.

A view showing the mode of pitching small cotton tents used on the Barren Lands.

our large party we took one such tent made of 8 oz. duck, 12 feet by 8 feet, with walls $2\frac{1}{2}$ feet high, and 6 feet at the ridge-pole. Such a tent weighs about 20 lbs., and is consequently too heavy to pack when constantly moving camp on land, but will be found very useful and luxurious in the moose-country, or where the long poles necessary for successfully pitching this form of tent can be cut. The dimensions here given for this class of tent may quite well be reduced by one or two feet in length, for the use of a single sportsman. I should, however, never advise taking one, even of this reduced size, on a trip to the Alaska Peninsula, where such tents are a mere nuisance, owing to the lack of poles with which to pitch them. Colonel Cane adopted the plan of having a gauze mosquito-net made to fit inside a tent of this description, and this is certainly a luxury, even if not a necessity, when shooting during the hot season in a country so infested as this is by the mosquitoes. One point is of vital importance, namely, that all tent-ropes should be made of cotton, which does not shrink when wet; a plan whereby one of the greatest curses of life in the ordinary British Army tents would be avoided. Any one who has had to spend hours in camp tightening and slacking-off ordinary hemp-ropes in wet weather will soon appreciate the advantage of cotton ropes. As a general rule, they are used in making tents by the Chinamen, but it is well when ordering camp-kit to emphasise this point. The total cost of these tents is absurdly small in Victoria; some £2 or £3 suffices to purchase the lot, and they can be made by the Chinese in two or three days, if required in a hurry.

With regard to the question of clothing, the matter may be briefly summed up as follows. Two complete suits of ordinary English shooting kit, and one change of underclothes, with a few spare pairs of socks, or stockings, will suffice. The question of boots *versus* shoes, etc., may be answered according to the fancy of their wearers. Personally, I swear by a pattern of field-boot made specially for me by E. Olsen, Bootmaker, Trondhjem, Norway. These boots, which are very light, durable, and waterproof, are exceedingly cheap, costing less than 30s. per pair. Most of the natives and miners in Alaska are provided with long "gum-boots,"—undoubtedly the most uncomfortable and tiring foot-wear on earth. If short ankle-boots are worn, the water is perpetually getting over the tops of them in marshes and small streams. Nine times out of ten long field-boots will get their owner across such spots with dry feet. On the tenth occasion my advice is, make the native carry you over the water. If he is wearing "gum-boots" he will not get wet, and if he has not such boots he will get wet in any case, and may just as well carry you over as let you get wet too. There is no doubt that field-boots are apt to be rather noisy when the wearer is crawling through thick brush in the moose-country. Putties or stockings do not make so much noise when striking the twigs; but perhaps the best form of leg-covering for this job is a pair of soft cloth gaiters, as they do not tear or get caught in the bushes. An exception is always to be made in favour of the native moccasins, which are far the best things for creeping about in, but are not popular with most Englishmen. A really good waterproof coat, such as is supplied by Burberry of the Haymarket, is a necessity, as also is a broad-brimmed soft hat, over which a mosquito veil can be hung. A pair of long gauntlets to aid in keeping off the attacks of mosquitoes, which, as the prospectors in the country declare, "look as big as rabbits, and bite like a dog," is also valuable.

As regards cooking pots, food-supplies, etc., I cannot do better than quote the following words from Colonel Cane's list :—" Two medium - sized axes, 1 small tomahawk, 2 frying-pans, 6 cooking-pots, fitting one inside the other to make a 'nest,' 1 gridiron (an unusual luxury), a coil of $\frac{3}{4}$-inch rope, 150 feet long, for towing, a ball of twine, and a small amount of light cord, a cup, plate, knife, fork, and spoon for each member of the party (with one or two spare ones), a small bag of nails, several small whetstones (most important) ; bacon, flour, baking-powder, beans, tea, coffee, or cocoa (the latter for choice), sugar, salt, and a few cans of preserved meat for emergencies. These articles are all necessities."

To this list I should add two or three good skinning knives, and a number of small bags of fine salt for curing skins. Most sportsmen buy an inferior form of coarse salt for this purpose, but the fine table salt is not ruinously expensive, and a small bag of it goes farther than one of twice the size and weight of coarse salt, and is of course much more convenient to carry.

In the place of a small tomahawk I should substitute a really good English bill-hook, or even two. This weapon is unknown in Alaska, but for cutting trails through brush, and for chopping up small wood like alder, it is far better than any axe ; and the number of times, while watching our men hopelessly chopping at small sticks with an axe, that we exclaimed, " Oh for a good old bill-hook ! " was beyond all counting.

For reasons elsewhere stated, it is hopeless to offer any advice on the subject of a sportsman's battery in Alaska. Suffice it to say, that we found both the .256 and the 8 milli-metre Mannlichers quite good enough. Glyn's Paradox was

SALDOVIA BAY, APRIL 1903.

not, in our opinion, a good weapon to use against big beasts such as bears and moose. On the other hand, we found one of the new pattern, .35 Winchester, a very good rifle for stopping heavy game. A small .22 Winchester came in most usefully for killing grouse and ptarmigan for the pot; and if it is intended to collect birds for specimens a small 410 bore collector's gun is the most convenient weapon. There is always plenty of sport to be had with a shot-gun at wildfowl if the sportsman is prepared to drag about such a heavy weapon merely for that purpose. It will be needless to enumerate all the small articles required for mending clothes or boots, simple remedies in the way of medicines, and accessories such as watches, a good compass, field-glasses, telescope, etc., all of which will occur to the mind of every sportsman before setting out on a trip of this kind.

Nearly every sort of supplies in the way of food can be obtained at any good local stores, such as are found at Saldovia, Kussiloff, Kenai, Kodiak, and Sand Point; but it is well to outfit with these things as near as possible to one's point of starting for the trip, and thus save the extra trouble and expense of dragging a lot of freight all the way from Seattle or Victoria.

CHAPTER III

THE GAME LAWS OF ALASKA

THE following remarks are chiefly extracts from letters of mine which appeared in the *Field* in December 1903 and January 1904, relating to the above subject. During the fall of 1903 there were no less than five Englishmen, including the writer and others, who were shooting in Western Alaska. Since it appears probable that others of our countrymen may be inclined to visit that country ere long, I take this opportunity of making the following remarks for the benefit of those who may intend to do so. As the law at present stands, no licence to kill game is required, nor is any payment necessary to obtain permits. Permits to export trophies from Alaska must be obtained. The proper mode of procedure is to apply direct to the Secretary, Department of Agriculture, Washington, D.C. The applicant should state the number of each kind of big game required, not exceeding the number allowed by the game laws of Alaska.

During a recent conversation with Dr. T. S. Palmer, the assistant chief of the Biological Survey Office at Washington, who is in charge of the Game Preservation Department, I was informed that there seemed to be a somewhat confused idea in the minds of English sportsmen as to the correct

27

mode of applying for permits to ship out trophies of big game.   He said that it would greatly facilitate matters if the applicants would state in what districts of Alaska they intend to shoot, as larger permits are issued for certain districts than for others.   He also stated that one or two instances had come to his notice where sportsmen had applied for permits through more than one source at the same time, some having even applied to the British Ambassador as well as to the Secretary of Agriculture, and in one case a duplicated application had found its way on to the table at a committee meeting of the Senate, thereby causing some amusement and unnecessary confusion.   I may add that all letters are answered with the greatest promptitude and courtesy by the Secretary of Agriculture, so that no doubts need be entertained on this subject.   It is probable that the existing laws may remain in force for some time to come, as they represent a carefully amended copy of the first game laws of Alaska, originally passed by Congress, June 7, 1902.   The latest amendment was passed in August 1903.   The authorities at Washington, who were responsible for framing this first Act, admitted to me early in the spring of 1903 that the law was then only in an experimental stage, and that it would be subject to various alterations in due course.

I was kindly invited to express my views on the Act then in force, and to make any suggestions bearing on the subject which might be of any assistance when framing any further amendments.   This I did to the best of my ability.

The present Act was a wise step, and taken in good time by the authorities for the protection of game in Alaska.   But even in its present state it does not cover the whole field, when viewed in the light of a protective measure.   It has, indeed, effectively protected the game from extermination by sportsmen, but these have been so few and far between in the country up to the present date, that they have not been to any extent a real menace to any kind of big game.

The real danger at present lies in the indiscriminate killing of bears, moose, caribou, and sheep by the natives for the sale of the hides and horns, and also for the sake of the meat of the last three species, which is sold by the natives and others to ships, canneries, and miners throughout the country. For the last-named purpose males, females, and young of all kinds of game have hitherto been killed at all seasons of the year.

Naturally this practice has in many cases entailed much wanton destruction, since the natives are so intensely lazy by disposition that they will often kill a beast and only carry away the haunches, leaving the remainder of the carcass to rot. I have known an instance of a native killing three moose in the evening, after he had already killed one in the morning, and leaving the greater portion of the first killed beast in the forest. On being asked why he did so he calmly said, " Because he saw the last three beasts nearer to the settlement than the first one, and it was not so far to pack in the meat." The new Act endeavours to make the selling of game animals for meat an offence, but according to the wording of the clauses such sale is only unlawful during the close season. Apparently any dealer can still buy or sell any number of hides, etc., provided that they are taken from animals which are killed in the open season ; and although it appears that he should have permits in order to send them out of the country, I know of several instances where large consignments of brown bear skins have been shipped out of Alaska since this Act was in force, without the owners holding any such permits at all. It is one of the objects of the authorities to restrict this form of killing big game, but according to the law in its present form it is hard to see how it can be efficacious.

During my late trip in Alaska I received several letters from Dr. Hart Merriam, the courteous and talented chief of the Biological Survey Department at Washington, in which he discussed various matters relating to the new game laws. In one of these letters he stated that it was not the intention of the authorities to prohibit the killing of game all over Alaska, but rather to restrict the numbers allowed, and to protect the game more strictly in certain districts such as Cook's Inlet and the Kenai Peninsula, which are easy of access and are therefore most visited by sportsmen. I replied saying that the intention of the Act was undoubtedly good, but at present it appeared that the killing of the game by the natives, as described above, threatened to exterminate the game in the country far more quickly than the small number of big heads annually killed by *bona-fide* sportsmen.

With regard to the clauses of the Act which concern sportsmen, there are several new ones which make it questionable whether or no the trip of 9000 miles to Western Alaska and the expenses entailed are adequately remunerated by the amount of trophies which it is permissible to obtain. The killing of caribou on the whole of the Alaska Peninsula west of Lake Iliamna is prohibited until 1908. This district is the best part of the accessible country near the coast in which caribou can be found, and they still abound there in thousands. It is also sufficiently adjacent to a good moose country to render possible the collection of both moose and caribou in one season under the old conditions. I only know of two districts near the coast of Alaska where both moose and caribou may now possibly be obtained in one trip, but both of these places are very remote and little known to hunters. The killing of walrus south of the Bering Straits is also prohibited. This means a special expedition into the Arctic regions to obtain even one specimen of this species. Furthermore, only one moose is allowed to be exported by each sportsman from the Kenai Peninsula, although by the wording of the Act any person may still kill two moose in any part of Alaska. Needless to remark, every sportsman or hunter in search of a good head, if on the Kenai Peninsula, exercises his right to kill two moose, and if he is unable to export the second head, the better one is taken out, and the other left to rot, or given to any person in the country who cares to accept it.

Assuming, then, that a sportsman intends to visit the Kenai Peninsula for shooting in the autumn, and possibly some other place for bears in the spring, the most he can hope to obtain of the protected game, after spending the whole season shooting, is comprised in the following list :—Four brown bears, four mountain sheep (*Ovis dalli*), and one moose ; or if he desire to get caribou, then he can substitute four caribou in the place of one moose, but to obtain both the latter in one season under the present local restrictions will be a hard matter. I do not wish to insinuate that either of the above bags should be despised, but to say the least of it, any one who goes out to Alaska and strictly adheres to the letter of the present laws will be somewhat disappointed if he views some of the collections made by the few pioneer sportsmen in Alaska who were fortunate enough to visit the country before this new Act was in force. Being myself numbered amongst these privileged ones, I can sympathise with any enterprising sportsmen who may venture to this far-off land under these altered conditions, since it is no mean undertaking, even with the prospect of a good bag in return for one's long journey, and a certain amount of hardships entailed.

Since the above remarks were written I have again heard from Dr. Palmer, and he says : " Congress is still considering the question of amending the Alaska game law. One of the provisions of the pending bill purposes to transfer the issue of permits for trophies to clerks of the courts in Alaska, and such permits, authorising the shipment of two deer, two moose, and two caribou, will be issued to non-residents, only on payment of $250."

If this idea be carried out it will, no doubt, have a good effect, although perhaps the price is rather stiff. It will probably put a stop to the issuing of permits to a number of men who have hitherto obtained them in order to trade the trophies thus sent out of the country. These men are likely to be known to the clerks of the courts in their own district, and permits may be refused such persons, but it is impossible for the authorities at Washington to identify many of the applicants who apply for the permits in writing.

The great drawback to this arrangement, from the point of view of an English sportsman intending to visit the country, appears to be that if he desires to receive a permit before leaving England (which is undoubtedly the wisest thing to do under these ever-changing regulations) it necessitates a very long delay between the time of writing for it, and the time of receiving the permit. Moreover, if permits are issued by clerks of the courts to export trophies only from their own particular districts, it may happen that the sportsman will find himself, at the termination of his wanderings in Alaska, many hundreds of miles from the place where he originally intended to be at that particular time, and probably in the district of another court, where possibly he may be subject to prosecution from some Deputy Marshal, who may not approve of him, or of the fact of his having received a permit from some other district. I presume, however, that a permit once issued would hold good to export trophies from any part of the country.

There is one remarkable fact about the enforcement of the game laws in their present state, and to illustrate this I will add these few final remarks. Writing to me in April 1904, one of the head authorities at Washington expresses himself as follows :—" The law specifically prohibits natives from selling skins of animals killed for meat, or from selling the heads and skins of any game animals." And yet in spite of this I can positively state that the natives bring in regularly a supply of brown bear skins to all the local stores, and if not already sold to the storekeepers, they offer these skins to any one who visits the local settlement. I can quote three instances occurring in 1903, at three of the largest stores on the coast of Alaska, when I saw a total of over 120 brown bear skins sold by the natives to the storekeepers, and afterwards shipped out of the country openly, and with the full cognisance of the local authorities. One only needs to pay a visit to the sale-rooms of Messrs. Lampson in London, where hundreds of Alaskan brown bear skins are always on offer, to see how loosely this portion of the game laws is enforced. Although personally I should be the last to complain, after the generous permits which were issued to me by the authorities at Washington, it must and does seem passing strange to sportsmen who have visited Alaska, to see such things, and to look back to the time when they were subject to all kinds of indignities for the unfortunate *faux pas* of shooting a beast out of season, or killing one

more than their permit allowed, when in dire straits for
fresh meat.

UNITED STATES DEPARTMENT OF AGRICULTURE

REGULATIONS FOR THE PROTECTION OF GAME IN ALASKA

U.S. DEPARTMENT OF AGRICULTURE, OFFICE OF THE SECRETARY,
WASHINGTON, D.C., *August 22, 1903.*

In the Act of June 7, 1902 (32 Stat. L., 327), Congress has provided a
comprehensive law for the protection of game in Alaska.   Prior to the
enactment of this statute the only protection accorded game in the Territory
was a prohibition of the destruction and shipment of eggs of cranes, ducks,
brant, and geese, contained in the Act of June 6, 1900 (31 Stat. L., 332).
The Act of 1902, commonly known as the Alaska Game Law, defines game,
fixes open seasons, restricts the number which may be killed, declares certain
methods of hunting unlawful, prohibits the sale of hides, skins, or heads at
any time, and prohibits export of game animals or birds except for scientific
purposes, for propagation, or for trophies, under restrictions prescribed by
the Department of Agriculture.   The law also authorises the Secretary of
Agriculture, when such action is necessary, to place further restrictions on
killing in certain regions.   The importance of this provision is already
apparent.   Owing to the fact that nearly all persons who go to Alaska to
kill big game visit a few easily accessible localities—notably Kodiak Island,
the Kenai Peninsula, and the vicinity of Cook Inlet—it has become
necessary to protect the game of these localities by special regulations in
order to prevent its speedy destruction.

PURPOSE OF THE LAW

The object of the Act is to protect the game of the Territory so far as
possible, but without causing unnecessary hardship ; hence Indians, Eskimo,
miners, or explorers actually in need of food are permitted to kill game
for their immediate use.   The exception in favour of natives, miners, and
explorers must be construed strictly.   It must not be used merely as a
pretext to kill game out of season, for sport or for market, or to supply
canneries or settlements, and under no circumstances can the hides or heads
of animals thus killed be lawfully offered for sale.

In addition to the animals commonly regarded as game, walrus and
large brown bears are protected, but existing laws relating to the fur-seal, sea-
otter, or other fur-bearing animals are not affected.   The Act makes no

close season for *black bears*, and contains no prohibition against the sale or shipment of their skins. Heads or skins of large brown bears, like those of other protected animals, can be shipped only in accordance with the regulations hereinafter provided. Regular hunting licences are not issued by the Department, but shipping permits are required for the export of all trophies, without regard to the circumstances under which such trophies were secured.

TEXT OF THE ACT

The Act reads as follows :

An Act for the Protection of Game in Alaska, and for other purposes.

" Be it enacted by the Senate and House of Representatives of the United States of America in Congress assembled, That from and after the passage of this Act the wanton destruction of wild game animals or wild birds, the destruction of nests and eggs of such birds, or the killing of any wild birds other than a game bird, or wild game animal, for the purposes of shipment from Alaska is hereby prohibited.

" *Game defined :* The term 'game animals' shall include deer, moose, caribou, sheep, mountain goats, bears, sea-lions, and walrus. The term 'game birds' shall include water-fowl, commonly known as ducks, geese, brant, and swans ; shore birds, commonly known as plover, snipe, and curlew, and the several species of grouse and ptarmigan. Nothing in this Act shall effect [affect] any law now in force in Alaska relating to the fur-seal, sea-otter, or any fur-bearing animal other than bears and sea-lions, or prevent the killing of any game animal or bird for food or clothing by native Indians or Eskimo or by miners, explorers, or travelers on a journey when in need of food ; but the game animals or birds so killed shall not be shipped or sold.

" *Seasons :* Sec. 2. That it shall be unlawful for any person in Alaska to kill any wild game animals or wild birds except during the seasons hereinafter provided : Large brown bears, from April fifteenth to June thirtieth, both inclusive ; moose, caribou, walrus, and sea-lions, from September first to October thirty-first, both inclusive ; deer, sheep, and mountain goats, from September first to December fifteenth, both inclusive ; grouse, ptarmigan, shore birds, and water-fowl, from September first to December fifteenth both inclusive : *Provided,* That the Secretary of Agriculture is hereby authorised whenever he shall deem it necessary for the preservation of game, animals or birds to make and publish rules and regulations which shall modify the close seasons hereinbefore established, or provide different close seasons for different parts of Alaska, or place further restrictions and limitations on the killing of such animals or birds in any given locality, or to prohibit killing entirely for a period not exceeding five years in such locality.

"*Number:* Sec. 3. That it shall be unlawful for any person at any time to kill any females or yearlings of moose, caribou, deer, or sheep, or for any one person to kill in any one year more than the number specified of each of the following game animals: Two moose, walrus, or sea-lions; four caribou, sheep, goats, or large brown bears; eight deer; or to kill or have in possession in any one day more than ten grouse, or ptarmigan, or twenty-five shore birds or water-fowl.

"*Guns and boats:* That it shall be unlawful for any person at any time to hunt with hounds, to use a shot-gun larger than number ten gauge, or any gun other than that which can be fired from the shoulder, or to use steam launches or any boats other than those propelled by oars or paddles in the pursuit of game animals or birds. And the Secretary of Agriculture is authorised to make and publish such further restrictions as he may deem necessary to prevent undue destruction of wild game animals or wild birds.

"*Sale:* Sec. 4. That it shall be unlawful for any person or persons at any time to sell or offer for sale any hides, skins, or heads of any game animals or game birds in Alaska, or to sell, or offer for sale therein, any game animals or game birds, or parts thereof, during the time when the killing of said animals or birds is prohibited: *Provided,* That it shall be lawful for dealers having in possession any game animals or game birds legally killed during the open season to dispose of the same within fifteen days after the close of said season.

"*Export:* Sec. 5. That it shall be unlawful for any person, firm, or corporation or their officers or agents to deliver to any common carrier, or for the owner, agent, or master of any vessel or for any other person to receive for shipment or have in possession with intent to ship out of Alaska any hides or carcasses of caribou, deer, moose, mountain sheep, or mountain goat, or parts thereof, or any wild birds or parts thereof: *Provided,* that nothing in this Act shall be construed to prevent the collection of specimens for scientific purposes, the capture or shipment of live animals and birds for exhibition and propagation, or the export from Alaska of specimens and trophies, under such restrictions and limitations as the Secretary of Agriculture may prescribe and publish.

"*Penalties:* Sec. 6. That any person violating any of the provisions of this Act or any of the regulations promulgated by the Secretary of Agriculture shall be deemed guilty of a misdemeanour, and upon conviction thereof shall forfeit to the United States all game or birds in his possession, and all guns, traps, nets, or boats used in killing or capturing said game or birds, and shall be punished for each offence by a fine of not more than two hundred dollars or imprisonment not more than three months, or by both such fine and imprisonment, in the discretion of the court : *Provided*, That upon conviction for the second or any subsequent offence there may be imposed in addition a fine of fifty dollars for any violation of sections one and three, and a fine of one hundred dollars for a violation of section two.

"*Enforcement :* It is hereby made the duty of all marshals and deputy marshals, collectors or deputy collectors of customs appointed for Alaska, and all officers of revenue cutters to assist in the enforcement of this Act. Any marshal or deputy marshal may arrest without warrant any person found violating any of the provisions of this Act or any of the regulations herein provided, and may seize any game, birds, or hides, and any traps, nets, guns, boats, or other paraphernalia used in the capture of such game or birds and found in the possession of said person, and any collector or deputy collector of customs, or any person authorised in writing by a marshal, shall have the power above provided to arrest persons found violating this Act or said regulations and seize said property without warrant, to keep and deliver the same to a marshal or a deputy marshal.   It shall be the duty of the Secretary of the Treasury upon request of the Secretary of Agriculture to aid in carrying out the provisions of this Act : *Provided further*, That nothing contained in the foregoing sections of this Act shall be construed or held to prohibit or limit the right of the Smithsonian Institution to collect in or ship from the District of Alaska animals or birds for the use of the Zoological Park in Washington, District of Columbia : *Provided further*, that such heads and hides as may have been taken before the passage of this Act, may be shipped out of Alaska at any time prior to the first day of July, anno Domini nineteen hundred and two.

"Approved, June 7, 1902."

REGULATIONS UNDER THE ACT

In accordance with the foregoing Act, conferring upon the Secretary of Agriculture authority to modify the close seasons for game in different parts of Alaska and prohibit killing entirely for certain periods, to make further restrictions necessary to prevent undue destruction of game, and to prescribe restrictions governing the collection of specimens for scientific purposes, capture of live animals and birds, and shipment of specimens and trophies, the following regulations are hereby prescribed to take effect October 1, 1903 :—

1. LOCAL RESTRICTIONS

Caribou.—Killing caribou on the Kenai Peninsula and on the Alaska Peninsula west of Lake Iliamna (except for scientific purposes under special permit) is hereby prohibited prior to September 1, 1908.

Walrus.—Killing walrus south of Bering Straits and Cape Prince of Wales (except by natives or for scientific purposes under special permit) is hereby prohibited prior to September 1, 1908.

Skins and tusks.—Shipment of caribou heads or skins or walrus hides or tusks obtained in the regions above mentioned is likewise prohibited, except under permits for scientific purposes or in extraordinary cases. Persons shipping walrus tusks from the port of Sitka or any sub-port of Alaska must present satisfactory evidence to officers of the customs at Seattle or San Francisco that said tusks were not obtained from animals killed in violation of these regulations.

Water-fowl.—The open season for hunting water-fowl on Afognak, Kodiak, Uganuk, and Wood Islands is hereby extended from December 16, 1903, to February 1, 1904.

2. HOUNDING

Hunting deer, moose, or caribou with hounds *or other dogs* in any part of Alaska is strictly prohibited.

3. PERMITS

Persons desiring to collect mammals, birds, nests, or eggs for scientific purposes; to obtain animals or birds for exhibition or propagation; or to ship game animals and birds killed in open season, should apply for permits to the Secretary of Agriculture, Washington, D.C. Applicants should state (1) the number of each kind of animal or bird they desire to kill; (2) the regions where they are to be obtained; (3) the port and probable date of shipment; and (4) the purpose for which obtained (specimens for scientific purposes, live animals for exhibition or propagation, trophies for personal use, etc.). All permits will expire on December 31 of the year in which issued, but consignments actually shipped before the expiration of the permit may be admitted on arrival at Seattle or San Francisco.

4. SPECIMENS FOR SCIENTIFIC PURPOSES

Packages containing specimens for scientific purposes offered for shipment must be marked "Specimens for Scientific Purposes," or words to like effect, and must bear the shipper's name and address. Inattention to these details will render packages subject to examination and detention by officers of the customs. Packages of specimens addressed to the U.S. Department of Agriculture, the Smithsonian Institution, or the U.S. National Museum, if properly marked, may be shipped without permit and without examination. Packages addressed to individuals, whether officers of Executive Departments or not, must be accompanied by permit.

5. Live Animals and Birds

Consignments of live animals or birds for exhibition or propagation must be accompanied by permits, except as stated in Regulation 6. Consignments offered for shipment without permit will not be refused transportation, but may be forwarded to Seattle or San Francisco and held there at owner's risk and expense until permits are obtained.

6. Parks excepted

Under the provisions of Section 6, live animals and birds consigned to the National Zoological Park, Washington, D.C., are not subject to the Act. Live animals other than moose and brown bear (not exceeding 3 in one consignment) and live birds (not exceeding 25 in one consignment) may be shipped *without permit* to the following public zoological parks, if shipped directly to said parks and not to some agent :--

> Golden Gate Park, San Francisco.
> Lincoln Park, Chicago.
> Menagerie of Central Park, New York.
> New York Zoological Society.
> Zoological Society, Philadelphia.

Consignments for these parks which exceed the above-mentioned limits must be accompanied by regular permits in all cases.

7. Shipment

Hides, skins, heads, horns, trophies, specimens, live game animals, or game birds shipped from Alaska to other ports of the United States or to foreign ports must not be accepted for transportation unless shipped *via* Seattle, Wash., or San Francisco, Cal., to be there subject to examination by officers of the customs or representatives of this Department.

8. Reserved Rights of Department

The Department expressly reserves the right to restrict the number of each kind of game animal which may be shipped under permit (within the limits fixed by law) whenever deemed necessary by reason of local or relative scarcity of the species, or other causes ; to examine at Seattle or San Francisco any or all hides, skins, heads, horns, trophies, specimens, live game animals, or game birds from Alaska, whether shipped as personal baggage or otherwise ; to detain, if necessary, at said ports any consignment of game animals or birds or any part thereof not forwarded in conformity with these regulations, and to require the return of the same either to original port of shipment or to the Collector of Customs at Sitka, Alaska. Owners and masters of vessels will accept all consignments subject to these conditions. In case of return all expenses of reshipment will be paid by the vessel transporting the goods from Alaska ; and the master of said vessel must file at Seattle or San Francisco a customs receipt for all goods returned to Alaska.

9. PACKING TROPHIES

All trophies (including hides, skins, robes, antlers, horns, skulls, and similar specimens not intended for scientific purposes) must be exhibited to an officer of the customs or packed so that they can be readily examined, and the package must bear the name and address of the shipper. Trophies must not be concealed in personal baggage so as to prevent examination ; and packages supposed to contain trophies improperly packed may be refused transportation until satisfactory evidence as to contents has been presented. Common carriers are enjoined to make every effort to carry out the spirit of this regulation.

10. SPECIAL MANIFEST REQUIRED

All consignments of trophies, specimens, or live animals, whether shipped as personal baggage or otherwise, must be declared before an officer of the customs and accompanied by a *special manifest* to be forwarded to the Collector of Customs at San Francisco, Calif., or the Deputy Collector of Customs at Seattle, Wash. In case the point of shipment is not a regular port of entry, the shipper will deliver the invoice to the master of the vessel, who shall declare the goods and surrender the invoice to the proper officer of customs at the port of delivery.

11. EXAMINATION OF SHIPMENTS

Hides, skins, heads, horns, trophies, or specimens arriving at Seattle or San Francisco, not covered by permits or shipped contrary to these regulations, will be held for examination by officers of the Customs, promptly reported, and released only upon instructions from the Treasury Department ; provided that all goods not released within sixty (60) days after arrival shall be returned to the port of shipment or to the Collector of Customs at Sitka (at the expense of the vessel bringing the same), for disposition in accordance with the provisions of Section 6 of the Act.

12. TRANSPORTATION IN CLOSE SEASON

Vessels plying in Alaskan waters must not receive for transportation out of Alaska, or for consumption on the voyage, any carcasses of game animals or birds during the close season. Owners and masters of vessels are enjoined to insist upon a strict compliance with this and all other regulations governing shipment.

All special rulings of the Department in conflict with these regulations are hereby revoked. JAMES WILSON, *Secretary.*

Since going to press I have received the following amendments to the game laws, which have been forwarded to me from Washington.

The primary object of the Alaska game law is the preservation of game for the use of the people of Alaska, native and white. This is accomplished chiefly by stopping the export of deer-hides and by restricting the killing and shipment of big game as trophies. Prior to the enactment of the law thousands of deer were slaughtered each year for their hides, and these hides were shipped out of the Territory. This export has now practically ceased.

There seems to have been some misunderstanding respecting certain privileges conferred by the law. Attention therefore is again called to the provision in Section 1 which allows Indians, Eskimo, miners, or explorers in need of food or clothing to kill game for their immediate use. Attention is also called to the fact that the clause in Section 5, prohibiting shipment of hides and heads, does not apply to bears, hence the skins of large brown bears and bears of all kinds may be shipped from any point in Alaska without the formality of a permit; and in view of a widespread feeling that the protection afforded bears is unnecessary, the open season is here materially extended. Certain other changes in open seasons which experience has shown may be made without injury to the game will be found in Regulation 2.

During the past session of Congress a bill was introduced making radical changes in the law and in the system of issuing permits. As this bill is still pending and will doubtless receive attention at the next session, the issue of permits will remain practically suspended for the present, and few if any permits for the shipment of trophies of moose, caribou, or sheep will be issued during 1904.

REGULATIONS FOR 1904

In accordance with the foregoing Act conferring upon the Secretary of Agriculture authority to modify the close seasons for game, to provide different close seasons for different parts of Alaska, to make further restrictions necessary to prevent undue destruction of game, and to prescribe restrictions governing the collection of specimens for scientific purposes, the capture of live animals, and the shipment of specimens and trophies, the following regulations are hereby prescribed to take effect August 1, 1904 :—

1. DISTRICTS

For the purposes of this Act, the following game districts are hereby established :—

(1) The Sitka District, comprising South-Eastern Alaska east of the 141st Meridian.

(2) The Peninsula District, comprising the Aleutian Islands, the Alaska and Kenai peninsulas and adjacent islands, and that part of Alaska west of the 141st Meridian which drains into the Pacific Ocean.

(3) The Yukon District, comprising North-Western Alaska north of the Peninsula District, including the area drained by the Kuskokwim, Tanana, Yukon, and Kowak rivers, and the area which drains into the Arctic Ocean.

2. SEASONS

Bear.—The open season for large brown bears throughout Alaska is hereby modified to extend from April 1 to December 31, both inclusive. There is no close season for black bears.

Deer.—The open season for deer in the Sitka game district is hereby modified to extend from August 1 to January 31, both inclusive.

Moose and Sheep.—The open season for moose and sheep throughout Alaska is hereby modified to extend from September 1 to December 31, both inclusive.

Caribou.—The open season for caribou in the Yukon game district is hereby modified to extend from September 1 to December 31, both inclusive. In the Peninsula District, killing caribou on the Kenai Peninsula (except for scientific purposes under special permit) is prohibited prior to September 1, 1908.

Goats.—The open season for goats throughout Alaska is hereby modified to extend from August 1 to December 31, both inclusive.

Walrus.—The regulation of August 22, 1903, establishing a closed zone for walrus, is hereby modified to read as follows :—Killing walrus south of a line drawn from the north end of St. Matthew Island to Cape Vancouver (except by natives or for scientific purposes under special permit) is hereby prohibited prior to September 1, 1908.

Ptarmigan and Water-fowl.—The open season for ptarmigan and water-fowl throughout Alaska is hereby modified to extend from September 1 to January 31, both inclusive.

.   .   .   .

4. Permits

The Department cannot grant permits extending from one year to another, as the law and regulations are subject to change ; neither can it issue indefinite authorizations to persons to bring out " any trophies which may be obtained during the trip." All permits will expire on December 31 of the year of issue, but consignments actually shipped before such expiration may be admitted on arrival in Seattle or San Francisco.

Permits to collect mammals, birds, nests, or eggs for scientific purposes will be issued only to regular representatives of public museums, or under exceptional circumstances, to persons who are known to be engaged in making special investigations. Applicants should state the region where specimens are to be collected and the port and probable date of shipment.

CHAPTER IV

THE BIG GAME OF ALASKA

BEARS

ALTHOUGH it has not been my intention to make this book in any way a scientific treatise on the game animals of Alaska, I consider that the work would not be regarded as complete without some passing mention of their places in scientific classification and the local distribution of the various kinds of big game. Starting, then, with the bears, I shall briefly attempt to throw some light on the subject, on which I must confess that I was hopelessly confused after paying one visit to Washington, where I examined numerous specimens of the brown bears that came from different parts of Alaska. I am indebted to Dr. Hart Merriam, Dr. T. S. Palmer, and Mr. W. Osgood, of the Biological Survey Office, Washington, for much useful information on the subject. The last-named gentleman earned my special gratitude by spending a considerable time in showing me the museum specimens, and supplying me with the substance of many of the notes which follow.

Mr. Osgood writes, in one of his letters to me: "We proceed very slowly in getting exact knowledge of these bears, and there are many points about them which we would be glad to learn ourselves."

I have referred elsewhere to the partiality of all American naturalists for describing new species or sub-species of animals, and there is no doubt that in the case of the large brown bears of Alaska they have given free scope to their sentiments in this direction. I do not mean to insinuate for a moment that they make assertions which they are unable to support with specimens to prove their accuracy, but I do think that in certain cases a very few specimens, brought probably by one man from a certain district, have been deemed sufficient to warrant the authorities in founding a new species, even although the variations between that species and one already known are only in very minute details. Some years ago Dr. Merriam published a paper on the bears of America, giving much valuable and useful information. This still remains the only general paper on the subject published in America.

Since this paper was published, three distinct names have been given to supposed forms of large brown bears. These are *Ursus kidderi, Ursus dalli gyas,* and *Ursus merriami.* The one called *merriami* is unquestionably the same as *gyas,* and the original specimens of each came from places within a few miles of each other. Which of the names should prevail depends on the question of priority of publication, as the descriptions appeared within a few days of each other, *gyas* being slightly in advance. According to the account given me by Mr. Osgood, a plain statement of the knowledge of the authorities at Washington as regards the subject is somewhat as follows :—

The brown bears of Alaska are all of one general type, and distinct from the grizzlies and other bears, and from the standpoint of any one who is not a professional mammalogist they might well be considered as one species. They are

distributed from the vicinity of the British line at Portland
Canal, northward along the coast, and along the length of
the Alaska Peninsula, and are found on Unimak Island, but
do not extend farther westward than this island.   In the
south-east they do not occur on Prince of Wales Island, but
are abundant on Baranof, Admiralty, and Chichagof Islands.
They are also found on Kodiak Island and the neighbouring
smaller islands.   They extend along the Bering Sea coast
for some distance northward, but exactly how far is not yet
definitely known.   In the interior they probably range at
least to the Yukon River, but very few specimens have as
yet been brought from that region.

The various different forms of brown bear which have
been named and recognised are of the nature of subdivisions
of the one group to which they all belong.

The following short list will give the distribution of the
various sub-species as they are known to-day :—

Ursus sitkensis occupies the south-east coast and part
of the islands of the Alexander Archipelago.

Ursus dalli is found on the coast at Yakutat Bay, and
doubtless somewhat farther north.

Ursus dalli gyas inhabits the Alaska Peninsula, and
probably extends on down the coast to merge with the true
dalli.

Ursus midd.ndorffi is found on Kodiak Island, and the
smaller islands immediately surrounding it.

Ursus kidderi frequents the same localities as *U. dalli
gyas* on the Alaska Peninsula, and, so far as known at
present, does not differ from it in colour, but only in the size
of its teeth and certain cranial peculiarities.

As regards the measurements and weights of these great
bears, the wildest yarns have been circulated.

Even in some of our own good standard works on big game measurements I have met with some astonishing statements, such as that bears have been killed in Alaska measuring 13 feet in a straight line from nose to tail, and having an estimated weight of 1800 lbs. or even 2000 lbs. To prove the inaccuracy of these statements I will quote the following example. Some years ago particulars were required of the largest measurements known of a Kodiak bear for publication in a well-known English book on sport.

Application was made to the head of a recognised commercial company at Kodiak for details. A rumour came from the mainland on the Alaska Peninsula that the natives near Wrangel had the skin of a very large bear. An old employé of the Commercial Company was sent over to get this skin, which *en passant* I may add was probably the skin of *U. dalli gyas*, and therefore not a true Kodiak bear at all. I happened to meet this man on a subsequent occasion, and he gave me details of the affair, saying that on arrival he found the skin in a native hut stretched over a beam in the roof, both ends of it strained with ropes, and heavy weights affixed to it. The measurements of this skin, which really did exceed 13 feet in length, were returned as the correct measurements of a large Kodiak bear!

In 1903 I had a unique opportunity of seeing laid together all the skins of the bears which had been killed during that season on Kodiak Island. They were then at the store which belongs to the Alaska Commercial Company, and the manager, Mr. Goss, kindly showed me the whole lot, saying that he certainly had some measuring over 12 feet unstretched. They were a fine lot of skins, of all colours and sizes, and about 60 in number, but the largest stretched skin did not measure 10 feet, and the largest unstretched

one, which my friend Glyn purchased for curiosity, did not
measure 9 feet in length when we put the tape over it.

The only two authentic measurements which I can vouch
for as regards the actual length of these big bears are the
following, and when we consider that Mr. A. J. Stone and
his party killed 10 bears, and our party accounted for 12,
all killed on the Alaska Peninsula, where the bears are
admitted to be the largest in Alaska, the two best specimens
from a total of 22 thus obtained should give a fair idea of the
size of these animals.

Mr. Stone's largest bear measured from nose to tail in
a straight line 7 feet 5 inches.

My largest one measured in the same way was 7 feet
$9\frac{1}{2}$ inches.

On comparison of the skulls of these two bears, mine
was found to be the larger, and as both our measurements
were carefully taken with assistance and in the presence of
witnesses, they are probably as nearly correct as possible.

The exact measurements and weight of my big bear are
given elsewhere. The measurements were taken not over
the skin, but on the stripped carcass after it had been skinned,
and the weighing was done two days after it was killed. No
allowance was made for weight lost, except 40 lbs. for entrails
taken out the first day by my natives to make cameleekas.
Had this bear been killed earlier or later in the season he
would probably have carried an extra 150 lbs. of fat at least,
but at that time of year, late in June, the bears are generally
thin, as this one was.

There is now to be seen in the National Zoological Park
at Washington a very fine specimen of an Alaskan brown
bear. I spent a long time in the park one day carefully
examining all the bears, and, through the courtesy of one of

the officials who accompanied me, was enabled to take notes of the relative sizes and weights of the bears in the different cages. On the cage containing the largest brown bear is a board bearing the following inscription :—

> *Kodiak Bear.*—Caught May 24, 1901, near Cape Douglas. Received
>   at Zoological Park, Jan. 9, 1902.
>   Weight when caught about 2 months old, 18 lbs.
>   Weight, Jan. 17, 1902, 180 lbs.
>   Weight, June 15, 1903, 450 lbs.

This beast looks enormous. We induced him to stand on his hind legs, and I am certain that his head must have been at least 8 feet above the ground when he was standing in that manner. Owing to his magnificent coat I should have guessed his weight at fully 800 lbs., but probably this was over the mark, as I doubt if he had put on 350 lbs. in five months. This bear will easily outstrip the largest grizzly in the park ere long, although some of the latter are a great age and consequently very heavy. The greatest weight attained by any grizzly there is about 950 lbs., as nearly as I could make out from the official list.

The curious part of this affair is that this brown bear is obviously misnamed by the authorities of the Zoo, since it was caught on the mainland near Cape Douglas, and is not therefore *Ursus middendorffi* at all, but either *U. kidderi* or *U. dalli gyas*. It is impossible to say to which of the latter two forms it belongs without an examination of its teeth, and for my own part I had no wish to take on a job of that kind. I have seen and killed these brown bears in various colours, from a dark brown to a very light fawn or cream colour.

The black bear, *Ursus americanus*, is plentiful all along the Alaskan coast, from the south up to a point on the Alaska

Peninsula where the timber line ceases. Beyond this to the westward it is not found, nor beyond the point where the timber line ends on the north side.

Like the brown bear, it appears to be more numerous near the coast than farther in the interior, and this is probably to be ascribed to the attraction of the salmon in the rivers and lakes near the coast.

There is yet another species of bear, *Ursus emmonsi*, commonly called the blue or glacier bear. It is found in the neighbourhood of Mount St. Elias near Kayak, and inhabits high and inaccessible places on the mountains. Bears of this species are small in size, not being nearly so large as the black bear, and in colour the skins which I have seen resemble those of the blue fox. The coat is remarkably long and fine, the extreme tips of the hair being silver-grey in colour.

Very little is as yet known concerning the habits of this animal, and although, from information given me at Kayak and elsewhere in that district, these bears appear to be fairly plentiful in that country, so far as I know a few specimens only have been killed by natives, and up to the present date of writing not one of these has found its way into England.

It was my original intention to try to procure a specimen for the British Museum, but the description and general appearance of the ground which these bears frequent frightened me into abandoning the attempt.

It yet remains for some keen sportsman to visit that country and bring out some good specimens, and some trustworthy information of these bears.

Any one contemplating a visit to that part should call on Mr. Stracey, the manager of the great English coal and oil company at Kayak. Being himself a good sportsman, he is always ready to assist a fellow-countryman ; and since he is practically king of the district, he is the man to make friends with before leaving Kayak.

Since but little is yet known of this bear, and as it appears likely to be of great interest to sportsmen who may visit the country near Yakutat or Kayak in the future, I append the following remarks made by Professor Dall after examining some specimens of *Ursus emmonsi* :—

" The general colour of the animal resembles that of a silver fox. The fur is not very long, but remarkably soft, and with a rich under-fur of a bluish black shade, numbers of the longer hairs being white or having the distal half white and the basal part slaty. The dorsal line from the tip of the nose to the rump, the back of the very short ears, and the outer faces of the limbs are jet black. Numerous long white hairs issue from the ears ; black and silver are the prevalent pelage of the sides, neck, and rump ; the under surface of the belly and the sinuses behind the limbs are greyish white, or even nearly pure white, I am told, in some cases. The sides of the muzzle and the lower anterior part of the cheeks are of a bright tan colour, a character I have not seen in any other American bear ; and this character is said to be invariable. There is no tint of brown elsewhere in the pelage. There is no tail visible on the pelts. The claws are small, very much curved, sharp, black above and lighter below ; the animal evidently can climb trees, which the brown bear cannot do."[1]

As regards the period of gestation in bears in Alaska, nothing appears to be definitely known by the natives. They declare that, although they have killed she-bears during summer and winter, and even in the holes and caves

[1] Dall, *Science*, N.S. II. No. 30, p. 87, July 26, 1895.

where they hibernate, yet they have never seen one which was carrying cubs. It appears certain that the she-bears drop their cubs whilst hibernating, and probably about the month of February, although the exact date when the event happens is not certain, nor is there anything to show if this occurs with all bears at the same time of year. It is the native belief that on the first occasion a she-bear usually has only one cub, but that subsequently she has two, or even three, at a birth. As a rule, in the spring the old bears remain with their cubs in the neighbourhood of the caves and hills where the cubs are born, and the following winter the latter again hole up with their mother.

I have myself seen cubs of more than a year old walking with their mother in the months of June and July. It is a well-known fact that the she-bear only breeds once in two years. Although, according to the natives, a male and female bear are often found hibernating in the same hole, it seems that the males do not mate with the females until the early spring. Then, as soon as they are strong enough after leaving their winter quarters, they roam the hillsides in search of a mate, and often indulge in sanguinary contests with each other for the possession of some favourite female. Most of the old males killed in the spring carry numerous traces of these battles on their faces and legs. I had a unique opportunity of watching the antics of two bears on the Alaska Peninsula in the end of May, and it was evident that these two had just paired.

A remarkable fact is the splendid condition in which these huge beasts emerge from their dens in the spring. Although existing for months without food, and their only form of amusement and sustenance being the licking of their paws, they are rolling in fat, but at first very groggy on their legs owing to lack of using them for so long. When first they begin to eat grass they scour considerably, and soon lose a lot of fat, so that by the early part of June they are quite thin; but after a long course of feeding on salmon they become very fat, before returning once more to winter quarters.

The following photograph shows seven of our picked brown bears' skulls, and a careful study of the photo will reveal a considerable difference between some of the specimens depicted. I venture to try to determine two of the different species now recognised by the American authorities; but I much regret that I did not submit the whole lot of skulls and skins to the Museum at Washington to have them properly named, as Mr. Lydekker, who has examined the skulls, informs me that there is not the material at hand in our own National Museum with which to make comparisons and a correct determination of these specimens.

I append herewith a list of the measurements of these skulls as numbered in the photograph, together with a few remarks on the locality where each was killed, and the form to which each belongs. The measurements were taken by Mr. Rowland Ward.

Skull No. 1.—Adult female. Hope Bay, Alaska Peninsula.
  Basal length from back to front, 15¾ inches.
  Width across the zygomatic arches, 9 inches.
  Weight clean, 4 lbs. 8½ oz.
  Zygomatic arches like No. 4, with which the specimen agrees in general characters.
  The dentition is similar to that of No. 2, and I am therefore inclined to think it belongs to *Ursus dalli gyas.*
Skull No. 2.—Very old male. Aniakchak Bay, Alaska Peninsula.
  Basal length from back to front, 17½ inches.
  Width across the zygomatic arches, 10⅞ inches.
  Weight clean, 8 lbs. 4 oz.

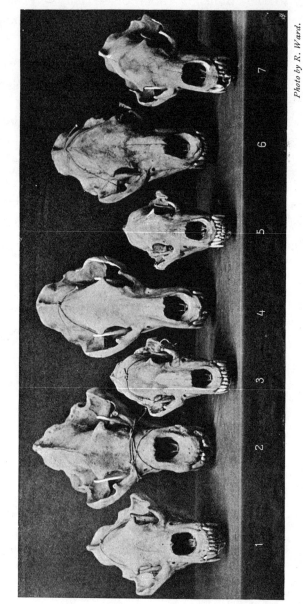

Photo by R. Ward.

GROUP OF BROWN BEAR SKULLS.

The zygomatic arches are very much higher than in specimens 3 and 4.

Sagittal ridge well defined and high, frontals concave.   First molar tooth in upper jaw $1\frac{1}{2}$ inch long.

The animal was very dark in colour, and appears to be undoubtedly *Ursus dalli gyas.*

Skull No. 3.—Young male.   Aniakchak Bay, Alaska Peninsula.

Basal length from back to front, $12\frac{5}{8}$ inches.

Width across zygomatic arches, $6\frac{3}{4}$ inches.

Weight clean, 2 lbs. 12 oz.

Conforms generally with No. 4.

The colour of skin was a light cream colour.   Believed to be *Ursus kidderi.*

Skull No. 4.—Adult male.   Aniakchak Bay, Alaska Peninsula.

Basal length from back to front, $17\frac{1}{2}$ inches.

Width across the zygomatic arches, $9\frac{1}{8}$ inches.

Weight clean, 6 lbs. 5 oz.

The sagittal ridge in this skull is not much developed.   Frontals slightly concave, but quite different from No. 2.

In colour the coat of this bear was considerably lighter than in either of the other adult males.

The dentition and cranial peculiarities are quite different from those of No. 2.   I believe this to be *Ursus kidderi.*

Skull No. 5.—Young male.   Bear River, Bering Sea coast.

Basal length from back to front, $12\frac{7}{8}$ inches.

Width across zygomatic arches, $6\frac{3}{4}$ inches.

Weight clean, 2 lbs. 8 oz.

Specifically undetermined, but probably the same as Nos. 6 and 7.

Skull No. 6.—Adult Male.   Bear River, Bering Sea coast.

Basal length from back to front, $16\frac{1}{2}$ inches.

Width across zygomatic arches, $9\frac{3}{8}$ inches.

Weight clean, $5\frac{1}{2}$ lbs.

Agrees generally with No. 4, but does not actually resemble either No. 2 or 4 as regards dentition.   Very dark-coloured skin.   Species not determined.

Skull No. 7.—Adult female.   Bear River, Bering Sea coast.

Basal length from back to front, $14\frac{1}{8}$ inches.

Width across zygomatic arches, 8 inches.

Weight clean, 3 lbs. $8\frac{1}{2}$ oz.

In general character similar to No. 6, and undoubtedly the same form.

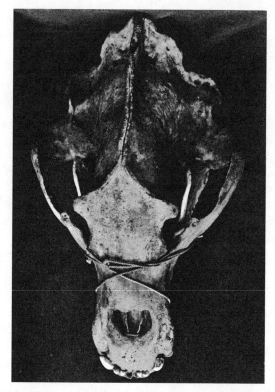

BROWN BEAR SKULL No. 2.

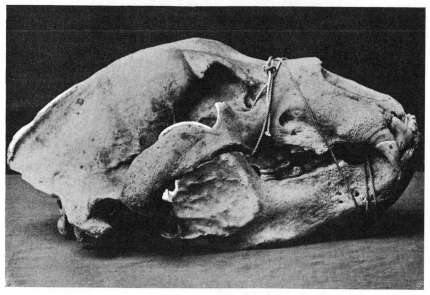

BROWN BEAR SKULL No. 2.

There is no doubt that the skull No. 2 is an exceptionally large specimen, and I was much gratified to find, on comparing it with one which Mr. A. J. Stone procured about the same time in 1903, that mine was considerably the larger.

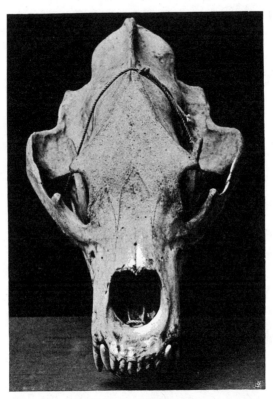

BROWN BEAR SKULL No. 4.

Mr. Stone considered his beast to be the largest he had ever seen, and as he has had several years' experience in Alaska and at the New York Museum, I think myself decidedly lucky in obtaining such a specimen on my first trip in the country.

Whether or no there is actually a difference even between those bears which I obtained from the Pacific and the Bering

Sea coasts is a matter for conjecture, and I may even go so far as to say that it is hard to define where such forms as *Ursus dalli gyas* and *Ursus kidderi* begin and end respectively, since there is at present nothing to show that all the Alaskan

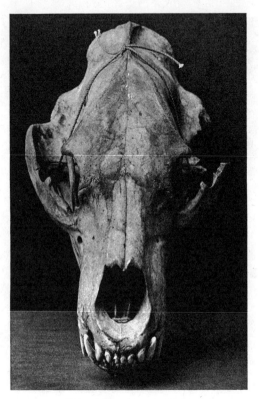

BROWN BEAR SKULL No. 6.

brown bears do not interbreed in the districts where they merge with each other.

MOOSE

Turning next to the Cervidæ, we find most conspicuous for its enormous size the moose of Alaska.

This species is known as *Alces gigas*, and is acknowledged

to be distinct from *Alces americanus*, which is found farther south in Canada and elsewhere. The former is by far the larger and finer animal as regards size, weight, and the spread of its antlers. In fact, during recent years the Kenai Peninsula has produced such heads as the old moose-hunters in Canada never imagined to exist even in their wildest dreams.

As regards their distribution, moose may be said to extend to the very limits of the forest line. Outside of this, on the barren lands they are not found.

In late summer and autumn the moose on the Kenai Peninsula assume a very dark colour, particularly the old bulls, whilst in winter they change their coat and become almost grey in the thick under-coat, with the longer hairs turning a light brown. The bull moose has a curious growth of long hair, which is called a bell, hanging from beneath the throat. In young bulls I have seen this bell as long as 15 inches, but in the older animals it is often worn away till it becomes little more than a pouch of slack skin covered with long hair, the long hanging tassel of hair having quite disappeared.

In ordinary seasons, on the Kenai Peninsula, moose have lost the velvet from their antlers by the end of the first week in September, the young bulls getting clean heads earlier than the old ones. In 1903, however, I saw several heads, both large and small, which still carried portions of velvet as late as September 15, and one even on September 20. The old bulls shed their antlers during December, but the young ones carry them much later, and according to the natives may be seen in February still carrying them, although the majority shed their antlers during January.

Space, and the nature of this work, do not admit of a

detailed account of the habits of moose, which indeed would
require a separate work on the subject, even provided that
the writer were qualified to give it. I shall not therefore
attempt the task, though a few facts may be gathered from the
actual account of how we saw and hunted them; and some brief
details of the size of antlers, and of the measurements and
weight of moose on the Kenai Peninsula, may be interesting.

In 1903 the total number of sportsmen hunting moose on
the Kenai Peninsula was ten, of whom five were Englishmen,
four Americans, and one German. Except for scientific
purposes, only one head was taken out of the country which
did not exceed 60 inches span. The twelve best heads
killed and taken out by these hunters measured respectively
as follows:—74, 72, 71, 70½, 70, 69, 69, 68, 64, 64, 64,
and 61 inches, and in addition to these the present writer
brought out one head killed by a professional hunter in 1902
which measured 77 inches when killed, but had shrunk
nearly 2 inches and then measured rather over 75 inches.
This latter head is the second largest authentic head ever
brought from the Kenai Peninsula. The world's record is a
head which was taken from a moose found drowned in the
Kenai River. The head and antlers were brought into Kenai
by a native who found them. They were purchased by Vein,
a Frenchman, commonly known in Kenai as "Frenchy."
This man "Frenchy" measured the head in the presence of
Mr. Mearns and other trustworthy men at Kenai, and they
all informed me that the exact span of the antlers was slightly
over 81 inches. During the winter the antlers, whilst hanging in a hut, shrank some two or three inches. "Frenchy"
told me that he wedged them out again to their original
measurement, using bits of wood forced between them and the
skull. He finally sold the head to a taxidermist in Chicago, and

HORNS OF MOOSE (*ALCES GIGAS*) AND WHITE SHEEP (*OVIS DALLI*).

Killed by English sportsmen on the Kenai Peninsula, 1903.

when in his possession I am told it again shrank to 78½ inches.
I believe this head has since been sold to a sporting club in
New York, but it still remains the record head, and is likely
to do so for some time to come.   It is an annoying fact that
all moose heads shrink considerably when the skull gets dry.
Big heads often decrease 2 or 3 inches in span.

Turning to the measurements of moose, I cannot do better
than quote the following table given me by Mr. A. J. Stone.
It is a record which he took of an adult bull moose killed on
the Kenai Peninsula in 1903.   Mr. Stone is sufficiently well
known as an authority on the subject to warrant my publishing
the measurements and affirming that they are correct.

MEASUREMENTS OF ADULT BULL MOOSE

Killed by A. J. Stone, Kenai, 1903.

Length.	Tail.	Tarsus.	Femur to Humerus.	Across the Chest.	Height at Shoulder.	Height at Elbow.	Brisket.
In.	In.	In.	In.	In.	In.	In.	In.
108	6	32½	58	21	75	40½	40½

I also append a table showing the weight of a large bull
moose killed by my friend Mr. David T. Hanbury on Kenai
Peninsula in 1903.

WEIGHT OF MOOSE.   Killed September 13.

	lbs.
Hide, paunch, entrails, heart, etc.	275
Rump and part of back	180
Neck and fore-part of back	215
One fore-quarter with leg and hoof . . .	115
Second do.	112
One hind-quarter, leg and hoof	135
Second do.	134
One side of ribs	50
Other side of ribs	55
Brisket	50

						lbs.
Kidneys and fat .	.	.	.	.	.	30
Scalp and fat	.	.	.	.	.	110
Head and antlers	.	.	.	.	.	115
			Total weight	.	.	1576

No allowance made for weight lost.

Mr. Hanbury measured the height of this moose as being 84 inches at the withers, but whether this was taken following the curves or between two upright pegs I am not certain.

I am convinced that the position of the forelegs when a beast dies makes an enormous difference in measuring. The shoulder has considerable play, and no doubt when the weight of the body is not supported by the legs, the animal often measures more when lying on its side than its actual height when standing.

I have myself measured a dead moose when stiff and cold, which I killed on the Kenai Peninsula, and try how I would, I could not make it less than 80 inches from the heel of the foot to the withers, although the measurement seemed too large at the time.

After reading an article in the *Field* of December 26, 1903, I began to think we must have under-measured our Alaskan moose, rather than otherwise. According to the letter referred to, a certain American sportsman killed a bull moose on the banks of Lake Superior, the exact weight of which when most of its entrails had been removed was 1632 lbs., and he estimated its live weight to have been close on 1750 or 1800 lbs. This bull measured 7 feet 6 inches in height at the withers, and 10 feet 6 inches from nose to tail. The writer naïvely remarks that unfortunately these were the only two accurate measures taken. After this I think that *Alces gigas* must be misnamed.

An interesting table, showing the measurements of moose from different parts of North America, is given by Mr. A. J. Stone in an article on the moose which he contributes to the book on *The Deer Family* in the American Sportsman's Library.

CARIBOU

The range of this animal in Alaska is so wide, and so many hundreds of miles of the country which it inhabits remain yet unvisited by naturalists or sportsmen, that we may assume not half of what will some day be discovered to be yet known about the caribou of Alaska. For all practical purposes as regards sportsmen it may be sufficient to classify caribou in two main groups :

The Barren Land Caribou, and
The Woodland Caribou.

Here again the Americans have been hard at work naming various local forms of these two groups.

An interesting and highly instructive little book entitled *The Caribou* has been recently written by Mr. Madison Grant, the Secretary of the New York Zoological Society, who has kindly sent me a copy of it. In speaking of the basis of classification, Mr. Grant makes a remark which expresses exactly the feelings of many sportsmen who are not actually scientific naturalists. He says : " Most of the distinctions between caribou species are based on size, colour, and antler development. The writer is perfectly aware of the uncertainty of any of these tests. Size alone does not often form a sufficient reason for specific distinction. Colour, especially in an animal subject to seasonal variations, is apt also to be an uncertain factor, and the warning of Linnæus—

ne nimium crede colori—has been too often ignored by zoologists.   Antler development is, if anything, a more variable quantity than either of the preceding characters."

All the caribou of Alaska, with the exception of perhaps a few *Rangifer osborni* found in the extreme south-east part, may be said to belong to the group of Barren Land caribou, and according to the American classification the species are as follows :—*Rangifer arcticus*, *Rangifer granti*, and *Rangifer stonei*.

Rangifer arcticus roams over the extreme northern part of Alaska, inhabiting the Barren Lands and extending far down into the interior of the country.

Rangifer granti is found on the Alaska Peninsula and Unimak Island.   There are many thousands of them still on the peninsula, in spite of the immense numbers killed in recent years by natives and others hunting for the meat market.   Speaking of this species, Mr. Grant says : " *R. granti*, inhabiting the extreme west of the Alaska Peninsula, has, thanks to the agency of man, been separated from its nearest relatives, so that we have lost whatever forms there may have existed intermediate between it and its close kindred on the Arctic coast."

I do not quite understand this statement, since I have myself seen caribou all along the Alaska Peninsula, both on the Pacific and on the Bering Sea side.   They still migrate along the peninsula from the direction of Lake Iliamna to the westward, and going east from Lake Iliamna caribou are found extending all the way along the divide between the head-waters of the west branch of the Sushitna River and the Kuskokwim River.   I have seen a number of good heads killed by natives from the last-named district.   Just where *Rangifer granti* ceases to exist, or merges with other

F

allied species, I cannot say, but I could see little or no difference in the specimens we killed all along the Alaska Peninsula in 1903, many of them being killed at places several hundred miles apart.

Rangifer stonei is, so far as we know at present, confined to the Kenai Peninsula. A very small herd of them is left there, and Mr. Stone only managed to obtain about three specimens for scientific purposes. This is the largest of all Barren Land caribou, and appears to be quite distinct, as regards its antlers, etc., from all other allied species. I have picked up its shed antlers, and seen a number of fresh tracks, but was never fortunate enough to see one of the animals during my trip on the Kenai Peninsula.

These caribou are now strictly protected under the recent Game Laws of 1903.

Owing to the restrictions now imposed by these Game Laws, any one wishing to get caribou near the shore in Western Alaska will be in future obliged to make an expedition up the Sushitna River, or travel farther round the coast into the neighbourhood of Bristol Bay.

BLACKTAIL DEER (*Mazama columbiana*)

This deer is found in great numbers all along the coast, and on many of the islands, as far up as the neighbourhood of Sitka, but does not extend farther north than that place.

Formerly great numbers have been killed on many of the islands by hunting the woods with dogs, which drove the deer to the water, where they could be easily killed by the hunters lying in wait for them. The use of dogs is now prohibited by the new Game Laws.

Sheep and White Goat

Perhaps the most highly prized animals from the sportsman's point of view to be found in Alaska are the mountain sheep, of which there are three forms at present known in the country. They have been named as follows : —

Ovis dalli, Ovis fannini, and *Ovis stonei.*

All three are distinct from the typical Rocky Mountain sheep, *Ovis canadensis.*

Ovis stonei, which is named after its discoverer, Mr. A. J. Stone, was first found by him on the mountains near the upper waters of the Stikine River. It probably merges in the south with the Rocky Mountain sheep, and how far north or into the interior of Alaska it extends is not yet accurately known.

It is darker in colour than either of the other two forms found in Alaska, and from all accounts has slightly larger horns. But I am unable to give any record measurements of them from personal knowledge.

Ovis fannini inhabits the interior of the country in the neighbourhood of Dawson, and I have seen a few specimens of this sheep. The horns which I have seen seem to have a slightly greater outward curve and are wider between the points than those of *Ovis dalli*—more, in fact, like the head of the Kamschatkan bighorn, *Ovis nivicola.*

The sheep itself is white, with the exception of a dark patch running from the back of the neck and along the centre of the back.

Ovis dalli is by far the most numerous of the three forms. These sheep are very plentiful on the mountains of the Kenai Peninsula, and all along the head of Cook's Inlet. They are reported to be much larger in the neighbourhood of

Mount McKinley and along the head-waters of the Sushitna River than nearer the coast. I have been credibly informed of heads brought out from that country which have a base measurement of 16 and even 17 inches, and exceeding 40 inches round the curve of the horns.

In 1903 a large number of heads were brought from the Kenai Peninsula by English sportsmen, but the American and German sportsmen were unfortunate in getting any good rams.

Out of some 25 heads killed by the Englishmen, the measurements ranged from 35 inches round the curve, with a base measurement of 13 inches, to some of $38\frac{1}{2}$ and $14\frac{1}{2}$ round the base. The largest spread between the points was 22 inches. A good average head for the Kenai Peninsula may be said to measure about 37 by $13\frac{3}{4}$ inches.

The *Ovis dalli* is white all the year round, although in its short summer coat it becomes slightly darker on the back. As winter approaches its coat increases considerably, and the long white hair gives it a very handsome appearance.

As a rule, except in places where these sheep have been much hunted by natives and others, they do not inhabit very bad ground, and may often be found in a fairly easy country, when they have drawn down in the mornings and evenings to feed on the grassy hill-slopes.

The ewes have small horns, which curve straight back over the head, and when full-grown the horns measure from 9 to 11 inches.

I much regret the absence of my weighing machine whilst in the sheep country, so that I have no accurate weights of these fine sheep, but at a rough guess I should say the rams are often close on 200 lbs. live weight.

Moreover, at the time of writing this I have mislaid the

exact measurements of a ram, although I distinctly remember measuring one which reached close on 3 feet at the shoulder. I append the full measurements of a ewe killed by Mr. A. J. Stone on Kenai Mountains in 1903.

Length.	Tail.	Tarsus.	Chest.	Femur to Humerus.	Elbow.	Brisket.	Shoulder.
In.	In.	In.	In.	In.	In.	In.	In.
51	4½	14	8	29	19	16½	31

It is a popular belief amongst hunters that the age of a ram can be determined by the number of rings which can be counted on one horn. Judging from a number of heads which I saw killed by sportsmen and natives in Alaska, I should say that this test is correct, since in all the cases in which I was able to tell the age of a ram by its teeth, the number of rings corresponded to the age of the animal. As most sportsmen know, the age of a sheep can be accurately estimated up to five years old by examination of its teeth—a yearling having two, a two-year-old four, a three-year-old six, and a four-year-old eight front teeth, respectively. The last is what is termed a "full mouth."

In the case of domestic sheep, which are fed on hard substances such as cake, etc., they often become what is known as "broken-mouthed" at about six years of age, when their teeth become broken or fall out. But I have observed in the wild sheep that as a rule they retain the full series of good teeth to a considerable age, the reason probably being that they are always feeding on soft grass and other kinds of food which do not damage the teeth. The careful observer will at once remark that there must be some explanation of these rings on the horn increasing in number each year. Many people who acknowledge the theory as being a correct basis of calculation have probably never troubled to reason out the cause of it. The simple solution of cause and effect in this problem appears to me to be this. During the fall and winter of each year the food of sheep is scarce, and after the rutting season the older rams are particularly poor. Throughout the winter, then, their horns cease to grow, but with the increase of good food in the spring the horns commence to grow again, and continue to do so until the following autumn, and hence the formation of a ring around the horn, which shows the point at which the growth of the horn was checked for several months.

The mountain goat, *Oreamnus montanus*, is found throughout a great part of Alaska, and is said to range as far north as latitude 60°. None of these animals are found in the neighbourhood of Cook's Inlet, nor to the westward on the Alaska Peninsula. They are numerous along the coast farther south, and although this goat is an ungainly-looking beast, it inhabits the most inaccessible places, over which it travels with surprising ease and fearlessness.

I feel some diffidence in approaching the following subject, but since most sportsmen who have visited the western coast of Alaska have probably heard similar yarns, I will quote a few statements which I gathered in regard to the fabled ibex of Alaska.

It is a popular theory amongst many prospectors and others who have been far into the mountains of the interior that an animal exists there which is neither a sheep nor a mountain goat. I had long talks on several occasions with one of the oldest and most trustworthy residents, who has lived for many years in the head of Cook's Inlet. He declared to me that he had seen some horns brought out by natives from the mountains some miles inland which were like the horns of the *Ovis dalli* ewe, but were more than twice the length of the sheep's horns and also larger. He said he imagined they belonged to some kind of ibex.

Mr. J. Folstad, the owner of the schooner *Alice*, in which we sailed along the coast of the Alaska Peninsula, who was a Norwegian engineer, and had travelled over a great part of the interior of Alaska, makes the following statement.

During the first great rushes to Dawson in 1897 and 1898 he was in the town of Dawson. There he saw, hanging outside a store (the owner of which sold meat such as moose, sheep, etc.), two animals with long horns which were unknown to him. On inquiry at the store he was told that numbers of people had been to look at the animals, and no one knew what to call them. But a sporting English doctor in the town, hearing of the episode, had been to examine them, and pronounced the beasts to be undoubtedly ibex. The only part of this story which I cannot understand is why this doctor did not obtain the horns of these beasts, and why the sporting world heard no account of his discovery.

On board the ss. *Bertha*, going down to Seattle in November 1903, we heard that there were two prospectors on board who had seen specimens of the fabled ibex. Mr. Vander Byl and I went to interview these men. They both described the animals as being darker than sheep, with shaggy hair underneath the throat and belly, horns brown in colour and curving backwards, about 30 inches long. One man claimed to have seen three of four dead ones killed by prospectors, and he said he had seen them in the mountains, sometimes in company with sheep, but that they were not so numerous as the sheep. We produced some photos of dead ibex killed in the Altai Mountains, and asked if he had ever seen a similar animal. He at once replied, " Why, that is the same beast, I guess." He declared these animals could be seen near the head-waters of a tributary on the east side of the Copper River.

I may mention that early in 1904 two sub-species of wild goat from British Columbia and Montana were described by Dr. J. A. Allen, but these, of course, have nothing to do with the reputed ibex.

Now the only explanation of the riddle appears to me to be this. Either there is some animal in Alaska as yet unknown to naturalists and sportsmen, or these animals are descendants of domestic goats which have escaped from old Russian or native settlements in former times. The latter theory is, I think, borne out by the so-called Mount St. Elias ibex. Colonel Cane, in his book *Summer and Fall in Western Alaska*, mentions a pair of horns which may be seen in the Post Office at Juneau, and are called the horns of a Mount St. Elias ibex. It is claimed that the animal was killed on the slopes of Mount St. Elias. I have seen and examined these horns, and entirely agree with Colonel Cane's remark that " they might at first sight have been taken for a very small pair of markhor horns; the twist of the spiral was, however, inwards instead of outwards."

On mature consideration, these horns certainly appear to have belonged to some form of a domestic goat, although I cannot say that I have actually seen any goat with a head closely resembling the one in question.

Doubtless some enterprising sportsman will ere long make an expedition up into the Copper River country, where there is also reported to be a particularly savage species of brown bear called locally the " bald-faced bear."

I have heard tales of these bears lying in wait for men

on the trails, and killing them without being previously wounded.

Any one who listens to half the yarns regarding big game in Alaska is likely to be led many merry dances on a fool's errand, but the stories regarding the ibex come from so many different parts of the country, and are all so very similar, that it leads one to believe that there really must be some " fire behind the smoke."

As regards the smaller animals of the country, there are still numbers of wolves, wolverines, lynxes, foxes, otters, and the smaller fur-bearing animals, such as marmots, marten, mink, ermine, etc. All of these, however, are rapidly decreasing in numbers, owing to the high prices and demands for their fur in the markets of the world.

List of Game killed in Alaska, 1903

The total list of game killed by Glyn, Little, and myself, including a few odd caribou or sheep which the natives killed for meat, is appended below :—

Brown bears .	13	Wolverine .	1
Black bears .	2	Porcupine .	6
Moose .	6	Rabbits .	31
Sheep .	15	Eagles .	3
Caribou	7	Grouse and ptarmigan .	108
Seal .	3	Geese, ducks, and various	
Fox .	2	varieties of other birds, in	
Otter .	1	all about .	60 species

All the specimens of animal and bird skins were carefully skinned and cured under the personal supervision of Little, and as the majority of them have met with an untimely fate since I commenced to write this work, a few notes on the disaster may serve as a timely warning to others.

On arrival at Seattle, in order to save the heavy expenses of freight by rail across the continent of America, we decided to send home all the trophies by sea, *via* Yokohama. For this purpose the whole lot was packed in two large wooden cases, the latter unfortunately not being lined with tin. In addition to this omission, we foolishly did not insure all the valuable specimens. Glyn and Little, who personally superintended the loading of our cases on board ship, thoughtfully saw that they were placed last in the hold and on top of the other cargo, thus avoiding the chance of getting damp at the bottom of the hold. The vessel conveying these things belonged to a big Japanese steamship company, and as she was a large and fast boat, by the fortune of war, on arrival at Yokohama, she was at once commanded to unload her cargo in order to be used as a transport by the Japanese Government during the war which had just commenced between Russia and Japan. In consequence, our cases and the other cargo were transferred to another ship, and owing to their position on top of the cargo in the first vessel, they became the bottom cases in the other ship. This second ship was named the *Bingo Maru*, and after escaping capture by the Russians and other perils at sea, she safely arrived in the London docks. Here, however, by the irony of fate, she caught fire. The fire was eventually extinguished, but for some extraordinary reason the cargo was left under water in the hold for many days afterwards. Although not damaged by fire, our cases were full of water when opened, and the result was that all our skins, including a fine collection which we hoped to present to the British Museum, were practically ruined, little save the horns and skulls being left for us. It has truly been since well described by a friend of mine as "the disaster of a lifetime."

CHAPTER V

THE COMMENCEMENT OF THE TRIP

PERHAPS one of the smartest deals ever done by a proverbially smart nation was the purchase of Alaska in 1867 by the American Government from Russia for a paltry sum of $7,000,000. In spite of the fact that, at the time of Secretary Seward's scheme for the purchase, a number of Americans were pleased to ridicule what they designated as " Seward's folly " in buying a mass of icebergs, many of those men lived to recall their words, and the Russians to realise that they had " got hold of the dirty end of the stick."

Regarded as a financial investment it was good, since the country has never yielded less than 5 per cent on the purchase price, and its future possibilities in mineral wealth, etc., are practically unlimited. From a sportsman's point of view the country is still a paradise, for big game of various kinds still abounds ; and owing to the stringent Game Laws passed by the U.S. Government in 1903 it appears to be well protected for many years to come.

In its present form the Alaska Game Law is certainly, as we have seen, open to some amendments, but viewed as a whole it is a step in the right direction, and opportunely taken. It would be sad to think that the noble moose, caribou, and bears now roaming over the country might be

75

subject to the persecution and utter extermination which overtook the unfortunate buffalo on the prairies of North-West
America within recent years. Hitherto the actual hunting
in Alaska has been carried on chiefly by miners and
prospectors, for the purpose of obtaining food for themselves,
and also by the natives with the same object, and that
of trading in the meat, fur, and heads.

To this general rule the few exceptions have consisted
of small parties of English and American sportsmen, who
have visited Alaska to collect specimens for science and
for sport. Of the former perhaps my friend Mr. J. T.
Studley may be called the pioneer, and his first trip to the
Kenai Peninsula in 1898 furnished such trophies that it
inspired a few others to follow his example. Foremost
amongst these may be reckoned Mr. F. Paget in 1901 and
1902, Colonel Claude Cane in 1902, and Mr. A. S. Reed in
1900 and 1901. The last-named sportsman has undoubtedly
the greatest experience of the country, and the finest collection
of big game trophies from Alaska of any hunter who has yet
visited that district for sport, and to him the present writer
is indebted for a store of useful information and kindly
assistance impossible to obtain elsewhere, for which he is
duly grateful. The same remarks apply to the information
supplied by Colonel Cane, whose account of his expedition
finally decided me to undertake this trip in 1903. Another
party of English sportsmen, consisting of Messrs. Lister
and Cowan, visited the Cook's Inlet country in 1901. Of
American hunters in Alaska the best-known men have been
Mr. Dal de Weese in 1898 and 1899, and Messrs. Kidder
and Blake, who also spent two seasons in the country.

Mr. A. J. Stone, representing the New York Museum, has
done good work collecting for several seasons in Alaska.

From Southampton to Western Alaska is a far cry, and a glance at the map suffices to give a fair idea of the distance to be travelled.   But nothing short of the actual experience of passing over the route can convey to the mind of the hitherto uninitiated the immense variety of country and scenery through which one has to pass, and the vastness of the territory which is reached at last.   The comforts of travelling in these days of Pullman cars and fast trains afford ample leisure, but perhaps too much of the kaleidoscope effect for real observation of the country *en route*.

Racing along by day and night across America, the traveller views an endless panorama of great cities, vast prairies, and the lofty Rocky Mountains, past which he flies with a speed which would have surprised the hardy old frontier-men of a generation ago, whom it cost many weary days to cross the lands which the Great Northern Flier now traverses with its freight of passengers from St. Paul to Seattle in less than three days' journey.

For the benefit of those intending to make a shooting trip in Alaska, it may be here stated that as the present Game Law is subject to probable alterations, and as permits to kill a certain limited number of big game are necessary, it is wise to travel *via* Washington, and there to visit the office of the Minister of Agriculture, whence the permits are issued. On the occasion of a recent visit there I found myself treated with the greatest courtesy by all the officials.   Permits were granted us as requested, maps of Alaska presented by the authorities of the Geographical Survey Department, and a large amount of useful information on scientific and sporting subjects kindly furnished by Dr. Merriam, the talented chief of the Biological Survey Department.   The prompt and willingly given assistance which we received in each depart-

ment was, indeed, as welcome as it was unexpected. For
general information a copy of the Game Laws of Alaska,
1903, has been given in this volume.

It should be borne in mind that in all matters, except
such as relate to one's own particular fancy in rifles and
ammunition, it is best to equip the expedition from a place
as near the end of the journey as possible, thereby saving
considerable expense in extra freight, etc., across America.
For this purpose the town of Seattle will be found most
convenient, since it is there that the Alaskan steamers
embark their passengers. Touching the matter of ammunition, when travelling across America, a warning may be
taken from the fate of a box containing all the bullets
which we conveyed with great care as far as Washington.
There it was lost, and the following was the manner of
its losing. All heavy baggage being usually forwarded from
one place to another by Express Companies, it is usual to
deliver it to the agents of these Companies, who undertake
to hand it over safely on arrival at your destination. In our
case no demur was made by the Express Company from
New York to Washington to conveying the ammunition,
but to our dismay, on arrival at Chicago, a telegram was
received saying that the authorities refused to forward it by
express from Washington, and that the box must follow us
by freight train. As this meant in all probability a delay of
weeks, we had to leave Seattle without it, and to equip
ourselves with other rifles for which we could obtain ammunition until our own arrived, since we found it impossible to
get bullets there for our .256 Mannlichers. The moral of
this tale is, Never let your ammunition out of your sight, even
if it means carrying it on your person or in your hand-bags.

As regards camp equipment, the outfit should be as small

and light as possible, since the only means of transport over the country is on your own and your men's backs, and unless you are prepared to make a big outlay, in a country where a native demands anything from a dollar to two and a half dollars per diem, a large camp-following is likely to be expensive.   Small tents made of cotton or light drill will be found best.   A tent similar to those used by prospectors in Alaska, which will accommodate two men, weighs less than 10 lbs., and will answer the purpose well.   A light stove will be found a useful addition, especially when shooting on the western part of the Alaska Peninsula, where timber is scarce and the only fuel obtainable is driftwood and scrub bushes.   For the rest, a good pair of high "gum-boots," which are often required when wading streams, and a rain-proof coat, together with a complete change of clothes, should suffice.   Such tinned provisions as suit the taste of the individual may be taken, but a good quantity of fresh meat can generally be obtained where wild-fowl and ptarmigan are abundant, as is the case in most places along the coast. One great drawback to the pleasure of a trip in Alaska is the incessant rain in the spring and the fall of the year.   Another is the pest of mosquitoes, and the myriads of vicious biting flies or gnats, to guard against which the hunter should be provided with a supply of mosquito netting and a pair of long gauntlets.   As already stated, the allowance of cooking-pots, etc., should be cut down to the smallest and lightest limit possible.

It is impossible to name the exact date in the spring when the snow will have sufficiently disappeared to commence hunting operations in Alaska.   It is, however, better to be too early than too late, if bear-hunting is intended, since the pelts are at their best when the bears first come out after

hibernating.   In an ordinary season, if the hunter is on his
ground by the first week in May, he will be in good time to
commence work.

It was the intention of my friend Mr. R. F. Glyn and
myself when we left England on March 11, 1903, to be in
Alaska even earlier than the date mentioned.   March 26
found us safely arrived in Victoria, B.C., after spending three
or four days in New York and Washington to get the
necessary shooting permits and other indispensable things.
In Victoria we were fortunate enough to secure the services
of Mr. Clifford Little as a hunter, taxidermist, and companion on our trip.   He had already made two trips to
Alaska on similar expeditions, and his former experience was
naturally of great assistance.

Here also we were kindly elected temporary members of
the Union Club.   This excellent Club can show quite a host
of well-known sportsmen amongst its members, and fortunate
indeed were we to find many of them there on our arrival.
Amongst others was Mr. Reed, to whom I have already
referred, part of whose magnificent collection of trophies
adorns the Club walls in great profusion.   There may be seen
his record moose head, a grand specimen of 76 inches span.
There too is the world's record caribou head, together with
bear, walrus, and the white bighorn sheep (*Ovis dalli*) galore,
all showing what Alaska can still produce, and raising in the
heart of a hunter *en route* for that happy hunting-ground
the wildest dreams and endless possibilities of the result of
his own trip.

Once in Victoria, the only thing to be done was to await
the departure of a steamer from Seattle.   Since it appeared
that we could not get away before April 7, it was decided to
pay a visit to Cowichan Lake on Vancouver Island, where

WINDFALLEN TIMBER, COWICHAN LAKE, VANCOUVER ISLAND.

R. F. Glyn sitting on fallen log.

chances were reported of picking up a black bear. After a
matter of 40 miles by rail from Victoria, and a further 20
miles by road, in a bone-shaking conveyance which rejoiced
in the name of a stage-coach, and was drawn by a pair of
horses at a best pace of about 6 miles an hour, we found
ourselves in the comfortable but isolated little hotel on
Cowichan Lake. Three or four days spent partly in fishing,
and partly in climbing over miles of huge fallen timber and
up steep little mountains, resulted in the capture of one
rainbow trout, and the sight of a few black-tailed deer
which carried no horns at this time of year. On our final
return to Victoria we had our host's assurances that we
had come too early for good sport, and in this we thoroughly
agreed with him. But, in justice to the lake and its
charming surroundings, it should be stated that it can produce good fishing and decent shooting, in due season for
each.

On the evening of April 7 we found ourselves on board
the steamer *Bertha*, outward bound from Seattle, with fine
weather, and a cheerful but mixed lot of passengers on board.
The latter were composed of a collection of mine-owners,
prospectors, and heads of some of the great salmon-canneries
situated on the Alaskan coast. Here, then, we had ample
material from which to furnish ourselves with the most
thrilling yarns of shooting, fishing, and mining exploits, and
of the nature and customs of Alaska as it was and as it now
is. It is a big country, and some of the stories were in
proportion to its size!

If the sportsman has any doubts on the subject of Alaska
being a marvellous country, he need only step into the
smoking-room on board such a ship as the *Bertha* and start
the ball rolling by putting a few leading questions, and then

sit down to listen, since all the information required is readily forthcoming.

In answer to the question, " I suppose it rains more in Alaska than any place you know ? " the following information was given :

" Wal, I guess that's so. There is a wooden pier right here, at my salmon-cannery, and on it the planks are about 15 inches wide, and about an inch space between each plank, and when it rains real hard, the water stands about 4 inches deep on that thar pier. If you don't believe it, come and see the planks."

" I suppose it is a job to get any dry clothes to put on when it rains every day ? "

" Why, certainly ; but then when it rains hard with a wind, you just go right along and hang your coat out in the rain, and it goes through the coat so fast that it dries itself, you see."

" Mosquitoes ? You bet ! Why, there is a place near us called Mosquito Bay, and one day we ran in there with a small vessel and tried to anchor about 100 yards from the shore, but a cloud of them mosquitoes just came out so thick that we had to give it up ; we could not see the shore and did not know where we were."

" Big ones, are they ? I should say ! Why, not long ago there were two men coming down the Yukon in a small covered boat, and they saw one of them big ones coming towards them from the bank. They got scared and hid themselves in the bottom of the boat, and that mosquito was just mad and started on gnawing at the top of the mast. They heard the sawdust and chips falling down into the boat ; but presently the mosquito quit that and flew back to the shore, and when last they saw it, the brute was killing a native dog on the bank."

"Bears ain't what they used to be? No, sir! Why, some years ago I was walking along a narrow sort of pathway on the face of some steep rocks, sort of prospecting for coal, when I heard something coming. It turned out to be a bear, and I had to shoot it to get it out of the way. The path was not very long, but darn me if there were not six of them bears following each other like dogs, and I had to shoot the lot before I could get on." The remarkable thing about the last yarn is that the writer has good reasons for believing that the main facts are true.

The trip from Seattle to Sitka in fine weather, early in the spring, is one of which the beauty beats all description. The route lies through a long succession of narrow channels and fjords which closely resemble those of Norway, but are on a grander scale. On each side of these fjords rise towering mountains, with their heavily timbered slopes deep in snow, running right down to the water's edge. Here and there a huge glacier intervenes, one end of which reaches to the sea, and the other goes winding away out of sight behind the snow-clad peaks in the far distance. As for the Alaskan mountains (to use the words of a writer on the Italian heights), "they are so utterly unlike any other hills in the world, and so extremely beautiful in their own peculiar way, that to describe them would be an idle and a useless task, which could only serve to exhibit the vanity of the writer and the feebleness of his pen."

The amount of snow still lying on the ground did not look hopeful for the early appearance of the bears, and on arrival at Valdez it was not comforting to see the snow piled up some 15 feet high in the streets of that small town, nor to be gravely informed that they had experienced a record severe winter, during which the total snowfall had rather

THE TOWN OF KODIAK (ST. PAUL), KODIAK ISLAND, APRIL 1903.

exceeded 64 feet. Since the *Bertha* did not run farther north than Kodiak Island, this had to be perforce our resting-place for a while. After numerous delays, whilst waiting for favourable tides to negotiate bad channels, and also to unload cargo at various small ports, we finally arrived at Kodiak on April 22, and were soon established in comfortable quarters at the head office of the Alaska Commercial Company, where the hospitable manager, Mr. Goss, did all in his power to assist us.

Here again the news was bad, as heavy snow was reported on the south side of the Alaska Peninsula, which we intended to make our first hunting-ground for bears. Moreover, our only way of getting from Kodiak to the mainland was by means of a small schooner named the *Alice*, which was then lying on the shore almost a wreck ; and although the services of this boat and her owner were placed at our disposal, we saw it would be many days ere we could hope to leave the island. As none of the celebrated Kodiak bears were yet to be seen, we were obliged to content ourselves with walking round the island and collecting a few specimens of the Kodiak birds, which I had promised to obtain for the British Museum, and in the meantime all available hands were set on to repair the disabled schooner. Here we had our first sample of Alaskan rain, since it rained and blew hard for thirteen days out of the fourteen which we spent at Kodiak. It was during this enforced waiting at Kodiak that a second stroke of misfortune fell upon us. It had its origin in the arrival from the mainland of a man who had lived for several years on the Alaskan Peninsula, and, according to all accounts, had done considerable hunting there. His reports of the number of bears around a certain lake in the neighbourhood of Aniakchak Bay, near which place he lived, induced us finally to decide on abandoning our original scheme of going direct to Unga Island, and thence on to the western portion of the Alaska Peninsula, where we knew from trustworthy evidence that bears were still numerous.   However, as our informant was well known by many of the residents at Kodiak, and pronounced to be a person of credit, we were inclined to believe his assurances that if we reached the lake which lay some miles inland we should get all the bears we required.   So then, in an evil hour, on May 5, we decided to set sail for Aniakchak Bay.   Arrangements had been made to engage the services of a native Aleut, by name Nicolai Picoon, living on Afognak Island, a hunter of some repute, who had previously accompanied Messrs. Kidder and Blake on their shooting trip in 1901.

One day's sailing took us to Afognak, where we shipped this man on board with his bidarki, or native canoe. These small boats are made of a light wooden frame, somewhat on the lines of the Rob Roy canoes.   The frame is covered with the skins of hair-seals, and two or three open hatches are made according to the number of persons which the bidarki is capable of carrying.   The natives paddle them with single-blade paddles, sitting in a peculiarly cramped position on their heels in the bottom of the bidarkis.   They are very light, and when empty can be easily carried on the shoulders of two men.   Although very easily capsized, it is surprising what a heavy sea they will stand when handled by experienced men.   They travel very fast, and can easily keep up a pace of five or six miles an hour in good water.   I have been many miles a day in one through heavy seas and breakers, scarcely daring to breathe, much less move hand or foot, with the feeling that one's hair should be parted in the centre to keep the bidarki balanced, and have lived to tell the tale, suffering no worse fate than a good wetting when we went clean through the big waves. For river work these small boats are excellent, since they draw very little water, are easily taken out when passing bad places, and are capable of carrying several hundred pounds of freight.

Our voyage from Afognak onwards was not productive of any very noteworthy events, except for the fact that the weather was about as bad as possible, and in consequence

THE AUTHOR AND NATIVES IN BIDARKI, BEAR RIVER, BERING SEA COAST.

some eleven days were spent beating against head winds, or running into shelter, on a voyage which under favourable conditions should have occupied three or four days at the most. This is the common state of affairs along the coast of Alaska, and any one wishing to attempt sailing there, particularly early or late in the season, should be prepared beforehand with a plentiful supply of patience and spare time to waste. The ideal method of travelling the coast on such a shooting trip would be to charter a small tug or steam launch from San Francisco or Seattle, sufficiently large for comfort, and small enough to run into any of the bays where it is required to stop and hunt. By this means it would be possible to make certain of getting to the right place for the different kinds of game at the right season, a thing which our expedition failed to do, although we covered the whole extent of country from Saldovia to a point many miles along the northern coast of the Alaska Peninsula in the Bering Sea. Whilst passing along the shores of Kodiak, Afognak, and Uganuk Islands, a sharp look-out was kept for any early bears which might have made their way down to the shore in any of the bays which we passed, since the sight of bears is by no means an uncommon one from the deck of a vessel coasting along the islands. In our case the search was fruitless. At a small place called Old Woman's Bay, on Uganuk Island, we rowed ashore to the mouth of a small salt lagoon. Here there were great flocks of harlequin and other ducks, a number of which we bagged with the gun, standing behind a rock at a narrow neck between the lagoon and open sea, where the ducks afforded some fine shots as they came flying in from the sea with a strong wind behind them. Near this place also we took the eggs of a pair of bald-headed eagles which had foolishly built their nest in a low tree. Glyn managed to bag one of the old birds with a good long shot from his rifle.

Matters were slow until our arrival at Aniakchak Bay on May 16. The next day found us busy unloading stores from the ship, and finally established in a base camp at the mouth of a big river up which we were to travel. Two days later we started off up the river. The bidarki and a dory (a good-sized flat-bottomed boat) were loaded up with stores and tents, two natives towing them up the stream. The going was by no means good, as the river teemed with sandbanks and shallows, over which it was necessary to haul and push the boats by getting into the water. The weather also on several days was vile. It alternated between gales of wind and storms of rain and snow, with now and then a fine warm day, and once following close on frost and snow, a hot day ending in a thunderstorm in the evening. The thunderstorm was regarded as a rare occurrence in those parts. The lack of timber along the river-banks made it hard to find suitable camping-places, and when found, the gales of wind were a constant source of annoyance, frequently blowing down our tents. The frost was, indeed, barely out of the ground, certainly not more than three inches below the surface, and in consequence to peg down the tents securely was a matter of sheer impossibility. Taken as a whole, the days spent towing up this river were not an unalloyed joy, but fortunately they were the only ones on which we suffered any real discomforts from the Alaskan weather, which we had been led to expect far worse than the realisation. The actual towing up to the head of the river occupied some four or five days, but it was the 27th of the month before we finally pitched camp by the side of the lake. For several days previous to this a sharp look-out had been kept along the hillsides of the river valley, in the vain hopes of seeing bear, and several wide reconnaissances had been made in front and on each flank of the line of advance. Our only rewards were a few old tracks of bears on the snow patches in the hills, and many old signs of the previous year where bears had been digging for ground-squirrels, etc. We had been led to expect plenty of caribou in the valley, and were counting much on this form of meat. On the third day up the river it was therefore with some relief that I saw through the glasses six or seven of them feeding near the

river.   Little and I started off with our rifles to stalk them.
This was not a matter of great difficulty, since, given the
right wind, they are the most stupid and easy brutes to
stalk.   Our intention had been to kill two of them, but of
course, as often happens, we both put a bullet into the same
beast ; and as the magazine of my Mannlicher then jammed,
I could not fire at any of the others.   There was, however,
one unfortunate fact for the caribou, which had not been
altogether unforeseen by me.   This was that Glyn, who
had been away all day looking for bear on the hills, had
also spotted the caribou on his return journey, and was at
that moment stalking them from the opposite direction.   As
the remainder of the small band galloped past him, he
dropped an old buck with a long shot.   It was probably a
fortunate event for Glyn that I was unable to fire again,
as he was almost directly in the line of fire, and he afterwards informed us that he heard passing over his head the
familiar song of a bullet, which Little had sent after the disappearing caribou, but added that he was soon perfectly safe,
since, profiting by recent experiences in the South African
campaign, he at once took cover behind a convenient rise
in the ground.

On arrival at the lake the outlook was not promising.   It
was a singularly desolate and forsaken-looking spot, particularly at this time of year, when it lacked even the relief of a
few patches of green grass to vary the monotony of the endless waste of volcanic ashes and tundra which covered the
valley, backed by its snow-clad mountains rising on either
side, devoid of any form of timber, save only a few clumps
of stunted alder-bushes still half buried in snow.   The lake
itself was circular in shape and about one mile in diameter.
On the north side rose a single conical-shaped mountain

about 3000 feet high, still covered with snow down to its lowest slopes. On two sides of the lake lay a boggy marsh, inhabited by nothing except a few seagulls, terns, and a number of various kinds of sandpipers. These latter birds are very numerous, and in great variety all along the river valley, and nothing but the fact of our having no small shot cartridges prevented our making a fine collection of their skins. There were also great numbers of ducks along the river, the harlequins predominating, but considering how seldom they can have seen a human being, their wildness was remarkable, for it was seldom they could be approached within gunshot after they caught sight of a man. In consequence, such as found their way into our cooking-pots were bagged with a small .22 rifle, and then only after much crawling along the river-banks to get near them. Along its upper reaches, for a distance of some twelve miles, the river followed a very winding course, through a wide valley some five or six miles across. The bed of the valley was a large desolate plain, covered with volcanic rocks and ashes, for the greater part devoid of vegetation, though here and there grew patches of scrub willow, and in places closely resembling an Irish snipe-bog. The whole was intersected by numerous small streams running into the main river. These, thus early in the season, were still covered with deep snow, which, as it began to thaw, made the travelling decidedly bad, and often dangerous in places where the snow was thin, since the sides of these streams were very steep, and a fall through the thin crust of snow often meant a drop of 30 feet or more before reaching the bottom of the gully. When clear of snow, the crossing of these streams was a constant source of wet feet to those unprovided, as was the writer, with a good pair of long field boots. These boots will be found invaluable in Alaska, where a day's walking invariably necessitates wading through endless streams and marshes about half-way up to the knee, and the only alternatives are the wearing of long thigh "gum-boots," in which walking is a misery, or everlastingly filling one's short boots with ice-cold water.

Our first business after reaching the lake was to search for any fresh traces of bear. Signs there were in abundance, such as well-worn trails around the lake, places where bears had pulled out salmon on its banks, and great excavations where they had been digging along the sides of the foot-hills. But, alas, not one of the signs was fresh, the evident fact being that all these traces dated from the previous season. Further search on the hills revealed a few tracks on the snow, all many days old. That there were bears here at certain times of the year was evident, but that there was probably then not one within miles of the lake, we were fully satisfied. Where, then, could they be?

Now the position of the lake was curious. Although situated close to the head of the river up which we had come, there was no stream connecting lake and river. It was exactly on the divide between our valley and another through which a large river flowed into the Bering Sea. We estimated that sea to be between 30 and 40 miles distant on the other side of the Peninsula. Out of the lake flowed a small stream into the Bering Sea river which was not shown on any map then issued, but I afterwards discovered that this river flowed into Port Haiden in the Bering Sea and was called by the natives the Meshik River. By this route the salmon reached the lake, but not till late in the summer. Here then was, as we believed, the solution of the problem, and therewith the utter blasting of our hopes of obtaining a good lot of bear skins in the spring before their pelts became

thin and rubbed.   We soon came to the conclusion that the
bears had made tracks towards the mouth of the river to
await the run of salmon some time in June, and would then
probably follow the fish up to the lake, where they could
easily catch them late in the fall, when salmon are weak after
spawning.   All this looked doubly certain because, in that
exceptionally late spring, all the hillsides were still quite bare
of any young grass or other food for bears.

CHAPTER VI

BETTER FORTUNES WITH THE GREAT BEARS

EXACTLY how the mistake of which we had thus been made victims arose, I never knew, but it is certain . that our informant must have visited this lake late in the season, when no doubt it was possible for him to see and shoot as many bears as he said he had done, but nothing will induce me to believe that there were many bears round that neighbourhood in the spring of 1903. The general outlook of affairs was not bright at that time, and the feelings of our party at having been so utterly fooled, were freely expressed but are best not stated in print. We were stranded there without hopes of getting away for some time, as on landing we had sent the schooner back to Kodiak with orders to return in about a month, by which time we hoped to have all the bears we wanted, and then to sail farther to the west in the anticipation of getting a walrus or two on the Bering Sea coast. Here let me add a warning to all sportsmen who may visit Alaska in the future, lest they should be ever led astray so far as to visit the shores of any lake in search of bears during the spring. Look for them rather on the seashore, and along the slopes of the hillsides where the young grass is beginning to grow in sheltered spots.

The most annoying part of the whole business was that

we knew of several other places, and had even passed close
by them, where we might have made certain of picking up a
fair number of bears.   But as we required a good many to
fill our permits, and as I was particularly anxious to secure
an extra large specimen of the Alaskan brown bear for the
British Museum, we had decided to go far away from the
beaten track of all former hunting parties in the hopes of
getting what we sought.   The foolish part of the affair
was that we had put all our eggs into one basket, and
that basket had broken down badly, as we had fairly burned
all bridges behind us in sending away the schooner.   On
May 29, Glyn decided to make an expedition down the river
which flowed towards the Bering Sea, and with this purpose
in view he and the two natives set out down stream in the
bidarki, taking with them supplies for five or six days.   There
were at least hopes that he might meet with some caribou,
as we could see none round the lake, and the food supply
promised to become ere long a serious question.   I remained
near the lake with Little, where for two days and nights we
were treated with samples of what the wind can do on the
Alaska Peninsula.   It blows there in a peculiar way of its
own.   The wind seems to come simultaneously from all four
quarters of the globe, rushing up and down the valleys, and
even if you think you have defeated it by getting on the
leeward side of a mountain, it comes rushing round the
corner and still hits you in the face.   No matter what
you may be doing, nor in which direction going, the prevailing wind of the Alaska Peninsula is always a head wind,
that is, excepting when stalking an animal, and for that
purpose the wind seldom seems right.   The only engine of
discomfort approaching it, which I have ever seen, is a dust
storm on the veldt in South Africa; but in Alaska rain takes

STARTING TO TOW UP THE ANIAKCHAK RIVER.

the place of dust.   In both countries I have remarked the
surprising ease with which the wind will flatten the best-
pitched tent, and compel its unwilling occupants to face the
elements in their futile attempts to fix ropes, etc., securely.

May 31 dawned at last, a fine warm day, a harbinger of
the long-expected spring, which was then some three or four
weeks overdue.   I remarked to Little before leaving camp
in the morning, that if we were going to kill a May bear we
must make haste about it ; and furthermore, that as it was
now some five weeks since we first set foot on Kodiak Island,
during which time we had not seen a bear at all, I felt rather
like my Norwegian boatman and gaffer on the Namsen
River, Norway, who has a quaint saying when the river is
in bad fishing order.   His morning greeting on such
occasions is, " I have generally a good hope, but I have not
a good hope to-day."

We took our daily tramp across the desolate plain in
front of the camp, and sat down on a small sand-hill to scan
the hills with our glasses.   After looking in every direction
without success, and being on the point of returning to camp,
about 2 P.M., I saw with the naked eye what appeared to
me to be two foxes playing on a snow patch high up on the
face of a hill opposite where we sat.   Turning our glasses
on them, one beast appeared to be nearly white, and we said
at once, " They are only caribou," and too high up to be worth
going after.   This seemed more particularly true as there
were a wide river and several streams to wade which lay
between us and the hills.   After watching them closely for
some time, the animals began to walk along the hillside, and
with such an unmistakably clumsy gait that we both jumped
up, exclaiming, " Bears at last."   Such was undoubtedly the
case, but we were over two miles from the foot of the hill,

and the bears were some 1000 feet or more above us.   They might go miles ere we could reach them.   However, it was worth a trial, and not hesitating to think of the cold, we rushed down the bank of the river and plunged into it.   It was here a raging torrent about 60 yards wide and as cold as the ice and snow from which it sprang in the mountains far above.   With some difficulty in keeping on our legs, we crossed it ; then, running fast across the level plain, panting and blowing, we started up the mountain side, still keeping the bears in sight.   By the irony of fate, it had now of course turned very warm, and when half-way up, I thought I should burst a blood-vessel.   Throwing myself on the ground, I asked Little, who was in better condition than I was, to go ahead and try to keep the bears in sight, as they were gradually going higher.   This he did, and as I laboured painfully after him, he located them in a hollow some 500 feet higher than where we first viewed them.   How I managed to get over this last 500 feet I don't know, but I repeatedly sat down utterly beat, and urged Little to go ahead and shoot at the bears.   This he refused to do, saying if I could not get up to them, he would not take the honour of killing our first bear.   It was fortunate for us that the two beasts were so occupied in their attentions to each other that they did not travel very fast.   It was soon obvious to us that they were a male and she bear which had paired off, and although the opportunity of studying them was freely given us, I feared that ere long they would receive an unexpected interruption to their amorous gambols.   At last, on reaching a ridge whence we could look down on a hollow below, we saw the two bears about 80 yards away, and slightly below us.   We had previously arranged that Little should take the dark-coloured animal, whilst I had a predilection for the light-coloured male.   So utterly beat was I, and so afraid of a further repetition of our climb if the bears got over another ridge, that, without stopping to get my wind or a steady aim, I fired hurriedly, putting in two shots from my Mannlicher as fast as I could load.   It appeared to me that I hit my beast with the first shot, as, startled by the report of the rifle, he almost fell.   Subsequent examination, however, proved that neither bullet touched the bear.   Little, on the other hand, did better, as with his first shot he broke the hind leg of the she-bear, and turning he put a shot into the other bear, thinking it was going away wounded.   As the latter was still going, but pretty sick, I gave him another shot, this time in the neck, and he fell like a log without moving.   We afterwards found that this bullet had smashed a bone of his neck clean in half.   Little then started pumping lead after the other bear, which was shuffling off downhill at a good rate with a broken leg, and giving forth terrible snarls and groans.   Five or six shots seemed to have no result, except one bullet which, we could see, hit the bear in the nose.   Finally, taking my rifle, in which there still remained two cartridges, Little gave her a bullet in the shoulder which settled her.   On examining the bear, we found that nearly all the bullets had gone through her feet and legs, and this was owing to the fact that after firing the first shot, the back-sight on Little's rifle had fallen down, and in the excitement of the moment he had not noticed that he was shooting without it.

Both bears were small ones, the female being the larger, but her skin, when taken off and spread on the ground, only measured 7 feet 8 inches, and the actual body, from nose to tail, was much shorter.   No measurement of the skin alone can give an accurate idea of the size of the beast from which it was taken. The male was a few inches smaller, but carried a remarkably fine coat, which was of a very light fawn colour, and looked in the distance almost white. Both skins were in fine order, and we judged the male to be a two-year-old, and the female one year older. Their bodies were rolling in fat, and as they could not have been long out from winter quarters, it showed how remarkably fat these animals keep all through the long winter months when they "hole up" and eat nothing during the entire period.

Our day's work had been satisfactory but was by no means over. We had next to skin both bears and pack home the pelts on our own backs, as the only two natives were away with Glyn. The skinning was one of the coldest jobs I ever remember. The wind was blowing bitterly cold off the ice and snow around us, and we were standing in snow slush many inches deep, with our boots already full of water and wet to the skin above the waist. To make matters worse we had but one skinning knife between us, no whetstone, and no rope or straps with which to make a neat pack of the skins. The packing of them afterwards, with the skulls and feet, etc., back to camp, was no child's play.

The picture of two weary men, covered with blood and grease, toiling slowly down the mountain side with their burdens, through swamps and rivers, five or six miles to camp, to a constant accompaniment of the smell of bear's grease, lingers yet with me in a vividness which is only possible to one who actually took part in the scene.

Next day Little and I were busy cleaning and "fixing up" the skins and skulls. This is a job essentially for natives, but being also one which will not wait, we had to do our best, which was by no means bad.

The following day Glyn returned from his trip down the
river. He reported that the river ran down a great valley
which was one vast swamp, and that to cover a distance of
some twenty miles straight the river flowed nearly twice that
distance. He had been unable to reach the sea owing to
lack of provisions for the return journey, but as he drew
nearer to the coast, there were many fresh tracks of bears on
the hills and river-banks. He had not actually seen a bear,
but all the signs tended to show that the bears from the
mountains and the neighbourhood of the lake were making
their way towards the Bering Sea. This was indeed what
we had surmised after a few days spent near the lake. There
is little doubt that the favourite food of these bears is salmon,
and as soon as the fish are due at the river-mouth in the early
part of June, most bears work towards the sea, there to await
the run of fish and follow them up as far as they go. Distance
is no object to a bear, and it is surprising how far these beasts
will travel in a day, even in such mountainous country as
this, especially early in the season, when all kinds of food are
scarce.

Glyn had managed to bag two caribou, which put the
meat question at rest for some time, and although rather thin
at this season of the year, they were excellent eating and a
pleasant change from the inevitable bacon and Yukon straw-
berries (as beans are called in Alaska), which form the staple
food of a hunting party there.

As we were convinced that we had bagged the only two
bears that had lived within a radius of many miles from the
camp, nothing then remained but a sorrowful return to the
coast to await the arrival of the schooner *Alice* from Kodiak.
For a wonder we were favoured with bright sunshine and a
pleasant day for our trip down, which was easily accomplished

in a day and was a very different matter, as we floated down the stream in the dory and bidarki, from the tedious under-taking of towing the boats up the river.

On the way down we happened on the camp of two Aleuts, who had come up the river from a neighbouring settlement to hunt for meat. They had just killed a small caribou, the skin and flesh of which lay by their tent. They were a quaint-looking couple with their small figures, rather large heads,

CAMP OF ALEUT NATIVES HUNTING CARIBOU.

and a peculiar likeness to the Japanese. Their language was different from that of our two natives from Kodiak and Afognak, who had great difficulty in making them understand. But we gathered that they had seen no bear up the river, and they thought our best chance to see one would be to visit the next bay to the westward, where they had seen some bears a short time before. On this Glyn, who was now getting desperate, at once engaged them to take him round to this bay in their bidarki for a few days' hunting until our schooner arrived.

I decided to remain in Aniakchak Bay and do a bit of hunting round a large salt marsh and lake there, where we thought it possible a few bears might come to prospect for salmon and clams along the shore.   Leaving Little and one native in our base camp at the river-mouth, I crossed the bay some five miles with the native Nicolai, and camped near the shore on the edge of the salt lagoon.

Two days later I heard from Little, to the effect that whilst walking along the shore he had caught sight of a wolverine on the beach.   Having nothing but a shot gun with him, he ran to cut off the animal from the only place where it could get away up the rocks.   He managed to get near enough to bag it with a charge of buckshot.   This was a stroke of luck, as, although fairly numerous in those parts, a wolverine is not often seen in daylight.

I spent several days without seeing anything, regularly scanning the bay in the early morning and evening in the hopes of spying the schooner.   It was a performance which constantly recalled to my mind the title of the well-known old song, " Alice, where art thou ? "

On June 13 I saw the first fresh traces of a bear which we had come across for a fortnight.   We struck the tracks of a very large one leading back towards camp.   As these were quite fresh and evidently made during the day, we followed them three miles, hoping in vain to see the bear which must have passed close by the camp during our absence.   He had followed a well-worn trail leading past my tent within full view of it, and only about 200 yards away from it.   The next day it rained so hard, and the fog was so thick, that it was impossible to see 500 yards.   I spent the whole day until 9 P.M. watching the trail in the hopes of seeing my friend returning along it.   A faint hope, but one which might have been realised, as my rage was great when I found early next morning that the brute had actually passed back again on the trail during the night.   His huge hind feet had left a track which exceeded 14 inches in length—truly a beast worthy of sitting up for all night on the bare chance of getting a shot at him.   Another day of fog and rain followed, and I had given up all hopes of ever seeing this bear.   On the 16th, however, the fog lifted a little in the afternoon, and taking Nicolai, I walked about four miles from camp to a small hill, where we sat down to look round.   The persistent attentions of mosquitoes soon brought out my pipe.   Shortly afterwards, happening to glance at the side of a steep mountain opposite, I saw, about 500 yards away, a huge bear galloping along the side of the hill away from us, evidently having caught the scent of my tobacco smoke in a large patch of alders where he had been lying down wind of us.   I was furious, as it looked hopeless to follow him, but there was just one chance. The mountains along which the bear travelled were so precipitous that he could not get up more than a few hundred feet, and the range ran in a V-shape.   There was a low neck in the hills somewhere about a mile and a half distant, in a straight line from where we sat.   To get there, following the hillsides, the bear would have to travel nearly twice that distance, and as it appeared to be the only spot he was making for, I decided to race for it.   I am at the best an indifferent runner, and was then in a pair of high gum-boots reaching to the thigh, probably the most uncomfortable things on earth to run in.   But, quickly telling Nicolai to follow, I started at a run, both of us throwing away coats and waistcoats as we went.   My object was to get as far ahead as possible at first, since we started with a cross wind blowing from us to the bear, which only served to make him go faster.

Our pace could not have been great through swamps, streams, and scrub willows, but it seemed to me like record-breaking; and soon we had the satisfaction of seeing the bear gradually slacken his pace, then stop and look round. By that we knew that we had got a point on the right side of the wind, but we had to strive hard to keep it, as he was soon off again though not moving so fast as before. The bear was much hampered by low and thick alders, and numerous deep gullies running down the mountain slopes. In the distance lay the neck which we strove to reach, and here the valley along which we ran ended abruptly in a cup-shaped basin. At this spot there was a narrow open clearing across which it appeared that the bear must travel if his object was, as we surmised, to reach the top of the hills. Putting on a final spurt, I dashed up to within 20 yards of the high alders on the edge of this clearing, and threw myself panting on the grass in the open. Nicolai, who was hopelessly done up, arrived a few seconds afterwards and followed my example. We had beaten the bear by about 200 yards, and could hear him coming crashing through the bushes towards us. Very soon I saw the high alder-tops moving, about 40 yards from where we sat, and we knew then that the bear was coming straight towards us. When about 10 yards from the edge of the clearing, he stopped and remained perfectly motionless, evidently listening and trying to wind us. He was perfectly invisible in the dense brush, and this was the critical moment, since, if he turned round and retraced his steps, we could not possibly see him or get a chance of a shot. For fully two or three minutes we remained sitting perfectly still, scarcely daring to breath, and then we saw a huge head slowly emerge into the open. Taking a couple of paces forward, until he stood at a spot (which we afterwards measured) only 18 yards from where we sat, the bear stopped and looked at us fairly face to face. I had previously raised my rifle to fire on first seeing his shoulder, but curiosity to find out what he would do, mastered my murderous intentions.   Slowly lowering my rifle on to my knees I sat watching him, and bitterly regretted the absence of my camera in camp.   Keen as I was to obtain his skin, I would have gladly risked the chance of killing him, could I but have got a good picture of this magnificent brute as he then appeared.   He looked splendid, standing there in the full glare of a bright sun, against a dark background of alders.   Nicolai thought I had gone mad, and kept whispering frantically in my ear, " Hurry up, hurry up, shoot quick, he run soon."   But I wanted to see which way he would run, as we had heard so many conflicting yarns about the Alaskan brown bears charging on sight, and the reverse. This one seemed in no hurry to run either way, and after looking steadily at us for a few seconds, he slightly raised his head and gave vent to his surprise by uttering a deep " woof." Whether this was a token of rage or fright I cannot say, but the noise was deep and loud enough to scare anything. Once more he repeated this deep growl, and then took one step towards us, evidently bent on making a closer inspection. This was more than Nicolai could stand, and he fairly shouted in my ear," Shoot, shoot."   Thinking " discretion the better part of valour," I gave the bear a bullet right in the centre of his chest.   He turned a complete somersault towards us, and, getting on his legs a few yards away, gave out some of the most appalling growls and snarls I ever heard, at the same time biting savagely at the small wound in his chest.   I sat quite still, waiting a second till he turned sideways, and then planted a second bullet in his shoulder.   This settled him, and the good little Mannlicher had inflicted the most frightful wounds in both places, as we afterwards found on skinning the body.

Of course I thought at once that we had secured a record, as this was by far the largest bear I had ever seen, alive or dead, but to make sure I said to Nicolai, " Have you ever seen a larger bear than this one ? " After a short inspection he replied, much to my disgust, " He big bear all right, me see bigger bear killed Kodiak Island." Nothing remained to be done except to send back word to Little, who arrived in our camp that morning, reporting our luck and calling for his assistance to help skin and pack the hide back to camp. Whilst skinning the beast, we noticed that he had recently been fighting and had got badly mauled by another bear, as the scratches and fresh blood on his face and feet clearly showed. I remarked to Little that if there was another bear round that neighbourhood large enough to give this one a thrashing, I should like to meet him. Unfortunately we had no tape with us at the time to take the exact measurements of this beast, as Glyn had our only tape away with him, and although I took several measurements with string at the time, none of these can be accepted as accurate. This beast was, however, only a few inches smaller in every measurement than my largest bear, which we measured carefully with the tape soon afterwards. The actual skinning did not occupy much time, as Little and Nicolai were both adepts at the task. The biggest part of the undertaking was packing the skin and skull back to camp. It was a job that fell to the lot of Nicolai, and although only provided with some strong cord which must have cut his shoulders badly, he proceeded to make a pack of the skin and started off with it to camp.

MY FIRST BIG BROWN BEAR.

I did not envy him the task, as the four or five miles back to camp lay over very rough ground, which entailed pushing our way through thick alders, wading several streams, and crossing long stretches of very boggy ground. In these latter spots I, without any pack, often sank in up to my knees, and what Nicolai felt like with his big pack I cannot say, but there is no doubt that his burden was not a light one.   Although small in stature, and with no appearances of great strength, it is surprising what big loads a good Aleut can carry.   It took this man some two hours to cover the journey back to camp.

The following day all hands in camp were busy cleaning the skin and skull. At this work the Aleut again excels, nor do I think it possible to find any natives better at the business, since long experience in preparing furs for the market, and the great number which they have handled for years, make them masters in the art of cleaning skins. Their method is to sit down like tailors, with the skin resting on their knees. They hold a corner of the skin in their teeth, and placing one hand beneath it, and using their knife in the other hand, with great rapidity and dexterity they soon remove every particle of fat and blood from the hide. No white man can compete with them, and I must confess that although I tried it myself on more than one occasion, I felt rather ashamed when I looked at the cleaned part of a skin which represented my own labours, and compared it with a piece cleaned by the natives in the same time. Not only did they do three times as much, but it was also twice as well cleaned as mine. A further damper to my own efforts was the taste of bear's grease, which lingers indefinitely in one's mouth after attempting to hold the skin in one's teeth according to the approved Aleut style.

The next day Little, Nicolai, and I went out in the direction of our last kill. When about two miles from the spot where the carcass lay, we saw a bear feeding on the young grass a few yards from the spot where I first saw the other bear two days before. Even at that distance this fellow looked enormous through the glasses.

It was evidently a case of another smart bit of running, and off we went, Little leading with his advantage of 6 feet 2 inches, and legs in proportion. Both of us were more than a match for Nicolai, who was very blown before we had gone half a mile. On reaching a small knoll about a mile from where we had viewed the bear, we were delighted to see that he was still in the same place, and were just in time to witness a most curious thing. After feeding some time, moving slowly along, the bear reached the exact spot where I had first seen the other one. Here he stopped suddenly, apparently smelling the ground. Taking a look all around, he suddenly whipped quickly to the right-about, and dashed off at a gallop over the brow of the hill. This manœuvre puzzled me, and I at first imagined he must have winded or heard us. This, however, was impossible, and I knew there must be some other reason for the brute's behaviour. I appealed to Nicolai for an explanation, and he said, "Me think he smellum other bear tracks. He run little way, then lie down." There was nothing for it but to make our way to a point whence we could see the ground lying on the other side of the hill over which the bear had gone. This we did, and on looking down from the spot where we last saw our quarry we could perceive nothing but a dense patch of alders, many acres in extent, covering both sides of a deep ravine through which ran a small mountain torrent. So dense was the brush that it was hopeless to push a way through it with a view of getting a shot at the bear, even if we were fortunate enough to walk almost on top of him. At the head of the ravine, and on both sides, the hills towered up some 1000 feet with steep sides. There was just a chance that, by getting to some high point which overlooked the ravine, it might be possible to spot the bear if he was still in the alders. Giving Nicolai my glasses, I told him to hurry up the mountain side, and if he could see anything, to wave his hat. He and Little both started climbing, whilst I remained on the look-out below. Shortly afterwards I saw Nicolai standing on a rocky eminence some 500 feet above me, and after a long scrutiny with the glasses he began waving his hat. The next move in the game was for me to get up to him, and after much puffing and blowing, and scrambling over rocks, I reached the *coin d'avantage*, only to find that I could see no sign of the bear, although both Little and Nicolai declared that he was lying down in a place which did not appear thick enough to hide such a big beast. Then the problem to be solved was how to get a chance of a fair shot at the creature. As the wind was blowing up the ravine towards us, I decided to send Nicolai round to the far side of the alders, to a spot where he could get up wind of the bear and within 150 yards of him, with instructions to light his pipe when there, and remain quietly smoking. This I hoped would have the effect of rousing the bear and make him take off up the hillside, in which case he would give me a good shot in the open. But I had not then, nor have I even to-day, mastered the principle on which the wind blows in Alaska, especially in the gullies along the mountain sides. On this occasion it appeared to be blowing from the low ground upwards, at an angle of about 45°, for after Nicolai had vainly smoked his pipe for five minutes without effect, he proceeded to make a large heap of dead grass and set fire to it, with the result that I could smell the smoke distinctly, but that it appeared to be passing too high over the bear, which never moved. It was clear that some other plan must be tried, and Little, who was some distance from me, shouted to know if he should throw down a rock from the hill. I shouted " No," as I feared that this would drive our friend in the wrong direction. However, our voices had the same effect, as a moment afterwards I caught sight of the head of the bear as he stood up for a moment listening, and then dashed off through the brush—but in the wrong direction for me, as he was heading straight for Nicolai and his fire. Seeing no hope of getting a shot in the open under 500 yards if he kept on in the same line, I lay down as best I could on the sloping ground, judging the distance at about 200 yards, and fired three shots at the small part of the animal's back, which I could see occasionally as he moved through the bushes. He gave a dreadful squeal after my first shot, rather like a pig with its throat cut, and at the third shot stopped on the edge of the stream below us, and appeared too sick to cross it. Here Little got a view of him from his position and fired a shot at him. After going a little farther through the alders, the bear lay down. Nicolai meanwhile, who could see nothing that was going on in the bushes (and presuming, I imagine, that because I had stopped shooting the bear must be dead), started to run into the brush. I shouted to him to stop, but was too far off to make him hear. I then shouted to Little, who was making his way down the hill, to go to the rescue of Nicolai in case the bear should have life enough in him to give chase. Whilst I was blundering down the hillside, I saw Nicolai come running out of the bushes, and momentarily expected to see the bear after him. Fortunately, however, the latter was so sick that he could barely stand, and on Little shouting to say that he could see the bear in the brush, I told him to finish the business, which he did with a bullet in the shoulder. On reaching the spot, I knew that I had got a bear at last, and one that any one might be proud of, even in Alaska. Little said it was the largest he had seen, and, turning to Nicolai, I repeated my question of two days before regarding his opinion, fully expecting the same reply as before, since I suspected Nicolai of having caught the American trick of not liking to be beaten on his former experiences. However, I was agreeably surprised when he at once said, " No, me never see bear so large before." The task of skinning this great brute was not easy ; in fact it took us all we could do to haul the carcass out of a small hollow in the ground where it lay. When skinned, it looked like the carcass of some great bullock, and I guessed its weight at 1400 lbs., since we had heard such tales about these Alaskan bears exceeding 1600 lbs. in weight. Little, on the other hand, said he thought the weight was under 1200 lbs., but as I had provided myself with a weighing machine, in order to get some idea of the weight of the fabulous monsters inhabiting the country, we decided to return on the following day and then weigh the carcass. It was not, however, till two days later that we did return to do this, since it streamed so unceasingly with rain during the next day that none of us cared to face it. As soon as the skull and skin had been made into a pack, and the natives had removed part of the entrails for making cameleekas, we started for home. Nicolai fairly staggered under the weight of his pack, and on his arrival in camp some hours later, I could scarcely induce him to stand up with his pack and be photographed. On placing the skull and skin on the scales, we found the total weight to be 148 lbs., and I sympathised with Nicolai when he subsequently remarked that he hoped I should not get many more bears as big as that one. Two days after we returned to the scene of the kill, and, chopping up the carcass with axes, weighed it carefully. The weight, including the skin, etc., was 968 lbs., and allowing 40 lbs. for the entrails removed, and blood lost during two days, this gives a total weight of about 1010 lbs. I am told that my estimate, and allowance of 40 lbs. for wastage, is well under the mark, but I prefer to err on the right side in such matters, since it is my earnest desire to get the weight of these great bears definitely determined, and as nearly as possible correct. There is no doubt that if this bear had been killed in the fall of the year, just before holing up for the winter, when rolling fat, he would have been heavier on the scales by at least a hundred pounds more than was the case then, when he was in very poor condition. Taking it for granted that this was a fair specimen of the largest Alaskan brown bear—since every one who subsequently saw the skull and skin pronounced it to be so—I assume that it is very unlikely that Alaska produces many bears which exceed 1200 lbs. live weight. One thing is certain, that this bear was of great age, as was evident from the worn and split teeth in his skull, and from the short thick coat which these brown bears only assume in old age. I am therefore certain that he would never have increased in measurements or weight.

As we returned to camp on the evening of our last successful hunt, my joy was great on seeing, far out in the bay, what was unmistakably the good ship *Alice* slowly beating her way towards us. She anchored near the shore

that night, and early next morning Glyn arrived, with his
two natives, in a bidarki from the next bay.

I was delighted to hear that he had at last broken his
run of bad luck, and he produced the skins of a large she-
bear and three cubs. The latter were evidently yearlings, as
they were of considerable size, and were quite disposed to
show fight after the death of their mother. Consequently
Glyn was obliged, much against his sporting inclinations, to
give them their quietus. The incident, as described to me
by Glyn, was rather curious. It appeared that after leaving
our camp about a week before, he had made his way in the
bidarki, with his two natives, a distance of some thirty-five
miles by sea into the next bay, where his men reported good
prospects of finding bear.

Several days of fruitless search were the result, and Glyn
reported the mosquitoes as being absolutely terrific in
numbers and fierceness in the vicinity of his camp. There
was a large tract of swampy ground which is always dear to
the hearts of these venomous pests, and in fact is about the
only place where they are found in great numbers along the
Alaska Peninsula. It is a country bare of the timber and
trees beneath which they swarm along the coast of Alaska.
One rainy morning, during the dense fog peculiar to that
district, which seems to hang like a sheet around your camp,
Glyn was sitting in his tent when one of his natives ran up
explaining that he could see several bears moving about at
no great distance from the tents. Glyn, doubting the statement, and not clearly understanding his native, who could
only speak Aleut, took his rifle and went to investigate.
He soon saw two or three large cubs moving around some
object lying on the grass, and on a closer inspection this
proved to be a large she-bear fast asleep. He decided to

bag her, and leave the cubs to their own devices, knowing that they were quite large enough to be capable of making their own way in the world. Consequently he got within easy range of the sleeping bear and planted a bullet behind her shoulder. She never moved or gave any signs of being hit, and Glyn was uncertain as to the result of his shot. He described how the cubs, on hearing the report, ran to the old bear and tried to rouse her, but without success. She was stone-dead, having been shot right through the heart. Glyn imagined that the cubs would soon leave her and take to the bush, but such was by no means the case. They appeared inclined to assume the offensive on his approaching their mother. He said afterwards that the idea of trying to capture them alive occurred to him, but on mature considera-tion he thought the proceeding too risky, and to save further trouble expended a bullet on each, which settled the matter.

CHAPTER VII

A MOVE TO THE WEST AND THE BERING SEA

On the evening of June 20 we found ourselves once more on board the *Alice*, and heaving anchor, we bid adieu to Aniakchak Bay for 1903. I doubt if I shall ever be induced to visit it again, since the bears are few and far between there in the spring, although, as I have already stated, all along the valley of the river there were abundant traces that they are pretty numerous in the fall, when the lakes and small creeks are full of dead and dying salmon. As a happy hunting-ground for the ornithologist I can recommend this district, since nowhere in Alaska did we find such a variety of sandpipers, waders, and ducks as frequent the rivers of of that district. Also I should say that a good trapper could earn a small fortune in the winter along the banks of the rivers, since the otters and foxes absolutely swarm.

Making our way slowly towards the west with failing winds, and the usual Alaskan head winds when it did blow, we found ourselves on the evening of the 22nd lying in an exceedingly picturesque and sheltered spot, where we dropped anchor and remained whistling for wind. We lay near a spot called Three Star Point, and here the skipper of the *Alice* informed us we were at one of the most celebrated places on the Peninsula for the run of oolichan or candle-

MOVING CAMP ON THE ANIAKCHAK RIVER.

C. E. Radclyffe, C. Little, Aleut native with red fox, and R. F. Glyn.

fish. He added that two friends of his had come over from
Unga Island some seasons ago, and established themselves
here for a few weeks in May during the big run of candle-
fish, at the time when the bears come for miles to feed on
those thrown up by the tide, being particularly partial to
this form of food. These two men were stated to have
killed over thirty bears there in a few weeks, and on making
inquiries afterwards at Unga, I found this to be correct.
The run of oolichan being then over, it was useless for us
to attempt a landing here on the chance of seeing bears,
so we headed for a place called Ivanoff Bay, where bears had
again been reported plentiful. The next evening we made
a landing in this bay, and found a very good barabara or
native hut, which had been built by some white men who
came occasionally from Unga to hunt caribou for meat.
Two rivers run into this bay, and coming as they do across
a large open plain, with numerous creeks running into the
rivers, it appeared an ideal place for bears to come fishing
when the salmon were running. We had been told that
the Alaskan red salmon ran up one of these rivers, and a
large lake was shown on the chart at the head of the river,
which led us to believe the statement. Subsequent search
by Glyn revealed the fact that this lake did not exist, and
consequently the red salmon were conspicuous by their
absence. There were, however, a number of humpbacks
and dog salmon already in the mouth of the river, and
some good bear trails along the banks induced Glyn to stay
here with Little and one native. They spent the greater part
of the next day unloading stores and settling into their new
quarters, whilst I landed in the bidarki on the opposite side
of the bay to take a look round. On nearing the shore we
saw five caribou walking along the beach and looking very

unconcernedly at us in the bidarki.   We could not approach
within 300 yards of the shore without getting out to wade
and carry the bidarki.   I tried wading towards the caribou in
hopes of getting within decent range of them, but as the
wind was blowing every way except the right way, they soon
winded me and made off.   Shortly afterwards, having carried
the bidarki ashore, we carefully reconnoitred all the low ground
near the shore in the hopes of seeing more caribou, as the
meat question was getting rather serious with us on board
the *Alice*.   I caught sight of what appeared to be a single
caribou moving in an open glade which was surrounded by
dense alders and situated on the slope of a hill about a mile
from where we stood.   I pointed out the animal to Nicolai
who said, " Me think big caribou all right."   Before I could
bring the glasses to bear on the beast, it disappeared into the
alders and apparently lay down.   We decided to make a
detour and come over the top of the hill, whence we might
get a good view of the open glade below us.   Moving fast,
we soon reached this spot.   The mosquitoes were terribly
numerous and vindictive here, and compelled me to put on my
mosquito net and a pair of leather gauntlets.   Nothing being
visible from the brow of the hill, and the wind being
favourable, I determined to crawl through the thick alders
and make my way into the open glade on the other side.
Sending the native about 50 yards from me on my left, we
both advanced cautiously, making as little noise as possible.
I had not gone more than 30 yards when I heard a peculiar
grunting noise, but being slightly deaf, was unable to locate
the exact direction from whence it came.   I remained
stationary for a minute, listening, but could not hear the noise
repeated.   I then moved forward a few yards, and this time
the noise was so loud that I knew it was coming from only

a few yards' distance in the thick alders on my right. Peering through the bushes, I just caught sight of the head of a great brown bear about 15 yards away as he jumped up from a spot where he had been lying. It was only the work of a moment to tear off my mosquito net and right glove, but, hampered as I was with bushes which impeded every movement of my arms and rifle, there was no possibility of aiming steadily, nor was there much to aim at except a pair of great ears, as the bear dashed frantically away through the bush. I let go two bullets, one at the vanishing ears and another into the moving bushes which closed behind them as they disappeared. Hearing no sound from the bear, I was convinced that I had made a clean miss, and such was undoubtedly the case, for although we followed his great tracks for several hundred yards, no sign of blood was to be seen. This was evidently the animal which we had taken at a distance for a caribou, and perhaps we were fortunate to escape as we did, since tackling a brown bear in thick bush is no child's play if you wound the brute. Nevertheless I was furious at losing him, and returned to the schooner with the sole consolation of thinking that as I had blundered on a bear in my first hour on shore, therefore Glyn and Little stood a fine chance of picking up some good specimens if they remained there two or three weeks, as it was their intention to do. I did not see either of them on my return to the schooner, so was unable to tell them of this episode, as I was desirous of pushing on to the westward and seeking pastures new.

That evening we beat our way slowly out of Ivanoff Bay and shaped our course for Sand Point on Popoff Island. Another twenty-four hours of battling against unfavourable elements saw me safely landed at Sand Point, where I received a friendly welcome from Mr. Scott, the local post-master, storekeeper, and petty king of Popoff Island. Here I bid adieu to the good ship *Alice*, her pleasant owner Mr. J. Folstad, and her skipper Pavloff, who, by the way, is a grandson of the last Russian Governor of Alaska, and is now in somewhat reduced circumstances when compared with the position held by his ancestors. To him we owed the safe termination of a journey extending several hundred miles along one of the most dangerous and treacherous coasts in the world, of which as yet no correct charts have been made, but where each pilot or skipper relies entirely on his own knowledge of the route, and only a lifetime spent as Pavloff's had been, sailing this coast in all kinds of craft from youth upwards, qualifies a man to undertake the navigating of a vessel in those waters.

Arrived at Sand Point, I began to make arrangements to cross over to a spot called Portage Bay, which lay opposite, on the Peninsula, some fifteen miles distant. I took up my abode in a palatial wooden hotel, which had been built in the palmy days of the great fishing and seal-catching industry. Owing to the sudden falling-off in the profits of these under-takings, the great fleet of boats formerly seen at Sand Point no longer existed. The hotel in consequence remained empty, most of the costly furniture which had originally adorned it having been sold, and thus I found myself the sole occupant of the house, and slept under a roof once more for the first time during many weeks.

One day sufficed me to obtain a few stores, to engage the services of an excellent native called Nikita, and to strike a bargain with the owner of a small sloop who undertook to convey me, the two natives, and my bidarki, across to Portage Bay for the sum of $10. Once again we had all our work cut out to cross the narrow space from Popoff Island to the mainland. The weather was vile, and what with a choppy sea and dense fog, it cost us fifteen hours to traverse the same number of miles. It did not take long to land our few stores, the bidarki, and three small tents. On reaching the shore I was met by an Irishman named Burns, who occupied a lonely cabin on the shore, and here he hospitably invited me to spend the night, an offer which I gladly accepted. He had the reputation of being a great talker, and even admitted to me that such was the case. I can only say that he regaled me with all kinds of wonderful tales until midnight, when I dropped off to sleep in the middle of one of his anecdotes. The next morning, when I awoke and turned over in my bunk at 5 A.M., the first thing I was conscious of was the fact that my host was still walking round the room and talking just as I last saw him at midnight. Whether or no he had been doing this all night I never could make out, nor did I ask him. Burns informed me that a few days previously an expedition sent out by the New York Museum, and headed by Mr. A. J. Stone, had stayed one night at his house, having come across the Peninsula from Port Moller Bay on the Bering Sea, where they had been hunting bear for a few weeks, and had brought back one small brown bear cub alive, and the skins of ten others which they had killed. This decided me to carry out my original plan, which I had resolved on earlier in the season, namely, to cross to the Bering Sea. Time was now very limited, as I was obliged to be back at Sand Point by July 17 to catch the steamer *Newport*, which travelled once a month back to the Cook's Inlet country, which I wanted to reach during August. We had been told wondrous tales of the number of bears on certain rivers, and around one lake in particular on the Bering Sea coast. It was roughly a distance of nine miles across the narrowest part of the Peninsula at this spot. Early next morning I left Burns's house, having thanked him for his hospitality, and loaded myself with my two rifles, the tents, and a small pack of provisions—in all a total of some 50 lbs. weight. The two natives, Nicolai and Nikita, carried the bidarki, and thus we turned our backs on the Pacific and struck out for the Bering Sea. My only fear was that in the proverbially rough waters of that sea we should be able to make little, if any, progress in our sole craft, the tiny bidarki. However, the old saying that "it is an ill wind which blows no one any good" was about to be exemplified, and shortly afterwards I struck one of those wonderful series of lucky events which sometimes happen, and which completely changed the aspect of affairs. We had barely travelled two miles along the trail before we came upon a small and primitive kind of tent, beneath which I found a man asleep. He heard us and woke up. In the course of conversation I learnt that he was the owner of a schooner which was lying in Herendeen Bay with a broken rudder, having been disabled in a bad storm some time previously. He and the rest of the crew had left the vessel safely secured, and he was now making his way across to Sand Point to try to obtain materials, etc., to repair the damaged rudder.

My story was soon told, and he remarked that he knew something about the coast along which I wished to travel, and thought it impossible for us to get very far with the stores, etc., in our bidarki. Shortly after he said that at the end of the trail which we followed he had a large sailing dory moored, and that although he had never done such a thing before, nevertheless, as times were bad, and he was dead out of luck, he would lend me his dory and accompany us for a consideration.   I need not add that we soon came to terms.   His name I found to be Charles Schultze, and here let me say at once that I was more than fortunate to secure his assistance.   He was the finest hand at packing I ever saw, the most untiring, willing worker, an excellent cook, and a very pleasant companion in camp.   His experiences all over America were many and varied, and his accounts of them were a continual source of interest to me during our trip in the Bering Sea.

At one time, during the first great rush to Dawson and the Yukon, in 1897 and 1898, he had been the champion trail-runner, bearing the mails and other things, on foot and with dog teams, from Skagway into Dawson.   Some of his performances were truly remarkable for an amateur, and were quoted in most of the American papers at the time, and although large sums of money were offered by newspapers and others to find a man to beat him, Schultze remained undefeated so long as he retained good health.

One of the most remarkable of his performances which I have seen mentioned, was done on January 6, 1899, when he arrived at the largest hotel in Skagway shortly before midnight, having just completed a magnificent run over the trail from Dawson.   As he entered the saloon a man came to him and said that there had been a great discussion there that evening as to the relative merits of some of the trail-runners, and that one man wanted to back him, Schultze, for $500 to run eighty miles inside twenty-four hours over any of the snow-covered trails leading from Skagway.   The speaker added that he himself was prepared to bet against his doing it.   Schultze replied that if he would bet him another $500 he would try it straight away.   It ended in Schultze only getting a side bet of $100 himself, but, tired and hungry as he then was, just coming off the Dawson trail, he took some food in his hand and started out on the Bennet trail at midnight. Skagway is some forty-three miles from Bennet by this trail, but shortly after 11.30 P.M. the next night he arrived back at the hotel in Skagway, having run to Bennet and back, a distance of eighty-six miles, in 23½ hours.

His first performance for me was making two round trips in one day over the trail we followed, and each time bringing back a pack not less than 70 lbs. in weight. The total distance was thirty-six miles, and over half of it he carried a heavy pack. My two natives, who were both good packers, were utterly unable to live with him at this job.

We reached the Bering Sea safely, and camped on the shore of Herendeen Bay. That night, about 11 P.M., I was aroused from sleep by some one shouting at the door of my tent to know if it was inhabited. I replied in appropriate language, saying " Why, certainly," and wanted to know the name of my visitor. He replied that he was Mr. David Barstow, the U.S. Deputy Commissioner in that district, and about the only white man to be found around there during a great part of the year. He added that he had a yacht lying at anchor in the bay, and hoped I would pay him a visit next morning. Now a yacht is hardly the kind of luxury one expects to find in the Bering Sea, and I must confess that I was curious to see what kind of craft they called a yacht in that part of the world. It was with no small surprise, therefore, that on issuing from my tent the next morning I saw a beautiful white schooner of some 25 or 30 tons lying at anchor in the bay. After starting the men off back on the trail, to pack across the remainder of our stores, I took my rifle and strolled along the beach. I was soon sighted from the yacht, and a boat came ashore to take me out to her. My surprise was in no way diminished when I stepped aboard the *Volunteer*, as she was named, to find her a perfect copy of an English pleasure yacht, with her commodious cabin, brass fittings, and well-kept decks, on all of which the owner might have prided himself even had she been lying at Cowes instead of in the Bering Sea. Last but not least in the

THE YACHT "VOLUNTEER" IN BEAR RIVER.
The property of Mr. D. Barstow.

opinion of one who had lived for some time on beans, bacon, and tinned goods, there was a veritable alderman's lunch spread in the cabin, at which appeared caribou steaks, fresh salmon, and some of the finest prawns I ever saw, the last two items caught from the yacht herself. All these luxuries, accompanied by some excellent whisky, made me think that I had not struck such a bad spot for my first venture on the Bering Sea. Here at lunch I met Captain Du Can, a

retired officer of the French army, who was then manager of
a coal mine in Herendeen Bay, and he afterwards entertained
me most hospitably at his house on shore.

As soon as Mr. Barstow heard my plans of pushing along
the coast with our bidarki and the dory, he at once dismissed
the idea, by insisting on my bringing all our belongings,
together with Schultze and the two natives, on board the
Volunteer, and announced his intention of taking us anywhere south of the North Pole that we wanted to go.   He
would take no refusal, and as I did not require much pressing,
we went aboard the yacht next day.   That morning I sent
the two natives out to get a caribou for meat in our first
camp, and they returned with a fine beast in the evening.
I saw great numbers of caribou along the mountain sides of
some of the valleys, and although most of them are hidden
away at this period of the year, it only required a short walk
over certain parts of the ground, where their shed antlers
could be seen in profusion, to understand that later in the
fall the caribou are found in some of these valleys in herds of
several thousand at a time.   Whilst the natives were gone
after caribou, I decided to prospect on shore in a likely-
looking valley for a bear.   After rowing ashore, I had not
gone 500 yards from the boat before I saw a bear eating
grass about 1000 yards away, on the side of a hill which
sloped down towards the sea.   To get there I had to cross a
valley and travel to the next ridge.   I crossed the valley at
a run, losing sight of the bear as I went over the low ground.
Reaching a spot whence I could see the place where he had
been, I found that the brute had disappeared.   All around
me the alders were growing in small thick patches, and I
stalked up wind, searching every clump of bushes, but without
success.   I then crossed over the ridge and worked the

K

other valley in a similar manner with the same result. Having spent two hours in this way, and finding myself back near the boat, I got disgusted and rowed back to the schooner. My feelings can be imagined when, on stepping aboard, the ship's cook informed me that he had witnessed the whole affair from the schooner. The bear had crossed over the ridge of the hill, and while I was crawling up the first valley, he was coming towards me just out of sight on the other side of the ridge and making for the seashore. He had passed within 50 or 60 yards of me, and then walked along the beach for some time. Finally, as I crossed the ridge and, turning back, almost followed his tracks to the shore, he had similarly retraced my steps along the valley up which I went, and we again passed each other within a short distance, with only the crest of the hill dividing us. The cook had been a highly amused spectator of the whole performance, but he was too far away to make me hear if he had shouted to me. Thus ended my second misadventure with a bear. For two more days we remained in Herendeen Bay, where Mr. Barstow was making a survey of the coast-line, and on the following morning sailed out into the Bering Sea. Here we had an opportunity of seeing what a fine sea-boat the *Volunteer* was. On reaching the entrance to Port Moller and Herendeen Bay, we encountered a tide running out with a speed of 9 knots per hour, and at the point where this current met the full swell of the open sea, and also a strong head wind, there was a terrible tide rip. Our skipper, who was a Norwegian, said to me, " I guess this sea is real mean, and that is darn'd aggravating just now, when I wanted to show you what an elegant mover this craft is. However, it ain't what you want, but what you get in this country, so here goes," and clapping on all the canvas the yacht could carry, we dashed into a seething mass of great white-capped rollers, over which the gallant little schooner rose like a duck.   The motion of the boat was awful, and this, combined with flying scud and foam, made me feel decidedly queer, and drove me below decks, followed by the skipper's cheery remark, " I guess you don't feel particular good"; which was absolutely a true statement of the case. Our course lay in a north-east direction, and we skirted along the coast for many miles, making for a river where I was told bears were swarming.   The coast here has the most desolate and uninteresting appearance.   For miles and miles it follows almost a straight line, and the land for many miles back from the shore is flat, with numerous marshes, and absolutely devoid of any form of timber, even lacking the alders which abound along the Pacific coast on the opposite side of the Peninsula.   It is not until one reaches the foothills which run down from the divide that enough wood can be found to make a decent fire, and even on the seashore, driftwood, which is plentiful along the Pacific coast, is here very scarce.

Any one who intends to take a trip along this coast, and desires to make any form of bread on the way, should go provided with a light handy stove having an oven in it, as, owing to the small quantity of wood procurable, it is impossible to bake bread by any other means.

In due course of time we arrived at our destination, and, taking the schooner into the mouth of the river, we anchored. Near this spot there was a small native settlement where Mr. Barstow told me I could obtain a man who knew the country, and also another bidarki to tow up the river. Although it was late in the evening, I determined to find this settlement, and accordingly bid adieu to Mr. Barstow with a thousand thanks for his kindness and the services of his yacht, without which I should have had a terrible task, extending over many days, to reach this river in the dory and bidarki. We parted with a promise on my part to return and visit him at his house near the river-mouth, where there was a new salmon cannery which had just been started to exploit and fish some of the rivers along the coast. Having found the native settlement, which consisted of four or five huts, my next trouble was to explain to the chief exactly what we wanted. He appeared to be neither an Aleut nor an Esquimaux, but somewhat of a link between the two, and what language he spoke I cannot say, but by dint of Nicolai speaking to him in Aleut, and Nikita in Russian, I managed to engage the services of one man, and the loan of two bidarkis, for a small sum of money and some tea and sugar, etc.

I questioned him closely as to my chances of finding bears along the river. He replied that there were any number there, and that now the natives had ceased to kill them for the fur-market, since their skins only fetched a few dollars, the bears came down after the salmon to within a few miles of the village. He declared that he and his men had counted fifteen bears along the river-bank on one evening a few days previously. This made me crazy to be off, and although it was then 8 P.M., I ordered the men to hustle all our stores into the three bidarkis, and, leaving our big dory behind, we made about five miles up the river before camping for the night. Luckily, I had the forethought to take with us some dry wood, as there was not a vestige of anything to burn within several miles of our camp. We had already reached a spot where bears' tracks were fairly numerous along both river-banks. At daylight we were off again, and by 3 P.M. had reached a spot where two low spurs of foothills ran down on each side of the river. Here we came upon a large patch of alders, and the local native said that this was a favourite spot for bears to come fishing. A short walk along the river-bank convinced me that his statement was correct, as the whole place was covered with bear-tracks, from large ones

C. SCHULTZE, COOK, AND NATIVES AT DINNER, BEAR RIVER, JULY 1903.

down to small cubs. Leaving Schultze with two natives to pitch camp on the river-bank, and instructions not to light a fire till dusk, I took my rifle and Nicolai and climbed to the brow of a hill just above the camp, where I could see for several miles up and down the river, as it ran across a perfectly level plain. The wind was blowing across the river from the opposite side, and I knew it was here that we must look out for bears coming down to fish, since the foothills behind us were fouled by the wind blowing from us and the camp. The salmon were then running in millions up the stream, all making for the lake at its head, and the noise which they made, as they forced their way over a shallow in thousands just below our feet, was extraordinary. We had not been sitting long on the hill before I caught sight of something moving about half a mile away on the opposite bank, and coming along the foothill towards the river. I pointed the object out to Nicolai, who said, " He bear all right, big one, run quick." I did not quite know why we should run, nor where to make for, but as this was my first experience of a bear fishing, I thought it best to trust to Nicolai, and said, " You run, I will follow." It appears that Nicolai was experienced enough to know, what I afterwards discovered to be a fact, namely, that a bear always gets on the down-wind side of a river before starting to fish. Here they seem to smell the salmon by some extraordinary means, and then begin dashing in and out of the river at some shallow place, rarely failing to catch a fish. They bring it out on to the bank and devour it, if possible selecting some thick patch of bushes or grass in which to make their meal, which does not occupy them long. The quickness with which these huge and apparently ungainly brutes gallop into the water, catch a fish, and dash out with it, was a revelation to me when I afterwards saw the whole performance. In this case the particular bear in question was destined never to catch another salmon. By careful crawling through high grass, we reached a point on our own bank exactly opposite the spot where the bear appeared a minute later. The river was here some 70 yards wide, and as the bear stood for a moment on the far bank, I was sorely tempted to take a shot at him, more particularly as the whole scene was being enacted within 250 yards of our camp, and in full sight of it.   Luckily Schultze had seen us running, and soon after saw the bear, and had kept the men quiet in camp, although, unknown to me, our new man was then stalking behind us with his old-fashioned Winchester rifle, he having also seen the bear.

Nicolai whispered to me, " Don't shoot, he swim now," and sure enough he did.   After one look round, he plunged straight into the stream, and never have I seen any animal swim so fast and powerfully along the top of the water as this great beast.   The point he selected for landing was some 20 yards above where I sat in the high grass.   Just as his fore-feet touched the bottom and he began to raise himself from the water, I planted a bullet from my Mannlicher behind his shoulder.   He made a wild rush forward for a few yards on the bank, and I, thinking my first shot must have been wide of the mark, and yet scarcely believing I could have made so bad a shot at so short a distance, was preparing to give him another, when his legs collapsed and he fell on his side, apparently quite dead.   Having been repeatedly cautioned by older sportsmen than myself about approaching a dangerous animal in a hurry when he only seems to be dead, and knowing from previous experiences the tremendous vitality of these great bears, I was in no haste about walking up to him.   After reloading the rifle I stood up, and so, *mirabile dictu*, did the bear, for by some extraordinary manœuvre, which was too rapid for me to follow, he reared himself on his hind legs, thereby giving me my first correct idea of what these great beasts look like in that position.   It was all so sudden that I did not stop to think about spoiling the skin, but gave him a bullet in the side of the skull, and he fell like a log.   This should have sufficed for anything made of flesh

and blood, and so thought my new native, who had just
arrived on the scene, and now rushed past me right up to the
bear.   He was so wildly excited that I could not stop him,
and, standing between me and the bear, he placed his hand on
its back.   I never saw a man jump so high from a standing
position as he did when the bear gave vent to an awful
noise, something between a roar and a grunt, and raised
himself to a sitting position.   He was too far gone to stand
up, but the native, on reaching *terra firma* again, threw the
muzzle of his rifle against the bear's side, fired it, and bolted,
much to the amusement of Nicolai and myself, who stood
about five yards away waiting for further developments.   This
was the final act of the drama, and I soon got the men to work
on the skin.   The bear was a large male, some three or four
inches shorter in length than my record specimen.   He was,
however, such an animal as any man would have talked about
for years had he killed it anywhere else in America save
Alaska.   I was most curious to see the results of my two
shots, and on cutting open the beast found that the first
bullet had missed the heart by barely an inch, and expanding
had inflicted an awful wound internally.   The second bullet
had entered just below the right eye, smashing the cheek-
bone.   It had split the lower part of the skull and exposed
the brain.   After expanding, it had sufficient force to smash
away four inches of cheek-bone on the left side of the head, and
yet, with these two frightful wounds, the bear had managed
to get on his forelegs a second time and frighten one of my
natives nearly to death.

I returned to camp well satisfied with my first experience
of the river.   A large bear killed two hours after pitching
camp, and that within 250 yards of my tent, is a bag that one
cannot make everywhere.

The best times for seeing bears fishing are daylight and
dusk, and if I had to select one time, I should choose the
latter from personal experience, as, although we were up at
daylight about 4 o'clock every morning, I never saw a single
bear then, despite the declaration of the natives that the
morning is better than the evening.   On the other hand, we
never failed to see one or more bears any evening between
5.30 and 7.30, so long as we remained there.

The following evening I walked some two miles up the
river, and waited with Nicolai and the local native (whose
name I never learnt) near a good shallow place in the river
where tracks were fresh and numerous on the bank.   We had
not long to wait, for soon I saw, about a mile off and coming
leisurely across the open, a very large dark-coloured bear.
We were seated on a small knoll, and about 50 yards from
the foot of it ran a well-worn bear-trail along which it was
perfectly obvious the bear was coming.   There was a rise in
the ground some 80 yards away which hid part of the trail
from view, and directly the bear got out of sight behind this
hill, both Nicolai and the other native rushed down the little
hill on which we sat, saying to me, " Hurry up, run quick."
They were so sharp in starting that I could not stop them,
but I was furious with them for leaving a good position
whence a fine shot was certain, and rushing down to get
nearer the trail.   The wind was perfect on top of the brow,
but I had already learnt to distrust it in any hollows or
valleys in Alaska.   As the men were now between me and
the bear, there was nothing to do but follow them.   My
worst fears were realised, for on descending the brow, the
wind was undoubtedly blowing straight from us towards the
bear, and we were in a hollow of the ground, unable to see
20 yards right or left.   It was only 50 yards to the brow on

our right, behind which the bear was advancing, and Nicolai, discovering the awful blunder he had made, rushed towards the top of it with me close on his heels. I felt sure that, although still a long way off, the bear must have got our wind, and so he had, for on reaching the spot where we could again see the trail, we found the bear about 200 yards away standing on his hind-legs. Nicolai, by this time frantic, shouted, "Shoot quick, shoot quick." I think that my actual words, bidding him to shut his mouth, are not fit for publication; the result was a hurried aim followed by a bad shot. It was my only decent chance and I lost it, for the bear whipped round and dashed off, apparently untouched, although the men both said, "He hit all right." Suffice it, however, that he was able to gallop at a useful pace across a mile of open ground, and out of sight into the thick alders on the hillsides. Needless to remark, I emptied my clip of five cartridges after him as he galloped across the marshy plain. The only shot which appeared to annoy the brute was the last one at about 400 yards. This bullet struck a pool of water right under his nose, and so startled him that he stopped and half stood on his hind-legs before starting off again. Thus ended the third of my misadventures with bears. I returned to camp very disgusted, as we had undoubtedly lost a very large bear, and all through the men entirely losing their heads.

The next evening I moved camp some five miles up stream, and camped on a small island in the river. Taking Nicolai, I occupied a small hill commanding a good view of the river, and, as before, we had not long to wait before seeing a bear. He was a long time making his way across the open plain, but when once he smelt the salmon he began to gallop, and dashing into the river soon came out with a fish. He repeated this performance two or three times, all the while

moving fast up stream.   We followed, running, crawling, and
taking advantage of cover behind every tuft of grass, as the
bear kept stopping and looking round as if suspecting danger
from our quarter.   Finally I got within shot of him, and gave

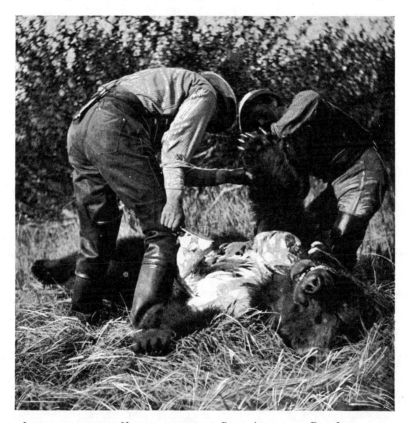

LITTLE AND NATIVE NICOLAI SKINNING A BEAR, ANIAKCHAK BAY, JUNE 1903.

him a bullet in the shoulder as he stood in the water.   He
never uttered a sound, but started swimming across the river.
I emptied the magazine at him, getting in two or three more
bullets, and these finished him as he crawled up the opposite
bank.   He was a small, light-coloured male.   The natives
pronounced him to be a two-year-old, but I am inclined to

think he was an early cub of the year before, and perhaps was about eighteen months old.

Having spent two hours after daylight the next morning looking in vain for more bears, I decided to make an expedition up to the lake which lay some four miles above my camp. The reports circulated by the natives and some white hunters who had visited this lake, regarding the number of bears to be seen there, made me curious to have a look at it, although it was the wrong time of year to find bears there, seeing that they were busy catching salmon in the various rivers all over the country and would not collect round the lake until the fall of the year, when the salmon would be dying after spawning and would fall an easy prey to the bears in the shallow water along the shore. An old hunter who spent a season hunting there some few years ago, when brown bear skins fetched a good price in the fur-market, told me that in a few weeks he and his partner had killed fifty-two bears around this lake, and on one occasion, late in the season, they had counted sixty-four bears in three days fishing along the shore. I was able subsequently to prove the first statement correct, so there is no reason to doubt the latter one, although it sounds a tall order.

The lake itself was some seven or eight miles long by three miles wide. At the head, and on two sides, rose high hills with dense alders growing on the lower slopes. It was a most picturesque spot, and I was glad not to have missed the opportunity of seeing it, more particularly as it furnished me with the most remarkable spectacle I witnessed in Alaska.

The men towed a bidarki up the river whilst I walked to the spot where the stream issued from the lake. As already stated, the Alaska red salmon were then at the height of their run, and it was no trouble to spear any number on the shallows with a pointed stick when in need of fresh food. We computed by the numbers passing our camp during the day and night that there must be already millions of fish in the lake. But I was utterly unprepared for the sight which greeted me on reaching its waters. The river issued from it over a shallow about 50 yards long and about 9 inches to 1 foot in depth. Over this shallow fish were running in countless thousands. As they forced their way up, with fins and tails out of water, they made a noise like a small waterfall. It would have been impossible to throw a stone into the river without hitting a fish at this spot. Once across the shallow, every fish turned sharp to the right and followed close along the shore of the lake. Although watching them a long while, I never saw any fish go to the left, nor straight out into the deep water of the lake. On the arrival of the bidarki I got into it, and told the men to paddle across to the other side of the lake. Here there was a high rock rising sheer up on the edge of the lake, at the foot of which the water was some 10 feet deep. Arrived there, I climbed up some 50 feet to a spot commanding a fine view of the water. On this rock a pair of peregrines had their nest, and our arrival disturbed the old falcon. She was soon joined by the tiercel, and the pair continued flying round, whilst we remained there, uttering their harsh chattering cry of rage which is so familiar to me as a falconer and lover of these fine birds at home. On looking down into the water below, which was clear as crystal, I could see the salmon swimming slowly past the foot of the rock, as they continued to follow the same direction in an endless stream of fish. They covered a distance of some 50 yards out from the shore, forming as it were a

solid belt of fish all around the lake. In many places they
were in layers of four or five deep, one above the other, and
almost touching each other side by side and head to tail.
I watched this extraordinary piscine procession with a kind
of fascination for fully an hour or more, then taking to the
bidarki again, we skirted along the shore, following the
course of the fish. Travelling faster than the salmon, we
constantly overtook fresh ones, and where the water was
shallow they would make such wild rushes, as the canoe
passed over them, that they lashed the water up over the
sides of the boat, and scores of them would get momentarily
forced aground on the edge of the shore by the mere weight
of numbers pressing on from behind. The whole time great
numbers of fish would keep breaking water, and it was the
most extraordinary sight as they did so to see on the surface
of the lake (which was as smooth as glass) the countless
noses and fins appearing and disappearing, as far as the eye
could reach. No fish jumped, except a few just as they
entered the lake. It seems wonderful to think that not
one of these salmon ever lives to return to the sea, but such
is undoubtedly the case.

No fresh signs of bears being visible around the lake,
and evening approaching fast, we decided to return to camp.
It took longer to reach the river again than I had calculated,
and here, as we crossed the shallow at its head, we went
bumping over the backs of the salmon as they came crowding
into the lake in their mad rush to certain destruction.

We were soon flying down stream at the rate of about
ten miles an hour, making two or three halts to scan the
plain on both sides of the river in hopes of seeing a bear;
but it got so dark that we finally decided to make for camp.
As the bidarki rounded a sharp curve coming down a rapid,

we nearly ran into a big bear standing on the bank. So
great was our pace that the men could not pull up until we
had shot past the spot where he stood. Seizing the rifle,
I jumped into shallow water and scrambled to the bank,
only to catch a fleeting glimpse of the bear as he disappeared
in the darkness over a rise in the ground. Knowing the
futility of attempting to follow it, we returned sorrowfully
to camp, having added one more lost opportunity to the list.

Next morning I had a particularly cold vigil from 4 A.M.
to 6 A.M., as we were enveloped in a typical Bering Sea fog
and mist. The result was again a blank, and we decided
to move camp down stream to our first camping ground,
which was accomplished at noon. As time was getting
short, we decided to make this our last evening on the river,
and as events turned out I narrowly missed making it my
last day in Alaska.

Craving the indulgence of my readers, I will inflict one
more bear episode upon them, and then bid adieu to all
ursine matters.

That evening Nicolai expressed a desire to try to get a
bear alone, so giving him my double-barrelled 450 Express,
I started him off to watch the bear-trail where he had made
such a mess of matters three days before. Taking the local
native, I went to the hill behind our camp whence we had
first viewed the bear three nights previously. An hour of
patient waiting rewarded me with a view of what was
undoubtedly a large she-bear and two big cubs moving along
the foothills on our bank, and evidently making for the
river. Here let me add that, although I always had a native
on the look-out with me, never once did he show me a
bear before I had seen it myself, and I observed the same
fact when moose - hunting with the natives on the Kenai

Peninsula. So far I had no specimen of a female bear, and the question arose in my mind as to whether or no these cubs could look after themselves if I killed their mother. Strangely enough, although fully aware of it, the element of danger in the undertaking did not then enter into my calculations. Turning the glasses on the animals, it was soon obvious that the cubs were yearlings, and big ones at that, therefore they were fully able to make their own way in the world. The native was carrying a 30.40 Winchester for my second rifle, and telling him to load the magazine, I set off at the double to get the wind right from the bears to us. A smart run of nearly a mile brought us to a small rise whence we could see the three bears busily engaged eating grass on the plain some 500 yards away. There was a small hillock about 100 yards from them, and seeing they were in no hurry to move, I made a dash for this, keeping well out of sight. Crawling to the top of this brow, I saw the old bear sitting down about 45 yards away, but protected by both the cubs, which were between her and me. At that moment one of the cubs walked up to her, and, being annoyed with it, she gave the most startling snarl of rage, and struck at it with her paw. Then, getting up, she started walking away from me. For a moment the point of her shoulder was visible, and, chucking up the rifle, I fired. She whipped round and stood facing me in the open, both cubs running close into her side. Standing up I fired again at her chest. Giving an appalling yell, she came straight at me, with the cubs keeping close on either side of her. As they were coming very fast, I knew it would be impossible to fire three shots before they were on me. Therefore I shouted to the native, " Shoot one little one," as, although I knew they did not mean fighting, the idea of being run over in the blind rush of

CAMP ON BEAR RIVER, BERING SEA COAST.
Bear skins drying on sand in foreground.

a beast weighing fully 300 lbs. did not appeal to me.   Whilst
loading again I heard a scuffle behind me, and turned to see
the native bolting like mad, rifle and all.   Bitterly I regretted
the absence of Nicolai, who would, I believe, have stood his
ground, but it was no time for regrets, and remembering I
had only three bullets left in the magazine, and moreover,
that if my next shot was a bad one it might be fatal to me,
I sat down quickly, resting my elbow on my knee, and let
the old bear have it in the chest at about 15 yards.   She
came on a few paces as if nothing had happened, and, as the
Americans say, " I guessed the game was up."   About five
yards away she turned a somersault and rolled over nearly
on top of me.   Meanwhile, having loaded again, I shot
the nearest cub in the chest, again being nearly knocked
over as he fell over my right leg.   Then, jumping up, I
waved the empty rifle in the face of the other cub and
shouted at him.   He swerved and dashed down the hill into
some bushes below.   Being furious at the scare they gave
me, I crammed in my last cartridge and clean missed this
cub at about 15 paces.   How it was possible to make such a
bad shot I cannot say, but probably when the real danger
was over I was rather jumpy.   Be that as it may, I felt like
sitting down on the dead she-bear and smoking a pipe to
think matters over, and prepare a suitable welcome for my
native, who was slowly returning from a distance.   He spoke
a little English, and after my remarks, telling him what I
thought of him and of various members of his family, and so
on, he replied smiling, " Me see old woman bear catchum
my brother same way; that no good, you bet."   Fearing
lest I should kick him if we prolonged the conversation, and
telling him to start skinning the two bears, I walked home to
camp, and sent my third native, Nikita, out to his assistance.

Shortly afterwards Nicolai returned furious with rage, as
he had seen a large bear coming along the trail near him,
and, so far as we could understand, had committed identically
the same error as before, which resulted in frightening the
bear away without his even getting a shot.

I need hardly say that I was well satisfied with the result
of my trip up this river, which had yielded a bag of four bears
in five days. Although it was now the first week in July,
every skin was in splendid order, a very unusual state to find
them in so far on in the season, and solely due to the lateness of the spring, which had prevented the bears from
coming out of winter quarters until fully three weeks after
their usual date.

SMALL ISLANDS OFF N.W. COAST OF BRITISH COLUMBIA.

CHAPTER VIII

THE LAST OF THE BERING SEA

THE next morning early saw us with our camp and skins packed in the bidarkis, and by noon we reached the native settlement. Here we left the local native and two bidarkis, making our way in the dory and the other bidarki to the salmon cannery, where we were welcomed by Mr. Barstow and his partner Mr. Ross. We were entertained hospitably and housed for the night; having spent the evening watching the fishermen, who were mostly Italians, shooting their seine-nets, and clearing the salmon-traps. The daily catch of fish was not heavy here, although the fish were swarming in the river. The manager, Captain Wagner, asked my opinion about the reason of their failure in making big catches. After looking at the traps, I concluded that the fish must be running under the bottom of the nets, as the river-bed was entirely composed of sand at that part, and this was always drifting down with the current, and thereby causing constant gaps between the bottom of the nets and the river-bed. I hear that this was afterwards discovered to be the case, but at that time the cannery had only just been started, and everything was in an experimental stage.

The fish caught were only salted in huge tubs and after-wards packed in barrels, as the cannery had not then been equipped with a plant for making its own cans and packing the fish in them, as is now done in all the complete establishments in Alaska.

The number of hair-seals swimming about at the mouth of the river was extraordinary, all being attracted there by the salmon. If it had not been for one curious circumstance I should have spent a few hours trying to shoot some of them. The fact I refer to is that during the spring and early summer the hair-seals are very thin, and if shot immediately sink to the bottom, whereas if killed in the proper season, when rolling in fat and blubber, they float. It is then that the natives hunt them to procure the skins for covering their bidarkis and making moccasins, etc. Glyn spent many days trying to bag an old seal, but although he killed several of them stone-dead, he was unable to get the bodies of any, with the exception of the young ones which were fat enough to float when killed.

While writing about the seals, it may be of interest to mention that there are a number of so-called fresh-water seals inhabiting Lake Iliamna on the Alaska Peninsula. These seals have been described to me, by men who have seen them, as being spotted like leopards, and it is claimed that they remain all the year round and breed in the lake. There is no reason to prevent these seals from going to the sea, nor, so far as I know, any conclusive evidence that they do not do so, since it is no very great distance to the Bering Sea down the Kvichak River. I have heard it stated that they are similar to the land-locked seals found in Lake Baikal in Siberia, but again I am unable to say on what authority this statement is based.

My next project was to visit some islands situated near the coast, and distant a matter of thirty-five miles from

the cannery.   Here I hoped to find walruses and obtain
a specimen.   The natives on the coast seemed to think that
owing to the late summer it was full early to expect walrus
on these islands.   However, as this was one of the great
inducements which led me to cross the peninsula, we determined to make the attempt.   Next morning, bidding adieu
to Mr. Barstow and other friends, we set out to sea, the two
natives going in the bidarki, whilst Schultze and I went in
the dory, accompanied by a Russian Finn named Andrew,
who lived in a solitary hut some twelve miles along the coast
in the direction that we were going.   He undertook to pilot
us as far as his place, and very glad we were of his assistance,
since neither Schultze nor I classed ourselves very high as
mariners, and it was not long after hoisting the sail of the
dory that it came on to blow great guns.   Fortunately the
wind was dead astern, and we ran before it with a big swell
following us, which soon kicked up a nasty sea and made such
a big surf on the shore that it was out of the question to run
the dory on the beach, where we should certainly have been
swamped.   There was nothing to do, under the circumstances, except to sit tight and run for the shelter of a sandspit some miles ahead.   The way in which the man Andrew
handled the dory, with nothing save an oar to steer her, was
a treat to see.   I doubt whether Schultze and I alone would
ever have reached land in safety.   As it was, we repeatedly
shipped big seas, and several times were within an ace of
being swamped ; but all the while Andrew steadily held on
his course, only giving way to an occasional smile at our
evident distrust of the situation.   Although the dory seemed
to be racing through the water, we had not gone three miles
before the two natives and the bidarki were clean out of sight,
and hidden from view by the big sea which was now running,

as the fiction-writers are pleased to call it, " mountains high."
I do not think that the sensation of placing my feet once
more on *terra firma* was ever so welcome to me as it was
when we made the friendly shelter of a long sandspit and
safely put the dory ashore, after running before the wind for
a distance of some twelve miles. Here we bade farewell to
Andrew, our skilful pilot, whose little wooden hut we could
see some two miles away from the spot where we landed, and
where also we decided to camp. A more desolate, dreary
spot than this it would have been hard to find. It took all
hands some time searching to find enough driftwood to
kindle a fire. Whilst engaged in this search I came upon
several fresh bear-tracks, all following the sandy shore. One
lot of tracks, which were only about twenty-four hours old,
were those of an old she-bear and two tiny cubs, the tracks
left by the latter being not much larger than those of a big
St. Bernard dog. I believe it is very unusual to see an old
she-bear with small cubs at so great a distance as this from
the mountains. The natives and all old hunters whom I have
met declare positively that the old mother remains for a
while in the hills near the spot where she has holed-up for the
winter, and stays there with her cubs often during the whole
season after they are born.

Towards evening the wind died away, the sea calmed
down very rapidly, and we were off again at daylight. Twice
during the day we remained for a long while almost stationary
in the dory, although there was a fair breeze for sailing. But
whilst crossing the entrance to a big bay we were caught
by the tide and remained floundering about doing what is
locally termed " bucking a tide rip," and a more unpleasant
sensation than this, in a heavily loaded dory, cannot be
imagined.

Nicolai on this occasion was alone in his wonderful little bidarki, which easily went clean away from us in the first few miles.   That evening we camped on a large island about one and a half miles from the mainland.   This place had formerly been a favourite haunt of caribou, which at certain seasons of the year would swim from the mainland to the island, and we found a great number of old shed horns lying all over the ground.   Here also I came across fresh bear-tracks, showing that the bears also did not mind a long swim. Not a sign of any brushwood was to be found growing, and once more it was a case of hunting for driftwood for cooking purposes.   Early on the following morning we crossed over to the mainland, and skirting the shore for some distance camped in sight of the walrus island.   The wind was blowing from there towards the shore, and as it is absolutely necessary to get a favourable wind in order to approach walruses, owing to their very keen power of smelling danger at a great distance, I determined to explore the island that evening. I feared the result would be a blank, since the island lay barely two miles away, and we were certain that if there had been any walruses on it we should have heard them making a noise.

Taking both natives and the bidarki, I crossed to one end of the island, and here from a small knoll surveyed the whole of it with the glasses.   As we expected, no sign of a walrus was to be seen.   The island was rather over a mile in length and about 200 yards wide, being merely a long low sand-bank with high rough grass growing all over it.   The walruses always hauled out on a sandspit at one end of the island, and on a closer inspection of this place it was evident that none had as yet visited the island during that season, since there were no great holes in the sand where they had been lying or sleeping. This was a bitter disappointment for me, as it was evidently hopeless to wait on the chance of a few odd ones arriving, which they might not do for many days. We felt certain they had not as yet come so far south, for if they had done so we should surely have seen or heard some along the coast. We had the melancholy satisfaction of finding numerous bones and remains of walruses killed here in former seasons by other hunters or natives who had been more fortunate than ourselves.

I was surprised at one thing on the island, and this was that it absolutely swarmed with red foxes. They had a great number of earths in the small sand-hills, and were so fearless that they remained standing at the mouths of their earths looking calmly at us often at a distance of not more than 50 yards. I could have shot a great many with the rifle, but would not do so, as their coats were then in a poor state and quite worthless. Their food must have consisted of dead fish and other refuse cast up on the shore by the sea, as there appeared to be no other living thing on the island. Doubtless a certain number of unwary ducks, etc., fall a prey to them, for we observed several huge flocks consisting of what I estimated at thousands of eiders, harlequin, and other kinds. There were also vast numbers of scoters, which were swimming and flying round the island. There was one immense mob of birds which could not have been less than 2000 in number, but just too far off for me to identify them. On first seeing them I thought my eyes had deceived me, as a moment afterwards I looked at the same spot and not a bird was to be seen. Another minute and they were all in the same place. On watching them closely I saw that, apparently on a given signal, the whole flock dived simultaneously and remained under water several seconds, not a

bird staying above the water.   Then all came up again about
the same moment, and kept repeating this performance so
often that I at last got tired of watching it, and we returned
dejectedly to camp, with the assured knowledge that a walrus
would not figure in our list of trophies from Alaska in 1903.

During that evening and all through the night we had
our first and only experience of what Alaskan mosquitoes are
like when they are thick.   Sleep was out of the question ; I
dared not close my eyes for fear of being eaten alive, but
started my strongest pipe in the hopes of keeping the insects
away.   Vain indeed were all such hopes, for although an
American had only a short time before remarked, on smelling
the smoke of this very pipe, " Say, cap, I guess that pipe of
yours would drive a dog out of a tan-yard," it had not the
slightest effect on the mosquitoes.   The natives even were
up all night trying to keep off their attacks, and next morning
I found the inside of their tent black with the pests.   In reply
to a joking question of mine asking if the men had any
mosquitoes in their tent, Nikita, who was well versed in all
the latest American sayings, replied, " Mosquitoes you bet
your life, they are buzzing round our tent to beat the band."

We had also another diversion during the night and
the following two days.   There is a large volcano on the
peninsula not far from Unga Island, and within view of our
camp.   This is called Mount Pavloff, and it suddenly burst
out with a series of terrific explosions, which were repeated
every five minutes, sending up clouds of steam and smoke,
and shaking the ground around for miles.   The nearer we
got towards it on our return journey the less I liked it,
expecting to encounter a tidal wave at any moment which
might send us and the dory to the bottom of the Bering Sea.
Nicolai also did not relish the situation, and appeared to

think Sand Point would have disappeared on our return, although it was separated by many miles of sea from the mainland, and some forty miles from the volcano. When the mountain grew rather more active than usual one evening, he confided to me quietly, " Pretty soon me think no more Sand Point." It was, however, merely a storm in a tea-cup, and had worked itself out before we recrossed the peninsula.

The return journey to Herendeen Bay was uneventful, except for the fact of our having to put in long spells of hard rowing in the dory to make headway against the dreadfully strong tides. Even then, with three oars out and the sail set, we had some severe struggles to round certain points on the coast. On one of these occasions we overtook Nicolai, who as usual had out-distanced us in his small craft, and was waiting for us under shelter of a sandspit. Here we found him sitting forward in the bidarki, his head on his arms, and fast asleep. The bidarki was rolling and tossing about in a heavy swell, requiring the utmost nicety of balance to prevent it from turning over, and yet we found this extraordinary native fearlessly sleeping like a duck on the water. So much for a life spent from childhood upwards in these canoes, during which Nicolai had earned the reputation of being the most fearless man in a bidarki, and also the most experienced and successful sea-otter hunter anywhere in the neighbourhood of Kodiak Island.

We arrived late one evening in Herendeen Bay, and ran the dory ashore near the coal station. Walking to the houses about a mile from the bay, we were received hospitably by Captain Du Can and his man, who gave both Schultze and myself a bunk in the house. The gallant Captain himself insisted on cooking us a supper, as we had come in tired and hungry.   I bade farewell to him next morning with repeated promises to look him up again, if ever the spirit which the Germans call *wanderlust* should lead my steps once more to that fine wild country.   A pitiless, desolate spot in winter, ice-bound and cut off from the rest of the world it is for many months in the year, but a sportsman's paradise during the months when it is possible to travel over it.   Owing to its remoteness, and the small number of the natives inhabiting the coast-line, the game which still abounds there may very likely continue plentiful for many years yet to come.

One more short trip in the dory, and we found ourselves at the spot where we had first embarked in Herendeen Bay. Here one evening and night were spent whilst everything was made up into suitably sized packs.   Two more days were occupied in conveying our camp equipment, the bear skins, and bidarki, etc., across the peninsula, and finally we found ourselves once more *chez Burns*, where I found the host still talking, but on this occasion he had a larger audience than myself, as there were two "outfits" or camps on the shore at Portage Bay, waiting for a favourable wind to cross over to Unga and Sand Point.   One party had been on a visit to some celebrated hot springs in Moller Bay for the benefit of the health of one of their number, who was crippled with rheumatism.   The water from these springs has the reputation of effecting marvellous cures for this complaint.   Whether or no it really does so, I cannot say, but such is the local tradition amongst the natives and whites in the district.   Probably some day, when Alaska is more accessible than it is at present, and when it becomes the Norway of America, some enterprising American will erect a summer hotel and hydropathic establishment there

which may make his fortune if he only advertises it
sufficiently.   One thing is certain, that ages ago the old
inhabitants of the country frequented these springs largely
for some purpose, since to-day there are a large number of
excavations in the ground which look as if they had once
been covered by native " barabaras," the dug-out huts still
in use throughout the country.   Around these holes are
ranged a large semicircle of the remains of old clam-shells.
Clams are very plentiful on the shore near by, and it
appears that the people inhabiting this settlement must have
eaten a great number of these shell-fish, and being too lazy
to carry away the refuse, threw the empty shells out at the
front of their barabaras and let them lie in a heap, even as
they are to be found there now.

The second camp at Portage Bay contained two men
who had crossed to the mainland to kill caribou for the
mining settlement at Unga.   This is quite a lucrative trade,
and an easy one at which to make money at certain times
of the year.   Also it is one which threatens to exterminate
the game far more quickly than will be done by the few
specimens annually killed by sportsmen in Alaska.   Mention
is made elsewhere of this subject, but I may further remark
here that I have known an instance, which came under my
personal notice, of one man returning to Unga Island with
seven caribou in his boat at one time, most of these being
females, and at that time when killed all with fawns by their
side.   Needless to say, the latter had also to be killed, or to
be left to starve to death.

CHAPTER IX

BACK TO THE KENAI PENINSULA

When landing at Portage Bay from Sand Point I had arranged with the skipper, Captain Harry, who conveyed me across, that he should make his way to the eastward as far as Ivanoff Bay, where he was to arrive on a certain date, and then pick up Glyn and Little. After taking them to Sand Point, he was to cross and meet us on my return to the Pacific coast. So well had we timed matters, and so propitious was Father Neptune, that on the morning after our arrival at Portage Bay Captain Harry was seen beating his way into the harbour. A couple of hours found our party safely on board, and forthwith we commenced another ding-dong contest with the wind and waves to reach the kindly shelter of Popoff Island. I shall ever regard that crossing to and from Portage Bay as about the longest and worst fifteen miles I have traversed on the sea, always, however, with the exception of the passage across Skelikoff Straits, which we made early in the season from Kodiak Island. It took us almost as many days, in the *Alice*, to cross that inferno, as there were miles of water to traverse.

It was late that night ere we reached Sand Point, and as soon as the sloop had dropped anchor, I made Nicolai launch the bidarki and we paddled ashore. I have never

seen such a curious effect as that caused by the phos-
phorescent light on the water in the bay that night. The
crest of every little wave seemed to be capped with fire,
and the water flying away from behind our paddles looked
like a liquid mass of flame. Although I have seen the same
phenomenon repeatedly in different countries, this was the
most vivid and brilliant example of it I have ever witnessed.

I soon found Glyn and Little established in a very
comfortable little hut, which was kindly lent to us by Messrs.

SAND POINT, POPOFF ISLAND.

Scott and Groswald, the local storekeepers and kings of
Popoff Island. Glyn and Little had just turned in for the
night, but soon got out of bed to hear my news and give me
their own. The latter was by no means good, and I was both
surprised and very disappointed to learn that they had only
seen three bears during the whole of the time at Ivanoff Bay,
and of these Glyn had only managed to bag one, an old male
which had such a poor coat that they did not trouble to keep
the skin. It appeared that Glyn had seen this beast walking
along the sea-shore, and had engaged in a great walking
match to try to overtake it. When he finally did so and

wounded it, the bear had gone some distance, and received seven bullets from his own and Little's rifle before it finally dropped dead at fairly close quarters. I do not quote this as an example of Glyn's and Little's powers with a rifle, since they are both good shots, but merely to show how tough these great brown bears are, and how great is their vitality if not hit actually in the right spot. Glyn had one more shot at another bear at long range, and failed to get it. The total results did not come up to my expectations after seeing one bear myself at Ivanoff Bay in the only two hours I spent on land there. They had killed one or two more caribou for meat, and also collected a few birds. I was more than sorry that Glyn had not accompanied me to the Bering Sea, where he could have got all the bears he wanted in a few days' time.

They described the mosquitoes as being terrific on several occasions during their stay at the bay, and this I had fully expected, as they fairly hunted me off the shore when I landed there. Glyn was not at all pleased with the results given by his 8-m. Mannlicher, not only in the instance of the bear, but also when using it for caribou. I do not profess to be an expert in such matters myself, but mine gave fairly satisfactory results, although the .256 Mannlicher is undoubtedly a harder hitting weapon. Personally I prefer the 8-m. Mannlicher to our English .303; the bullets from the former seem to mushroom better, and inflict more severe wounds than those of the .303. Every sportsman has his own particular fancy as regards some kind of rifle, and will continue to be of the same mind until the end of the chapter. But if every one reads and follows the various advice and hints to young sportsmen and others which are daily written upon these matters in the sporting press, he will everlastingly

be dissatisfied with his own particular rifle and want to
change it.   I have read with no small amount of interest and
amusement several learned dissertations on the effect of
small-bore rifles and bullets upon big game, in most of
which the statements made have been proved beyond all
possible doubt by some eminent young sportsman on his first
shooting trip.   The American sporting journals positively
teem with such articles, in which respects they are far worse
offenders than our own publications.

We hoped to get away from Sand Point two days after
my arrival there, as the steamer *Newport* was due to sail for
Cook's Inlet at that time.   However, we had long since
learned that Alaska is a country in which, as they say there,
" You must not figure on a boat being on time."   We had a
nine-days wait on this occasion.   During that time there
was little to relieve the monotony of walking down to the
store and back to our hut.   Glyn went off for two days and
crossed to a bay on Unga Island in search of hair-seals, which
were said to be numerous there.   He did succeed in killing
and bagging one young one, but failed to get an old one for the
reasons which I have previously stated.   A small excitement
was caused one night by an earthquake.   There was a bunk-
house not far from our hut, and this happened to be full at
the time of miners and fishermen who were, like ourselves,
waiting for the *Newport*.   The door of this house opened
outwards, and there was just room to open it without touching
the wall of an adjoining hut.   When all its inhabitants were
in bed, the bunk-house was suddenly moved a foot or more
by the earthquake, and it was then so near the other hut
that the door could not be opened at all.   It is no exaggeration to say that things were pretty lively inside that house
for a time, and the remarks from its caged prisoners, and the

M

way in which they shouted them out, soon aroused most of the dwellers in Sand Point.

As usual, there were plenty of reports flying around about bears having been killed which measured 12 or 13 feet from nose to tail, and as usual we tried without success to see even a genuine unstretched skin of these dimensions. It was reported to me that Mr. A. J. Stone had passed through Sand Point a few weeks previously with the skin and skull of a bear which had weighed 1600 lbs. I felt rather ashamed of my big one after this, and I was sure that if such a well-known collector as Mr. Stone had said his bear weighed 1600 lbs. he had weighed it carefully. In a subsequent conversation with Mr. Stone he admitted that he had only estimated this bear's weight, and when we finally compared notes and measured the two skulls of our respective big bears, I was quite satisfied to find that my skull, although the same length as Mr. Stone's, was some three-quarters of an inch wider, and considerably larger in circumference. Also, by careful measurements of the bodies, my bear was proved to be some $4\frac{1}{2}$ inches the longer from nose to tail. It does not by any means follow that the other bear might not have been the heavier, but to suggest the idea that there was a difference of nearly 600 lbs. between the two is asking me to swallow too much.

It was not long before we ran up against a local liar who, hearing about the visit of some English greenhorns on a shooting expedition, thought he might do some good business. One evening in the store he approached me and said, " Look here, I guess you reckon that bear's skin of yours hanging out to dry is a big one ? " I replied meekly that, in our opinion, it was fairly good. He then stated that in the spring he had killed a bear which was more than half

as big again as mine, and that the skin was so large that
he was hardly able to drag and carry it about a mile to his
boat.   A rapid mental arithmetical calculation convinced me
that to answer his description of it, this bear's skin should be
nearly 14 feet in length.   He added that the skin had not
been stretched, and he wanted $25 for it.   I replied saying
it was not my custom to buy trophies, nor had I ever done
such a thing, but that if his skin was really half as large again
as mine, and had not been stretched on pegs, I would give
$25 for it.   Spreading my big skin out I made him measure
it with a bit of string.   He next said, "Well, I guess my
skin is 2 feet longer than that one."   This was coming
down 2 feet with a jump, but I still replied, "Very well, if
yours is 2 feet longer I will give you $25 for it."   Finally it
came down to $25 if his skin was by 1 foot the longer.   He
disappeared for three days to bring this celebrated skin from
his home, which was situated some miles along the coast.
There was quite a small crowd on the wharf at Sand Point
awaiting the arrival of his dory when it appeared in the
harbour.   The local talent were quite certain that I should
have to pay over the deal.   When my friend appeared,
staggering under what seemed to be a tremendous load, I
began to have some misgivings, but these did not last long
when the first thing which Little and I noticed was that all
the sides of the hide were full of large holes where pegs had
been driven in to stretch the skin.   The climax arrived when
he triumphantly spread out the skin on the ground and careful measurements proved it to be some 3 or 4 inches shorter
than mine, which had only been salted and had consequently
shrunk considerably, whereas the other had been stretched
to its full extent and dried in the sun.   Needless to remark,
"the laugh was with me," and I did not part with the $25.

A good story, illustrating the undefeated powers of a first-class Alaskan narrator, came to me at Sand Point, but not feeling certain as to its originality I repeat it with some hesitation and apologies to the original inventor of the yarn. Two local skippers of some small fishing vessels, who were both notorious for talking big, were present one evening in the local store. One champion was holding forth to an admiring crowd on the subject of mosquitoes.

" Yes, gentlemen, those darned mosquitoes are pretty thick round about this neighbourhood. Why, not long ago we was lying off the shore and was just hoisting sails on my schooner. We got up the mainsail and foresail, and was just fixing up the topsail when by comes a cloud of them mosquitoes and carries the topsail clean away."

A look of admiration crossed the face of skipper No. 2 ; but, without turning a hair, he addressed the speaker, saying, " Pardon me, captain, but could you say near about where, and what date that happened ? "

Nothing daunted, the other promptly replied, " Wal, I should say we were 55° N. by 162° W. near about noon on June 27." Whereupon skipper No. 2 nobly rose to the occasion, and turning to the audience remarked, " Say, now, gents, that's right down queer, but I guess I can corroborate this gentleman's statement. On the very date in question I was laying off the coast about twenty-five miles to leeward of that identical spot, and a cloud of mosquitoes passed my schooner about 2 P.M., and every one of the darned brutes had on a canvas jacket."

Although a fairly good raconteur myself, it is heart-breaking to run up against such men as these, for, as the Americans say, they make one " feel tired," since they are capable of soaring to the most lofty pitches of imagination on

the slightest possible provocation, and as Alaska can produce
plenty of men who are reputed to be able " to give cards to
the best liar in Hades, and then snow under the other man at
his own game," the average Englishman feels himself rather
outclassed.

On July 24 the *Newport* arrived safely in Sand Point
harbour, but it was blowing such a gale that she was compelled to remain at anchor twenty-four hours before her skipper,
Captain Redfern, cared to risk the open sea passage.   The
Newport was not blessed with the best reputation as a good
sea boat, and one man, who had travelled often on board her,
declared to me that she was the champion boat to roll, along
the whole of the Pacific coast ; in fact, as he described it,
" She rolls that bad, you can see right down her smoke-stack
and out of the bilge-hole."   She afterwards gave an example
of her powers in this way, and I almost believed the statement
made by my informant.

When finally we bade farewell to the inhabitants of Sand
Point, the *Newport* was fairly crowded with passengers,
and amongst the number were a lot of fishermen and
miners returning from the westward, many of them fairly
lively from the effect of the numerous parting drinks
with friends at Sand Point.   Things looked like being
rather interesting on the lower deck before long.   I soon
discovered that Captain Redfern was most efficient in the
use of his fists, and on finding that I also had a sneaking
affection for the noble art, he enticed me into a conversation
on the subject, and told some most amusing anecdotes of
how he had been compelled to uphold his position as a mate
or skipper by sheer force of arms, amongst various crews of
all nationalities, in different parts of the world.   We were
standing on the bridge looking on to the lower deck, as we

approached the harbour of Unga. Captain Redfern said,
" The last time we came in here I had a bit of a scrap with
one of the passengers aboard, who thought he was boss of the
ship, but he soon found he was not." As he spoke I looked
below, attracted by hearing some one kindly offer to knock
some other person's head right off. The trouble seemed to
be between a burly fisherman and the first mate. The latter
being only a small light-weight, and surrounded by about a
dozen fishermen, the captain said we had better go and see fair
play, as there was certain to be trouble. I cannot say if he
was very long in persuading me, but we finally rushed down
the gangway, throwing off our coats as we went. The mate
and fisherman had started at it hammer and tongs before we
got there, and telling me to look after the interests of the
fisherman, whilst he attended to his mate, the captain and I
started clearing a ring for them as best we could. It was
not long before various members of the crew came rushing
on deck from below. The decks were as slippery as glass
owing to a thick fine rain which was falling, and as neither of
the combatants showed much science, they went tumbling all
over the place. Once as the fisherman went down a small
steward, who was a bosom friend of the mate's, took the
opportunity of rushing in and kicking the prostrate man in the
ribs. It was clearly my duty as a second to stop this, and
promptly tripping up the offender, I dragged him back into
his proper place amongst the spectators. At the same
moment a huge fisherman about 6 feet 2 inches tall rushed
to the assistance of his comrade. Before the captain could
interfere, this man was met by one of the ship's stokers, who
had a face like a bull-dog, and a fist like a leg of mutton.
Turning quickly, he landed the big man fairly on the jaw,
sending him over like a skittle to a distance of about five or

six yards, where he remained in a heap till the end of the contest. The end was not long in coming, as the little mate soon gave his opponent all he wanted. Afterwards, as no one seemed inclined to accept the captain's friendly offer that any other man who was "looking for trouble" could have a go at him, we went aloft once more. Glyn and Little were quite sorry to have missed this little diversion when told of it afterwards, since it was about the only amusing event on the whole trip.

At Unga we landed a few of the pugnacious passengers, and sailing again that evening reached Chignik the next afternoon. There we went ashore and spent an hour watching the men working in the salmon cannery, which was still operating at full swing.

Next day the *Newport* called at two places, Cold Bay on the mainland, and Uyak Cannery on Kodiak Island. The first place promises to be ere long a great oil-field, and from all accounts the various parties now working on different claims near the shore are daily and hourly expecting to strike oil in large quantities.

At Uyak we were informed that some natives had been there a few days previously with a small Kodiak bear-cub which they had offered to sell for a few dollars, but failing to find a purchaser, they had let it escape again. Had we seen this cub I should have bought it to present to the Regent's Park Zoo. On the following morning we found ourselves once more alongside the familiar wharf at Kodiak. Our friend Mr. Goss was on the quay when we arrived, and soon posted us in all the local news. The good ship *Alice*, with her owner Folstad, was away on some prospecting expedition. Here also we found the steamer *Tyonook*, which was running up and down Cook's Inlet and was due at Saldovia in four or five days, where we had hoped to meet her and thus get to Kussiloff. Here she was, however, laid up on the beach, with her propeller damaged and every prospect of our having to wait indefinitely for her at Saldovia. But as we had plenty of time to spare, and waiting for steamers being the usual rule in Alaska, the outlook did not worry us much.

At Kodiak we parted with Nicolai and his bidarki, not without regret on both sides. He was by far the best hunter I saw in the country, and, unlike the natives in Cook's Inlet, was nearly always contented and cheerful, nor did he assume the airs which the natives of the inlet put on at times when they wish to demonstrate that they are the equals of any white man.

At daylight on the day after leaving Kodiak we reached Saldovia. Here, after landing all our equipment, we bade good-bye to the *Newport* and our fellow-passengers.

Saldovia is a small settlement consisting of some twenty-five native houses, a Russian church, and two stores which are kept respectively by two men named Cleghorn and Herbert. Both the latter are excellent fellows, who are only too ready to help and equip parties of sportsmen wishing to hunt anywhere along the coast near Saldovia. Both Herbert and his partner, John Kilpatrick, are old hunters of some repute, and J. Cleghorn is the only white man I know who has any real knowledge of the Sushitna River country at the head of Cook's Inlet, up which it yet remains for some sportsman to make the first shooting trip. He could not do better in that district than secure the services of Cleghorn.

Our first job after landing at Saldovia was to try to find some spot in which to live for several days. Every hut, with the exception of two very dirty ones, was occupied. There was no clean and level spot suitable for pitching our tents, but there was a large scow or flat-bottomed barge, roofed on top, but open at both ends, which lay at anchor about 100 yards from the shore. On this abode we finally set our affections, and thither we conveyed our blankets. A prospector named Reese, who was on his way up the inlet, and like ourselves awaiting the *Tyonook*, joined us in this domicile. He was a cheery companion, and a type of the best American prospectors to be found in Alaska. It was seldom that we did not finally roll ourselves up for the night, and drop off to sleep laughing over some quaint saying of his, as he curled himself up in his own blankets.

The next question was how to employ our time whilst waiting for the steamer. There appeared to be no form of sport except sea-fishing, and the off-chance of getting a black bear which came down in the evenings to fish for the dog and humpback salmon that ran up two small streams not far from the settlement.

Glyn and I tried both forms of amusement, the fishing giving poor results and the bear-hunting still poorer. One day I made an expedition to a small stream some three miles away from the village. I paddled up with a local native in his bidarki. At the mouth of the stream we found all the men from the village of Saldovia living in a temporary summer camp, where they were busy catching the salmon with nets. When caught, the fish were split open, cleaned, and hung up in long lines on ropes, the branches of trees, or any available place. Here they remained to dry in the wind and sun, and were used as food throughout the winter months by the natives. The smell of rotten fish pervading the whole place was so awful that I was glad to get away from the spot, and follow up the stream for a couple of miles on the chance of seeing a black bear. There were evidently plenty of these beasts about, as all along the river-banks there were numerous fresh tracks, and spots where they had pulled out and eaten salmon.

But on both sides of the river grew a dense jungle of high grass, alders, salmon berry bushes, and that vile, prickly plant called in Alaska "Devil's Club," through all of which the native and I were obliged to force our way. It would have been impossible to see a bear at 10 yards' distance, as the undergrowth was over our heads. To make matters worse, the mosquitoes and a small kind of midges were swarming. About three hours' waiting patiently on the bank without seeing anything was enough for me, and we made tracks for the bidarki, and home again.

On arrival at Saldovia we heard that Mr. A. J. Stone was there, accompanied by a professional taxidermist from New York, and also an artist, Mr. Browne. Shortly after we met them, and had an opportunity of inspecting some of their trophies and specimens of small mammals and birds. They had been successful in making a very fine collection, and had also killed ten brown bears, and captured one cub alive in Moller Bay on the Alaska Peninsula. Mr. Browne told me a curious incident which happened when he killed one of the large bears. He said that close to the spot where the bear lay dead, he noticed a big excavation in the ground, and on examining it found the whole body of a large caribou which had just been buried there by the bear. A day or two previously they had shot at and wounded a caribou near this place, and he thought that this was the one which the bear had killed and buried. I had several long and interesting conversations with Mr. Stone, whose knowledge of the mammals of Alaska is perhaps more extensive than that of

any other man.   Like all other scientific naturalists he is very
keen on the discovery of new sub-species and varieties of
various forms of mammals.   The Americans have reduced
this science to a fine art, and whether or no they have carried
it a little too far, is a matter for some other than a mere
sportsman to decide.   I can only say that it appears from
conversations I have held with some of our own leading
authorities on the subject in England, that they find it
hard to follow some of the intricate points, and slight
variations, upon which the American naturalists base their
distinctions.

One form of amusement at Saldovia consisted of catching
some of the fresh-run dog and humpback salmon which were
crowding the mouth of a small creek near the village.   For
this purpose I rigged up a triangle of three large cod-
hooks, and with the help of a long pole, and some strong
line, we snatched a number of them on one or two fortunate
occasions.

As was to be expected from former experiences, the
steamer *Tyonook* was several days late in arriving at Saldovia
for her trip up the inlet.   It was August 7 before she finally
arrived there.   Leaving our bear skins and other trophies at
Cleghorn's store, we went on board, and reached Kussiloff
about midnight.   Here we landed, and were received by Mr.
Wetherbee, the hospitable manager of the Alaska Packers'
Cannery.   He put us up for the night, and next day gave us
the use of an empty hut where Glyn and I took up our
quarters.   Little in the meanwhile went on to Kenai to
collect natives and a fresh supply of stores for our trip up into
the sheep and moose country.   Three days later four natives
arrived with a dory from Kenai carrying a lot of stores, and
at once they started off to tow the dory some fifteen miles up

the river to Kussiloff Lake, which is otherwise known as
Lake Tustamena.   Here they were to establish a base camp,
and return again to tow up a second dory with the remainder

SNATCHING DOG SALMON, SALDOVIA CREEK, JULY 1903.

of our belongings.   On the second day, however, after leaving,
they returned without having covered more than half the
distance, as two of their number were taken ill with mumps,
and they came back terribly frightened with their heads

bandaged up.   On returning to cook our supper that evening
Glyn and I found the invalids and two other men making
themselves thoroughly at home in our cabin.   The two
patients were calmly sitting on our beds, and probably filling
the room with microbes of the mumps, whilst the other two
were peaceably cooking themselves a meal of the best
luxuries they could find in the house.   I was charmed with
their free-and-easy manners, and so was Glyn, who had never
previously had mumps, and daily expected them for some
time after.   I endeavoured to reason with them in a suave
manner, which ended in my almost kicking the lot out of the
house.   This meant a further delay to collect more natives,
and it was another five days before we finally started up the
river.

During our stay at Kussiloff we inspected all the wonderful machinery and appliances for canning the salmon.   The
cannery had stopped work a few days before, but all hands
were busy packing the tins in cases, and loading them on
steam-tugs, where they were conveyed across the inlet to
the big sailing vessel which was to carry the whole lot of men
and cases back to San Francisco.   There were countless
thousands of gulls flying round the cannery and river-mouth,
feeding on the offal and remains of salmon thrown out from
the cannery and carried backwards and forwards by the rise
and fall of the tide.   The noise made by these gulls screaming
by day and night was tremendous, and although we shot
a number of them and added the skins to our collection, no
amount of shooting seemed to have the effect of quieting or
keeping them away.   There were a fair number of mallards
on the marshes near the river, and we braved the mosquitoes
which swarmed there, in order to add some of these excellent fat birds to our daily diet of silver salmon, which

were brought every morning to our door by one of Mr. Wetherbee's men.

In the local store I found a good collection of furs caught by the natives in the neighbourhood. The mink, marten, and lynx skins being excellent, I could not resist the temptation of doing a small deal with Mr. Wetherbee for some of them.

CHAPTER X

IN THE SHEEP COUNTRY

ON August 15 we bade farewell to all those at the cannery who would be gone before we returned there in October. Towing boats up a rapid river like Kussiloff, where the trees and bushes overhang the banks, and numerous big rocks standing out of the water have to be circumvented, is no light task; and so our natives found it, even with three of them on the tow-rope and one man steering in the boat. The last had by far the best of the deal, and seemed to spend his time shouting to the other men, "Go ahead!" They meanwhile were often waist-deep in water, and kept floundering into innumerable deeper places, where they went almost out of sight. I will give them the credit of saying, that during the two days spent towing up the river these men worked hard and well. We kept making short cuts and walking through the forest wherever the river took a bend, and each day with the aid of a small .22 rifle collected enough spruce-grouse to make a good stew in the evenings. Although moose-tracks were numerous and fresh all along the river-banks, we saw nothing of the animals. We had, however, seen two young bulls early one morning before leaving Kussiloff, as they walked across the open marsh only a few hundred yards from the cannery.

175

The first evening we camped on the river-bank, and the second we pitched the tents on a long strip of land which runs out into the lake.   Yet another day was spent mostly in hard rowing, as we encountered the usual Alaskan head wind, which soon kicked up a big sea.   Kussiloff Lake is over thirty miles long, and on the third evening after leaving Kussiloff we reached the farthest end.   Here there is the headquarters of a mining company, and also the cabin of a man called Andrew Berg, who is the most celebrated hunter on the Kenai Peninsula.   We had previously met him at Kussiloff, and he kindly offered me the use of his cabin, of which we availed ourselves, as it was then empty.   The cabin contained a number of trophies of the chase, and many curious and ingenious appliances made by Berg himself for use in his various occupations.

Here we held a council of war, and it was decided to divide our parties, Little and Glyn with two natives going across the lake in a westerly direction.   They intended to pack some miles into the mountains, and hunt the ground on which Little and Colonel Cane had killed their sheep in the previous season.

Taking the other two natives, whose names were Pitka and Simeon, I started on the following morning in the opposite direction, making for the head of a stream called Indian Creek, where both Little and my natives had hunted in former seasons, and where the sheep were said to inhabit fairly easy ground.   It was this last consideration which decided me to go there, as I am a very poor hand at scaling dangerous places, and am utterly unable to negotiate a typical bit of ibex or chamois country owing to that deadly feeling of giddiness which no amount of practice seems to lessen.

INDIAN CREEK, IN THE SHEEP COUNTRY, KENAI MOUNTAINS.

As we had ample time before us, and the men were heavily loaded, we advanced by easy stages and camped the first evening near a small lake called Emma Lake, which is, I believe, named after Mrs. Dal de Weese, who accompanied her husband on his shooting trip in that country in 1901. Whilst on the trail I bagged half-a-dozen spruce-grouse and a porcupine with the little rifle, and so we had a good stew for supper. Next morning we followed a trail which led out of the timber line, and after two hours' slow crawling up hill, reached the summit of the first mountain range. From this point we could see Indian Creek below us, with a big glacier at its head. On each side of the creek rose steep hills, and on the mountain sides opposite to us we soon saw the first mountain sheep. The whole side of one hill was alive with small bands of them, easily visible to the naked eye for a great distance, as their almost snow-white coats showed up very distinctly against the green grass or the dark rocks on which they stood. There was no occasion here for a long and patient spying with a telescope to discover a beast; but I feared that owing to the great number of the sheep they were likely to be only ewes and lambs, since at this time of year the old rams usually get away in small bands by themselves. Turning the glasses on them, I soon found this to be the case, and although we counted eighty-six sheep within sight, not one of them was a ram of any size. However, we did not doubt that ere long we should discover the rams somewhere in the near neighbourhood. Pushing on farther, we descended into the valley of the stream, where our immediate object was to find a place suitable for wading across. Even when a place was found where the water did not reach above our waists, it was only with the greatest difficulty that we could keep on our legs against the stream, which ran with tremendous pace. To say that the water was cold, was hardly to express what it felt like ; but once safely across, I made the men pitch camp, and soon put on the only dry things I could raise in my kit. Here we were again below the timber line, and could find plenty of fuel for fires.

Next morning we were up at daylight, and after a hasty breakfast took what I judged to be the easiest way of ascent from our camp to the sides of the mountains where we had already seen some sheep. The sides of the cañon through which the stream ran were at this place some 1200 feet high, and although not really precipitous, it entailed nearly an hour's climbing to get out of the gorge. On reaching the top we saw before us a long stretch of undulating ground sloping up to a steep hill some three miles away. *Ovis dalli* inhabits the highest points of the mountains by day, but early in the morning and late in the evening the sheep draw down on the lower slopes to feed. We arrived on these slopes in time to see the ewes and lambs feeding, and as nearly as we could count there were over 130 of them scattered in bunches over the hillsides. These were not what I was looking for, and we pushed on to higher ground, avoiding, so far as possible, frightening the ewes as we went. Sending a native out on each flank, we walked straight ahead, covering a large extent of ground, but although we did not return to camp until thirteen hours after leaving it, during which time we found ourselves getting pretty hungry, no sign of a decent ram was to be seen. The men implored me to shoot a ewe for meat, but as I momentarily expected to find rams, I would not fire for fear of scaring away any that might be near although not visible.

The next day was a repetition of the first, except that, on

the return to camp, late in the evening, I shot a fine ewe. She suddenly jumped up from a hollow in the ground, and ran across our front about 100 yards away. The men shouted at me to shoot, for about the twentieth time in the past forty-eight hours. She appeared to me a big ewe, and as I wanted one to present to the British Museum, and furthermore held a special permit from the Minister of Agriculture at Washington, which empowered me to kill two sheep for this purpose at any time of year, I let fly a bullet at her. The date of this was August 21, and little did I think what a storm in a teacup that shot was to raise along Cook's Inlet at a later date. The ewe galloped away downhill and out of sight as if nothing had happened. I said to Pitka, " I missed her." He replied " You hit 'um all right ; me find 'um pretty soon, you bet." On looking over the brow of the hill, we saw a long gentle slope, and some 100 yards away the ewe lying dead. The men were delighted at the prospect of a " good few " meals of fresh mutton. I must admit that the same prospect appealed somewhat to me, as we had again got down to a diet of what the miners call " beans straight." My immediate interest was to skin and take out the leg-bones, etc., of the animal carefully, for a museum specimen. Unless I had personally seen it, I should not have believed the following circumstance, neither do I suppose that all who may read it will do so ; but on opening the carcass, we found that my bullet had taken the ewe behind the left shoulder, and expanding had passed clean through the heart, which was blown to atoms, then passing out on the other side, it had blown away part of the right shoulder and left a gaping wound over 3 inches large on the right side. And yet, with this awful injury, the animal had run some 140 yards before falling dead. How any living creature can have

enough vitality to run thus far with practically no heart left,
is a question I cannot answer; but the fact remains that this
one did it.

Late that night we roasted some ribs of the sheep on a
stick before the camp fire, and although freshly killed, the
meat, which was rolling in fat, was excellent.

At daylight the following morning we were off again,
working almost the same line of country. Leaving Simeon
in camp to clean the skin of the ewe, I took Pitka, and by
noon we found ourselves sitting under the brow of a hill
where we spent some time looking in vain with the glasses
for a good ram.

Suddenly I was roused by the well-known hum of a
ricochet bullet which passed over our heads. This was
followed by the sounds of several rifle-shots, and for a second
or two the fusilade was lively. I counted seven shots, but it
was impossible to tell exactly whence they came, owing to the
echo from the hills all round. However, as a string of lead
flying round is never very pleasant, I suggested to Pitka that
our position was getting "rather an unhealthy spot," to use
the words said to me by a celebrated American general on a
certain occasion when I was acting as "bear leader" to him,
and we found ourselves in the firing line which was attacking
a hill held by some 15,000 troops. It seems almost a pity to
have to add that this was only a sham fight during the great
English manœuvres of 1898.

In the case of Pitka and myself, the business was almost
too realistic for pleasure, but as there was not enough cover
to hide a mouse around us, there was not much to be done
save wait until we could see what or who was causing all the
trouble. Very soon I saw two small sheep coming over the
brow behind us; they were both yearling rams, so far as I

could judge.   One was limping painfully, and was evidently
wounded in the foreleg.   They both lay down about 200
yards from us, and I reasoned with Pitka as to whether or no
in self-defence I had not better shoot the pair of them and
save further trouble.   As we had no need of them, I decided
to remain quiet and await developments.   Shortly afterwards the heads of three men appeared on the sky-line, and
as all of them carried rifles, and were bearing down on us
with the sheep in a straight line between, I thought it wise
to stand up and wave my cap, showing them where the sheep
lay.   The nearer of the two men got up to within about 50
yards of the sheep and succeeded in killing one, although by
some means he managed to miss the wounded one as it
limped off over the brow of the hill.   On walking across to
them, I found that the party consisted of two Americans and
a native.   The leader of the party informed me that he was
Mr. Bonham of Denver, Colorado, and that he was collecting
specimens for the Denver Museum.   I told him I feared he
would have some trouble to find good rams there.   He said
he wanted anything—ewes, lambs, etc., to make large groups
for the museum.   These latter I told him he would have no
trouble in getting, since I could have killed twenty or thirty
in a couple of days.

The arrival of another party besides ourselves decided me
to abandon this country, and to move some miles farther up
the creek, where Pitka assured me we should find lots of
"big-horns," as he called the rams.   He believed they had
all moved to the precipices near the glacier above our camp.
This did not sound much in my line of business, but we
decided to try it.

Next day we moved camp and travelled as far up the
creek as we could go.   On one occasion we were compelled

to cross the stream, which was here very narrow, and a raging
torrent.   It was far too deep to wade, and we started felling
trees and floating them down until at last we got one to rest
on both banks.   This was only a small cotton-wood tree, and
to walk along the big end on our bank was about as much as
I could do.   To make matters worse, the water dashing over

MOVING CAMP IN THE SHEEP COUNTRY.
Glyn, Hanbury, and Natives.

it every second made the green bark as slippery as glass.
Pitka said that even he thought he could never get over, and
certainly not with his pack.   It was impossible to use a pole
so as to touch the bottom with it, as the weight of water
wrenched it out of our hands before we could move it six
inches in the stream.   I tried crossing on my hands and
knees, but had to give it up, as half-way across the tree was
so small that I could not get a grip of it.   At this juncture

Simeon came to the rescue.   He took a long pole, and using it to balance himself like a man on a tight-rope, crossed with ease.   He then came back again and said he would carry over one of the packs.   As this weighed about 80 lbs., I thought we might as well say good-bye to the tents and everything, but the clever native got first his own, and then Pitka's pack safely across.   It was now Pitka's turn, and he scrambled over, falling half into the water on the other side, where Simeon succeeded in pulling him ashore.   I knew that I could never do it, but the undefeated Simeon crossed once more, and pointing to his back said, " Me pack you all right."   I never believed he could achieve it, but said, " If you will risk your neck to pack me over, I will risk mine and go also."   He now had a load of some 185 lbs., but he never put a foot wrong, and got me safely over.   I would have given something to have been able to photograph the scene, as it was a remarkably fine performance, and one which I shall ever remember.

A further tramp of some two miles along the river-bank brought us to a spot where the river rushed through a deep gorge, the precipitous sides of which made it impossible to advance farther, as the natives could not get over the ground with their heavy packs.   Here, then, we decided to camp, as from this spot we could reach the glacier and mountains at the head of the stream.   There were a number of ewes and lambs visible on the crags far above us on either side of the creek.   Whilst the men were pitching camp, I searched carefully every crag and gully of the neighbouring heights with the glasses, and at last spotted one solitary ram.   He was standing almost straight above our camp, and fully 1500 feet above us, on a bare crag of rock, perfectly motionless, and apparently had already seen us.   To get

anywhere within shot seemed beyond my powers of climbing,
as the ground was very precipitous in places. There was,
however, a narrow strip of stunted alders running up a gully
towards the sheep, and hoping to be able to climb up by
clinging to these bushes, I started off, taking Simeon to carry
the rifle, and leaving Pitka below to watch if the sheep moved
his position. I shall long remember that climb, as it was
what the Americans call a "tough proposition." We soon
lost sight of the exact position of the ram, but at every halt
to get our wind we looked below at Pitka, who continued to
wave his hat as a sign to go higher. On reaching the end
of the stunted bushes we came on a very steep rock-slide,
and about 400 feet above us we could see the crag where
the ram had been standing, but no sign of the animal itself
was to be seen from our position. Hitherto we had been
hidden from view of this crag, but once on the bare rock-
slide it was another matter. So also was the climbing, and
after walking a few feet up it I had to go on my hands and
knees, being almost frightened out of my life at the way we
dislodged tons of small loose stones and rocks, which went
slipping down into the valley below in miniature avalanches.

At this juncture Pitka below us became wildly excited,
and waved his hat frantically. We guessed that the sheep
must have seen us, and telling Simeon to come quickly with
the rifle, I tried to get a firm spot on the slide to shoot from
if I could catch sight of the ram. A second afterwards the
ram dashed into sight as he crossed the head of the rock-
slide above us at about 120 yards' distance. For a second
he stood in full view looking at us. This was my only
chance. I could neither sit, stand, nor kneel, owing to the
ever-shifting ground around us. Exactly what position I
was in I never knew, but fired as best I could. The bullet

struck a rock about a foot over the ram's back, and he was
not long wishing us good-bye, as he vanished behind some
farther crags without giving another chance of a shot. I
was disgusted, and doubly so when on looking at the rifle
I found the 300-yards sight had been raised, which in the
hurry I had not observed, and which probably turned what
would have been a good shot, had the sight been down, into
a clean miss. I will draw a veil over my remarks on the
occasion as I handed Simeon the rifle and proceeded to
wend my way back through the brush to camp. He, on the
other hand, adopted a shorter but more dangerous mode of
getting to the bottom. He ran a few steps down the slide,
starting as he went all the small stones around him. Then,
sticking his heels close together, and leaning well back, he
let himself slide down with the moving mass of stones and
dust. It made me almost sick to watch him go down thus,
and I was vastly relieved to see him reach the bottom safely.
Former experience when crossing the slippery pole had
shown me that he did not suffer from nerves, but at this
exhibition I felt some fears for his ultimate fate, not unmixed
with similar feelings concerning my beloved Mannlicher rifle.
Late that evening a Frenchman named Vein, accompanied
by two natives, arrived at our camp. They were prospecting
for gold in the creek, and being short of grub were glad to
accept some of the mutton which we had hanging in camp.
Vein was a great raconteur, and regaled me with many of
his experiences in Alaska. He said that he had spent one
winter in a log-hut on St. Matthew Island in the Bering
Sea, and he and his partner killed during the season twenty-
one polar bears on the island.

He also said that he had spent one winter on Montague
Island near Valdez, about which place there is a yarn all

along the coast that the bears are so thick on the island that several parties of prospectors have been hunted off the place by them. Vein said he only saw two or three during his stay there. He can truthfully lay claim to being the man who sent out of Alaska the world's record moose-head, of which mention is made elsewhere.

On the following morning Pitka begged me to attempt the sides of the mountain near the glacier, and though not relishing the idea at all I left camp very early to try it. We had a long and arduous bit of climbing, and at last the men got me into a bit of country where I absolutely could go no farther. They tried hard to induce me to cross another very steep rock-slide, on nothing but a very sketchy kind of sheep-trail, which, not having four legs, I refused to try. Simeon held out an extra inducement by saying, "If you scared to walk, me pack you over." I was even more scared to risk that. Having seen no sheep I decided to return to camp. Pitka said, "Give me the rifle, me go catch 'um big-horns." Secretly hoping that he would fail in the attempt, I gave him the rifle and told him if he could locate any sheep on fairly easy ground not to shoot, as I would try to get there next day. It was late in the evening before the two natives returned to camp, very tired, hungry, and disgusted, as they said they had been miles all along the sides of the glacier, over very bad ground, and had not seen one single big ram.

Next morning early, Simeon came to my tent and said, "Pitka, he very bad." Suspecting it to be mumps, I went over to the tent and found Pitka looking very woeful with a swollen face. He said, "My face he hurt like hell. No can eat nothing. Pretty soon me die, I guess." He was terribly frightened, in spite of my assurances that I would pull him safely through the attack, having had some previous experience of the complaint myself. As he was afraid of being left alone, I sent Simeon out with the rifle to try to replenish our larder, since the meat supply had run out. He returned in the evening bringing back a fine young yearling ram, but still not having seen an old one with decent horns.

On the following day Simeon had to make a journey down to the base camp at the lake, to bring up a further supply of small necessaries, such as tea, sugar, etc. I remained in camp to discharge the mixed duties of cook and nurse. He had instructions to inquire, on his return journey next day, at Mr. Bonham's camp, to hear whether he had yet found any rams. The reply Simeon brought was that Bonham had got a number of ewes and lambs, but could find no sign of any decent rams. This decided me to move to fresh ground as soon as Pitka was sufficiently recovered. Two or three more days saw him crawling round the camp with his face in bandages. The weather during our stay at Indian Creek was magnificent, and on reference to my notes taken on the spot I find the following effusion, which was written on August 26 during one of my days of enforced idleness, and when evidently I must have been feeling somewhat sentimental :—

"Where now are the terrors of the Alaskan climate as I sit lazily at 10 A.M. 'neath the shade of a cotton-wood tree, in a grove of which my tents are pitched? The sun shines bright and warm overhead, scarcely a breath of air stirs the leaves or tall grasses which grow around in almost tropical luxuriance, and the smoke from a dying camp fire drifts slowly upwards towards the blue sky. On either side are lofty hills towering up some 1500 feet, with rocky summits on which are visible occasional mountain sheep.

The hills have between them a valley through which rushes a mountain torrent, passing close to my feet, and having its source in a glacier situated some two miles away, which now scintillates in the bright sunshine with all colours of a rainbow.

" A feeling of restfulness pervades in this Arcadia, with its vast panorama of magnificent scenery, and a great stillness is all around, save only for the splashing of the stream as it rushes onwards down its rocky course.

" The presence of several butterflies flitting midst the few remaining summer flowers, and the buzzing of numerous blue-bottle flies, tend strongly to remind me of a perfect English summer day. If further evidence of the general warmth and abundance of insect life is required, it is forthcoming, since one of my natives rushes up to where I sit, pursued by a swarm of wasps, and holding his face where he has been stung by one of his tormentors, after incautiously treading in their nest. His look of terror is comical to behold, and it takes some assurances on my part, and a plentiful application of Homocea ointment, to induce him to believe that the sting of a wasp is not fatal. The episode affords my other native, Pitka, some amusement, as he is likewise a spectator, and in his best style of English as he had heard it spoken, he confided to me the following statement. ' Me no like them flies. One time me find 'um little nest in tree. Me no savey what 'um is. My brother there, he savey, he say, " You catch 'um that." Me catch 'um alright. By 'um by lots of fly come round. Me fall down quick, no can get up for two minutes. All time fly he bite like hell. Next day, you bet you, my face big all same as mumps. That fly no good, no, sir.' "

And yet, with all its various attractions, this valley of

peace held not the one thing which would induce me to prolong our stay, since the big rams were absent.

On the morning when we finally decided to start back to the lake, Simeon began to develop the mumps, and this might have delayed us indefinitely except for the timely arrival on the previous night of one of our first invalided natives, whom we had left at Kussiloff, and who appeared just in time to carry Simeon's pack. We covered the return journey in one day, and paid a visit *en route* to the American's camp, where there was a great array of ewes' and lambs' skins and skulls, etc., in all enough to fill three or four cases for any museum ; and why so many were wanted at Denver I cannot say. Mr. Bonham had still failed to get any rams, nor had any been seen.

On arrival at the lake we saw that some fresh tents had been erected there, not far from our own tent containing our base supplies. My natives said they knew they were the tents of another Englishman who had come up from Kenai. Hearing this, I strolled across, and soon had the pleasure of meeting a fellow-countryman, by name Mr. David Hanbury, and one who on subsequent occasions I soon found to be a good sportsman and boon companion. Hanbury invited me to supper, an offer which I was not slow to accept, as the hour was late, and my men had as yet not arrived with the materials for cooking.

I found that Hanbury had been shooting near the head of another branch of Indian Creek, some ten or twelve miles from where we had been. He said that rams were very scarce there, and he had only bagged two, neither of which had a very big head. Like myself he was in search of a better country.

In our base camp we found one of Glyn's natives who had

TYPICAL VIEW IN THE SHEEP COUNTRY, KENAI MOUNTAINS.

been sent down from the mountains ill with mumps. He reported that Glyn and Little had found a lot of good rams in their country, and had bagged some good heads. Hearing this, Hanbury and I decided to join forces and go to the same ground. He was obliged to leave one of his men behind, as this man was also ill with the mumps. A hospital was started for our three sick men in an old hut near our tents, and early next morning we left them there, well provided with all the small comforts at our command. We set out in our two dories, and a row of some eight miles took us to the other side of the lake, at a spot where Glyn had established a small base camp. Here we found his cache tent, and in it a fine show of eight good sheep-heads which had evidently just been sent down from his camp in the hills. Here also was a small creek in which Glyn had moored his dory. The creek was full of dead and dying salmon, and all around its mouth on each bank were great patches of grass trodden down by bears, and heaps of salmon heads and bones, showing that bears came there freely to fish in the evenings. A long ascent lay before us up through the heavily timbered slopes of the hills which reach to the lake shores. Here the natives had cut a very decent trail, which made the travelling very much better than it would otherwise have been, owing to the jungle of high grass and quantities of fallen trees. The day was very warm, with scarcely a breath of air, and in consequence Hanbury and I regulated our pace in a leisurely manner to that of the men carrying their packs. On reaching the edge of the timber line, we saw Glyn's tents at no great distance, pitched in an open glade which commanded a view of the hills in front. The next thing we observed was that three sheep were lying down on the side of a green hill facing the camp, and less than a mile away from it. With the telescope we made them out to be rams, one with a decidedly good head. Moreover, they were on a very easy bit of ground, a place where even I could crawl up to them without the slightest misgivings. On reaching the tents we found Glyn and Little just getting out their rifles, preparatory to stalking these sheep, which they also had seen. Hearing of my previous bad luck, Glyn at once insisted that I should go after them, whilst he and Hanbury sat in camp to watch me stalk them. Little said that he would come also, as he knew the easiest way to reach the spot. Since the sheep had been lying down for some time, and might be on the move any moment, we started at once. On nearing the spot where we had seen them, and whilst climbing the last steep grassy slope which should bring us in view of them, Little said he would go a little higher and look down from a knoll above us. He made for this bit of high ground and reached it some distance ahead of me. The sheep had moved, and were then feeding away uphill towards us on the other . ᵕ of the brow. Little walked right into sight of them, and immediately I saw him crouch down and wave his hand, saying, " Come quick—run ; they are going." There was about as much chance of my running as of jumping over the moon. He was 50 feet above me, and the grass slope was so steep that I could only scramble up it. I reached the top just in time to see Little running at full speed about 100 yards away, to a spot whence he could see across the valley below. Into this valley the sheep had evidently disappeared, as they were nowhere in sight of me. Soon they appeared, galloping up the hillside on the other side of the valley, and about 250 yards from Little, who let fly a string of lead at them from his Mannlicher. At the fifth shot he killed the largest

o

ram, and it was no mean performance, as the beast must have
been fully 300 yards away and was going fast. He wanted
me to go across and look at the beast with him, but I was so
disgusted at losing another chance at a good ram, and all
through my own stupidity in not walking in front, that I said
I would return to camp and send out the natives to skin and
bring in the beast.

It turned out that Glyn had been getting his sheep at a
camp some six or seven miles farther up in the hills, and was
now on his way back to the lake, having merely camped at
this spot on the chance of picking up a black bear, of which
species he had seen several feeding on the blue berries that
covered the hillsides around this spot. These berries form a
very favourite food of the bears at this time of year.

Glyn undertook to pilot us next morning across the
mountains to his old camp, where we arrived soon after
noon. Here there was a small grove of cotton-wood trees,
which afforded the only decent fuel to be found anywhere
in the neighbourhood. The surrounding hills were by no
means difficult to climb, and providing that all the rams had
not taken to the precipices along the edge of the glaciers, I
had hopes of getting some good heads. Glyn did not inspire
me with great confidence when he said that towards the
end of his stay there the rams had all worked from the
hill-tops down along the precipitous sides of the mountains
overhanging a big glacier about three miles from the camp.
There even he had difficulty to get them, and his graphic
description of having to shoot whilst half hanging over a
precipice at rams standing on crags below, which, when he
killed them, went hurtling into space, and fell sheer some
2000 feet on to the glacier beneath, did not appeal to me as
being a pleasure. He said it was marvellous how the natives

would clamber down the apparently sheer face of the rocks on to the glacier after these sheep and return later with the horns, etc.   In the afternoon Glyn returned to his camp, he and Little meaning to strike out for the moose country in a day or two.

We were now camped at some considerable height above sea-level, and had a sharp touch of frost each night.   This in no way inconvenienced either Hanbury or myself.   He in particular was well accustomed to cold, since he had only recently come down from the Arctic Circle, where he had spent some three years living with the Esquimaux in the Mackenzie River country.   The touch of frost put an end to the few remaining mosquitoes, which fortunately are never very bad in the sheep country.   The last of these little pests which I remember seeing was on our first evening in this new camp, and it afforded some amusement to me if not to Hanbury, who was at that moment enveloped in a huge kind of mackintosh cloth which he tied round his head and arms in order to make a kind of dark room, in which he changed the plates of his camera.   Whilst busily engaged at this work the last mosquito of summer took him at a disadvantage, and having found some soft spot commenced to work its wicked will on him.   The awful flow of language coming in muffled tones from beneath the improvised dark room, and his futile efforts to get at the aggressor were so comical, that at the risk of making an enemy for life, I laughed most immoderately at his discomfiture.

At 5 o'clock next morning we were off to the hill-tops, and both walked together as far as the edge of the precipices overlooking the glacier.   One glance down was enough to convince me that all the sheep on earth would not induce me to go down the face of those rocks.   We saw a few rams in

the distance, far below us, but in such places that even
Hanbury, who is good at hill-work, could not get to them.
Here I left him to follow along the glacier. The view from
above it where we stood was very fine. Looking down some
1500 feet on to the great ice-field below, and then away into
the far distance where the glacier went winding between the
mountain-tops till it merged into a vast mass of perpetual
snow and ice, compelled one to realise what a mere speck on

THE GREAT SHEEP CREEK GLACIER NEAR LAKE TUSTUMENA.
Taken from 2000 feet above it.

the face of the globe is that mighty being man, when compared with many other of Nature's works.

After leaving Hanbury I made a wide detour of several
miles, and finally reached the summit of a mountain which I
estimated as being of an altitude of some 6000 feet, whence a
magnificent view of the surrounding country was obtained.
In front lay another big glacier, and away in the distance on
the far side of it I made out a few solitary rams, just visible
with the aid of a telescope, but utterly unapproachable from
our side. Moving farther on, we came across several small
bands of ewes and lambs, but still no rams. By this time,

having been over ten hours out of camp, and at a considerable distance from it, I decided to give up for the day. There was, however, one important matter to be attended to—namely, the lack of meat in camp, and I had promised Hanbury to repair the want on my return journey. Not wishing to kill a small sheep myself which would be reckoned as one of those allowed by my permits, I therefore gave the native my rifle and sent him after a small band of young sheep with orders to kill one, which he easily did. So far as I can see, this method which I adopted on two occasions is the only way by which a sportsman can obtain meat, when in need of it, without rendering himself liable to a charge of breaking the game laws at certain times of the year, and under certain conditions. I make this statement, having regard to the fact that at a subsequent trial held at Kenai the U.S. Deputy Commissioner informed the court that sportsmen could on no account be accepted as being included under the heading of " Explorers, or travellers on a journey when in need of food," these, according to the Act, being allowed to kill game for food. The Commissioner ruled that sportsmen were there for the express purpose of shooting, and therefore were practically outside the pale of the law. I maintained that the fact of having journeyed some 2000 miles in Alaska entitled me to some claim as a traveller, and this statement was subsequently upheld by the authorities at Washington, during the course of a conversation which I had with them on the subject. Nevertheless, as already stated, it is best to be on the safe side, and since the native is a sacred being in Alaska, who can do no wrong, and is not allowed to starve although certain white men may do so, when you feel hungry make sure that the natives are in the same state, and send one out to shoot meat for the camp.

On return to camp I found Hanbury, who had just arrived empty-handed, not having seen any rams in a place where it was possible to approach them.   We were both pretty tired and hungry, and it was not long before we had a good bit of mutton roasting in front of the fire.

The natives proceeded to cook enough meat for themselves to make what they called a good supper for all three of them.   If it had not been for my previous experiences with Kaffirs and Zulus I should not have credited the Alaskan native with the powers of eating which he possesses ; as it is, he is second only in this respect to the above-named tribes.

Hanbury had picked up two natives who were great characters in their own particular way.   One, who acted as his cook and personal attendant, rejoiced in the name of Sulivan. His great amusement seemed to be walking about the camp and whistling from morning to night what might be designated in musical parlance as a cavatina, which he had picked up at Kenai, and which after about forty-eight hours got on my nerves to such an extent that I found myself also whistling the dreadful tune on numerous occasions.   The other man was a tough-looking old customer who could hardly speak a word of English, and was reputed a mighty hunter.   I believe his name was William, but we at once christened him "Wandering Willy," and remarked that he looked what the Americans call " wild and woolly."

Late that evening Sulivan came to our tents and addressed Hanbury as follows.   " Willy he say he scared to go hunting to-day with you because he no talk English.   He say he take you to-morrow, he savey good place, you bet you catch 'um big-horns before 12 o'clock."   Hanbury said, " Very well, tell the old fool to come ; I don't care what language he speaks, if he only finds some rams."

Next morning Hanbury set off early with both his men again in the direction of the glacier. I climbed the hills behind the camp, and went several miles in the opposite direction until I found myself looking down from the highest point on to the great Kussiloff glacier. Although persevering for several hours, we failed to see anything except ewes and lambs, and towards afternoon I returned to camp.

On the opposite range of hills we saw Hanbury returning, and putting the telescope on the party I soon made out that his men were carrying two big sheep-heads.

It turned out that Willy had fulfilled his promise, and after being taken down some real bad places overhanging the glacier, Hanbury had bagged two good rams. He told me there were more rams in the same place, but that with my bad head it was hopeless to attempt getting them.

We were now convinced that all the rams in that district had got into similar places, and I decided it was best to leave the ground and give it a rest, intending to return later after doing some moose-hunting, when the first fall of snow had come. This generally drives the sheep from the highest peaks, to seek shelter and food on the lower slopes of the mountains.

There is no doubt that, for those who can really get over the ground, hunting *Ovis dalli* affords the finest sport which Alaska can offer. The magnificent scenery, splendid air, and healthy exercise experienced whilst hunting this wild sheep are such that the sport appeals far more to the genuine sportsman than the terrible monotony of still-hunting after moose in the dense forests, or even the more dangerous amusement of tackling the great brown bears in their haunts amongst the alder bushes and river-banks.

The following morning at daylight tents were struck, the

camp packed, and we started on our return to the lake. On passing Glyn's last camp we saw what was evidently a big sheep lying in the open, about a mile and a half away on the hillside, and not far from where I had previously made an unsuccessful stalk. Here was another chance for me, if only it was a ram. Hanbury and I got out our telescopes and examined the object, then both exclaimed, " Confound the brute, it has no head." Such was indeed the case, and a more careful study of the animal revealed the fact that it was

DEAD RAM (*OVIS DALLI*).

evidently a sheep which had been killed by Glyn or Little since we had passed the spot a few days before. Resuming our journey, we reached the lake, and once more set out in the dories to row across it to our base camp, where we arrived in the evening. We found some of our invalids recovering from mumps, and they told us that Glyn had gone on to the moose-country after leaving instructions where I should find him. He had left one more native in the hospital, this making a " total possible " of our men, who had now all caught the mumps in turn.

CHAPTER XI

AWAY TO THE MOOSE-GROUND

DURING the night the wind rose with tremendous force, and rushing down in violent gusts from the great Kussiloff glacier on to the lake, it lashed up a perfect inferno of waters. There is nothing like a storm on a big fresh-water lake for its suddenness and violence whilst it lasts; especially when, as was the case here, the wind comes tearing down three or four great valleys which converge on the lake. The outlook was not promising as Hanbury and I surveyed the waters in the early morning. It was far too rough to think of rowing, but the wind was blowing in the direction in which we wanted to go. We had no proper sails for the dories, but Alaska is essentially a country for new inventions, and we were not long in cutting some small spruce-fir trees and shaping out some masts. Then taking two tarpaulin sheets about 9 feet square we soon fashioned a couple of very serviceable sails. Previous experience in the Bering Sea had shown me that a dory when properly handled could weather a sea equal to the one now running on the lake. Setting a native to handle the sail, I took an oar to use as a rudder, and followed by Hanbury in his dory we set out. The wind was blowing great guns, and although dories are not notorious for their pace we made good time, and covered some ten miles in a short space of time.   Here we saw Glyn's tents on the shore, and running in with the two dories, we were just in time to catch him and Little on the point of starting to pack up into the forest.   They decided to stay another night, and during the afternoon the men reported a number of rabbits in a small patch of willows near the camp.   Thinking they would make an excellent addition to the larder, Hanbury and I, taking two Paradox guns and a few cartridges, posted ourselves outside the bushes, Little taking the natives and driving the rabbits towards us in the most approved style of English covert beating.   For a few minutes things were quite lively as the rabbits came out in all directions; and we bagged eleven of them without wasting a cartridge, returning to camp a few minutes after leaving it with materials for a good square meal for all hands.   Towards evening the gale died away, but Hanbury decided to remain with us for the night, and left early next morning to sail farther along the lake, where he meant to pitch his camp, some five or six miles away in a good bit of moose country.   At the same time we started off to pack into the forest, a distance of about eight miles from the lake, where the forest was not so dense, to a place where Little had previously hunted moose with Mr. Paget in 1901.   Following an old trail which they had cut, and which was still in good order, we finally reached a small lake which lay on the higher ground and at no great distance from the extreme edge of the timber line.   This spot was selected as our main camp for moose-hunting.   For an area of many miles around the camp a great forest fire had devastated the country many years before.   The gaunt and charred fir-trees still standing in many places bore evidence of this, and the still greater number of logs which had blown down and lay half hidden in the long grass made the travelling

in many places an arduous and tiring business.   On the other
hand the undergrowth of low willow bushes had grown up in
dense masses, thereby affording excellent feeding for moose
on the young shoots which they love so well.   In places
these bushes were so dense that to force a passage through
them without making considerable noise was an impossibility.
Moose-tracks were fresh and plentiful all along the trail and
around the camp, and every few yards we came upon fresh
beds beaten down in the long grass where they had been
lying down.   Towards evening we heard a shot some distance
from camp, and as Glyn had been working his way through
the forest without following the trail, we decided to send a
native on to a small knoll behind the camp, there to fire a
signal shot, since it was now so nearly dark that we estimated
Glyn had fired a signal to show that he was unable to find the
position of our new camp, which Little had tried to explain to
him before leaving the other camp in the morning.   This
surmise turned out to be correct, as shortly afterwards Glyn
arrived calling the little lakes in the neighbourhood all kinds
of strange names, and declaring that he had visited any
number of them, all answering to the description which Little
gave of the one where our camp was pitched.   He had seen
one young bull moose, but its horns were so small that he
would not shoot it, our fixed intention being to shoot at
nothing unless we estimated the head as being 60 inches
at least.

Our plan of hunting was to go out early in the morning
and work a big extent of country in different directions,
always walking until we got the wind in our faces and then
going straight forward, making as little noise as possible,
and keeping a sharp look-out ahead and on both sides as we
went.   A more monotonous, uninteresting, and often tiring

performance I have never indulged in, the only skill required
being such as is supplied by a sharp pair of eyes and ears, in
addition to the power of creeping about quietly—in fact the
most elementary principles of hunting, and the element of
chance existing so strongly that it is merely a matter of
"bull-headed luck" if you come across a bull moose with a
head measuring 40 inches or 70 inches.   I observe that Mr.
A. J. Stone, in a long article on the moose, has written as
follows : — " The man who has acquired so thorough a
knowledge of the habits of the moose as to enable him,
unaided, to seek the animal in its native haunts, and by fair
stalking bring it to bay, has reached the maximum standard
of the American big game hunter."   This may be so, but
personal experience has taught me that the natives on the
Kenai Peninsula are very bad at quickly seeing any animal,
and that they have invariably got their eyes on the ground
looking for tracks, etc., when often a moose is staring them
in the face, probably half hidden by a tree at no great
distance away.   Therefore, although two pairs of eyes may
be better than one, it will be found that the additional man
makes more noise than one alone, and I maintain that any
intelligent being can master the principles of moose-hunting,
as carried on in the Kenai forests, after two days' playing at
being his native's marionette, to such an extent that he is
fully capable of going and killing his own moose single-
handed.   Given the element of luck referred to above, it is
quite possible that his first beast may be a record head, or
nearly so.   To know thoroughly the habits of moose is
another affair, and a life's study might not suffice some men
for this purpose.   The only way in which such knowledge
can be acquired is by living summer and winter amongst the
animals in their native home.   How few men there are who

OUR MAIN CAMP IN THE MOOSE COUNTRY.

have done this, and at the same time made an intelligent study of the animals! One such I know, and he is my friend Mr. A. S. Reed, who has already been mentioned in these pages. Many years spent in the forests of North America, living as he did alone with the natives in their huts or tents, entirely cut off from civilisation, surrounded by various kinds of big game, he has accumulated a store of valuable information on the habits and wild life of the game which it is granted to but few white men to acquire. I would that I had his stock of knowledge to draw upon, and then indeed there might be some notes on the habits of moose which would be worthy of the reader's attention when glancing at these pages.

My first day in the moose country gave promise of better things than subsequently followed. Taking Pitka to instruct me in the approved style of Alaskan moose-hunting, I set out, and worked my way through the timber for a considerable distance. Innumerable recently used beds, fresh tracks, and droppings of moose covered the ground. Finally we reached a high point on the very edge of the timber line, beyond which lay a large open tundra stretching far away to the foothills of the sheep country whence we had come. Below us lay a deep valley thickly timbered, with here and there an open glade. At some distance away on the open tundra a large brown bear was busily eating the blue berries which covered the ground in masses. Having no intention of going after this beast, I was not watching him so closely as Pitka. On glancing at the valley below, I saw some 300 feet beneath us a single moose standing in an open space. Turning the glasses on the spot, I found it was a cow. Shortly afterwards we made out two more cows, each with a calf, and one young bull carrying a small head. Here was my opportunity of seeing something of the habits of these animals by day. Telling Pitka to sit down and be prepared for a long halt, I did likewise.

The solitary cow soon began browsing on the young shoots, and when tired of feeding proceeded to lie down. Before doing so she took a quick run in a semicircle and then lay. This manœuvre she repeated several times after getting up and browsing a short time in various places. The flies were very bad around the animals, and it was curious to see their great ears working backwards and forwards in the endeavour to keep the pests away. The little calves seemed to be particularly worried by them, and kept dashing through the bushes in a circle round their mothers. Occasionally the noise they made would startle the solitary cow and the young bull, both of which would then jump up and run a short distance, turning to look back and sniff the air for danger. It was here I first observed that a moose when startled nearly always runs in a semicircle, so as to get to leeward of the spot whence the noise comes, and thus satisfy itself by means of its marvellous power of smell as to the cause of all the trouble. From about 11 A.M. until 3 P.M. the moose did not move very far, and spent the greater part of the time lying down. Afterwards they began to move off, slowly feeding their way out of my sight and into the denser forest. I enjoyed the few hours spent watching them, and nothing would induce me to shoot at any of them, although Pitka thought I was temporarily mad, and kept saying, " You shoot one, plenty good meat there, you bet." We returned to camp without seeing anything more. Glyn had failed to see a beast all day.

After this we hit upon a series of blank days, and oh the weariness of that endless crawling about over fallen logs, through high grass and thick brush, all streaming with water in the early mornings, after a heavy dew or rain during the night! During five days I only saw one small bull moose, and Glyn did not manage to see even so much as this during the same period. Little did, however, succeed in killing a small bull moose on a day when we all set out with the intention of getting some meat, of which we had been destitute for several days.

On the day following I also managed to get a moose with a fair-sized head, so that we then had too much meat on hand at once. On this occasion I was walking up the side of a steep hill, and through high grass above my waist, followed by a native. He was not my own trusty man Pitka, whom I had left in camp. My attendant on this particular occasion was called Ivan, and considered himself something of a hunter, but so far as I could make out his greatest exploit had occurred in the previous season, when he and another native were following a wounded moose in some high brush. Ivan saw something move in the high bushes and fired at once. He was somewhat surprised afterwards to find that he had shot his companion dead on the spot.

As we walked along, I told him to keep a sharp look-out on each side, whilst I kept looking ahead. On stopping to take breath, I turned and glanced back, and there, standing in an open clearing, about 200 yards away below us and exactly in the line where Ivan should have been spying, was a fine bull moose, evidently listening to the noise of our approach. He was not looking straight at us, so that it was hard to see exactly the spread of his horns. We dared not move nearer, as, although the grass was high, we were fairly exposed to view on the steep slope of the hill. The first thing to decide was whether the moose bore a sizable head. I judged it about 60 inches, and said to Ivan, " What do you think? " He replied, " Big horns all right ; hurry up, shoot quick." The last four words he kept repeating about every second, and growing furious, I cursed him freely. There was I, not liking to risk a standing shot at the distance, as I am a poor hand, when standing, with a rifle, not able to see over the long grass when sitting or kneeling, trying my best to get into a steady position, and at the same time to keep the fool of a native quiet. Finally I managed somehow to get off a shot, aiming where I believed the beast's heart to be. It will give some idea of the accuracy of my aim, and the steadiness of my position, when I say that the exact measurement of this beast from nose to tail in a straight line was about 9 feet; he was standing broadside on, and my first shot broke his hind-leg just above the hock. Everything considered, it was fortunate for me that I was shooting at a beast so big that it was hard to miss some part of it. With his three remaining legs, the moose made off at a tremendous pace, followed by two more bullets, neither of which touched him. Ivan dashed wildly down the hill after him, shouting, " Come quick. Run." Down I went, falling over logs, with a loaded rifle, expecting every moment to blow a hole through Ivan or myself, but it was no time for trifles of that sort to worry us. As we followed the tracks some way into the high timber, we kept stopping from time to time to listen. A wounded moose will lead one through the thickest brush it can find, and here we had a sample of this habit of the animal in its worst form. Falling and crashing through the bushes, we made noise enough to scare every moose for miles. Suddenly Ivan, who was in front, shouted, " Come quick. He run." Dashing ahead, I saw the hind-quarters of a moose

P

disappearing behind a tree, and fired at once. Result, bullet planted well into the tree. This started the hunt again, and off we went at full speed, following the wounded beast partly by sound and partly by tracks, blundering over fallen trees, splashing through deep soft places covered with moss under which lay yielding mud and slush, tearing the skin off our hands and faces as we raced through the thick scrub in which the small twigs kept flying back and hitting us viciously in the face. Verily, it was a merry chase. My progress was, I regret to say, punctuated here and there with short halts to get my wind, and expend some of it in swearing at the bushes, trees, and everything which seemed to combine to annoy us and retard our progress. To make matters worse, I caught a glimpse of the moose moving through the trees ahead of us, just as I was hung up by the legs and arms in a more than usually thick place. Nothing daunted, I let go two more bullets after him, and we found eventually that one of these had passed through the fleshy part of his neck. But the end was approaching, and soon the poor brute, which must have been suffering intensely with its broken hind-leg, lay down in a thick cover. Here we ran almost on top of him, and Ivan, jumping behind a tree as he stood up and faced us, shouted, " Shoot quick." I must confess I should like to have had the chance over again, when I would have delayed shooting a little, to see if he would charge us, as the moose is reported to do when wounded and cornered. But since we had at last " brought him to bay " (which I take it is not exactly what Mr. Stone meant when using this term), I thought it best to plant a bullet in his shoulder; and so ended what will ever be to me a memorable chase, entirely brought on by a disgracefully bad shot in the first instance. He was a very large animal

although not carrying a pair of horns remarkable for their
size. Their spread was 57 inches, and the total number of
points only 23. It was a gracefully shaped head, and one
with which I was satisfied for a beginning, although it was

My first Bull Moose, Kenia Forest.

a very small specimen for the Kenai Peninsula. The horns
had still small shreds of the velvet hanging from the tips,
and these had misled me into thinking the head to be larger
than it really was.

Ivan and I skinned as much of the beast as we could
get at, but to turn over the body was more than we could

manage with our united efforts. We had no machine for weighing the animal, and I have not much opinion of estimated weights. I remarked at the time that the weight was probably about 1500 lbs., and judging by later experiments made by my friend Hanbury this estimate was not far off the mark. I sent Ivan back to camp to get help to finish the skinning and pack home the head, etc.

On return to camp I found Glyn very disgusted at not having seen a moose; but he had shot at, and severely wounded, a black bear which had got away into some thick alders, where he and Little had been unable to follow it. They had left it, deciding to return with the natives and track it next day. Of course, as always seems to be the case, it rained hard during the night, and next morning, when Pitka went with Glyn to try to follow the trail, all the blood-marks had been washed away and they found nothing.

The date of my killing this first moose was September 11, and for nine days afterwards I did not fire a shot, nor did we see a sizable bull during the whole time.

I questioned Pitka closely as to his opinion why we did not see more big bulls. He gave an explanation which I think was correct, saying that the big bulls did not get their horns out of velvet so soon as the smaller ones; and it was obvious, from the fact of my beast of September 11 still having velvet on the horns, that many of the larger animals were sulking in the dense thickets, where they would remain until their horns were clean. Furthermore, he said that owing to the late spring and summer the moose were very backward in getting their horns clean. In ordinary seasons on the Kenai Peninsula the bulls begin to run round looking for the cows, and then fighting with each other, from about the middle of September. That is the best time to pick out the good heads. But I am convinced that in 1903 in the forest around Kussiloff Lake the big bulls did not commence to run much before the end of September, and I was even counting on getting the best heads in October. A sudden and unexpected ending was, however, put to our trip, just after the moose had begun to run freely. Pitka would frequently return to camp after a blank day, saying, " Old man moose, he no walk around yet."   On September 18 I moved camp to a fresh bit of country, leaving Glyn and Little in the old camp. We pitched our tents in a very dense part of the forest at a spot in which we afterwards dis-covered that it was no easy matter to find the camp after dark.

On the evening of the 19th I had a message saying that Glyn had bagged his first moose, but that he was disgusted to find he had not seen a good view of his horns, and that they did not measure 50 inches, although the head had appeared to be much bigger. On one of my blank days I had an annoying experience with a black bear. A number of these beasts came out on the open tundra from the timber every morning to eat the blue-berries.

Having gone out early one morning as far as the edge of the timber line, with the express purpose of looking for black bear, I soon saw one feeding about two miles away on the open tundra. The beast was at no great distance from a deep gully, which was full of dense brush. It was my object to cut him off from this, and calling Pitka, who accom-panied me, we started running at our best pace. Before we could get within shot, the bear had disappeared somewhere into the gully. I decided to try a drive, and leaving Pitka at the head of the gully, with instructions to walk along it when I had reached a place where I might be able to see a clearing in the brush, I made a wide detour, reaching the gully some 400 yards below where Pitka sat. My drive would certainly have given me a good chance of bagging the bear if it had not been for one circumstance. This was that I did not go far enough down the gully, but happened to select the very spot to take up my position at which the bear was then feeding behind a dense clump of thick willows. I started pushing my way through them, and when well tangled up in the middle of the clump, Pitka began whistling and pointing frantically down the gully towards me. I stopped, naturally thinking he could see the bear somewhere on my left, between him and me. After looking that way in vain, I began to move again. At this, Pitka began whistling and gesticulating afresh. I was furious, since at that distance and angle I could not say where he was pointing, and dared not shout and ask the fool where the beast might be, as that would only have the effect of driving it the wrong way. Utterly unable to see five yards, for the jungle of bushes reaching just above my head, I started to move again. Suddenly, close at hand, but on my right side, and only a few yards away, I heard some big beast crash into the bushes in front of me. Making a frantic dash I pushed through into the open, only in time to see the bushes moving as they closed behind the bear, which had disappeared down the gully below me. Pitka soon arrived, and explained that, after he first whistled, the bear had been standing on its hind-legs not ten yards from me the whole time. If he had had the sense to shout saying where the bear was, I might have caught a glimpse of part of his body, by looking in the right direction. As it was, my back was almost turned to the animal, and I was intent on looking in exactly the wrong direction. So ended my first misadventure with the black bear.

Glyn and I were so unlucky in our attempts to get these black bears, which are very numerous in certain parts of the moose and sheep country, that we began to regard them with a kind of superstition. In fact, after a subsequent misadventure with one of them, which is referred to later, I turned to Pitka, who was present, and said, "After this, if a black bear stands up in the open and looks me in the face at ten yards away, I will be d—d if I shoot at it"; nor did I do so, but chiefly because I never had the chance.

A really fine night in the depths of the Alaskan forest has a peculiar charm for those who love silent nature and solitude. As a rule the ordinary sportsman is so dead tired after a long day in the forest, that on return to camp his first idea is to get something to eat, and his second is to roll himself in the blankets. My two natives were no exceptions to their race as regards their powers of eating and going to sleep, and during a spell of particularly fine weather, when all was quiet in camp, being alone and perhaps feeling somewhat sentimental, I would take my pipe (my best friend, and sole comforter in rain or sunshine), and seating myself under a very large spruce tree near the camp, would listen to the various forest sounds by night. Doubtless if this work was intended to bristle with sentiment, this would be a very appropriate place to work in an apt quotation from Gray's dear old *Elegy*, but presuming that, like myself, the majority of my readers are all lovers of the poem, and all rather tired of seeing one man quote another's words to try to express their own sentiments, in similar circumstances, when their vocabulary and powers of stringing words together are not equal to the task of expressing what they think is hurting them; then I only beg to state that if you, kind reader, will consider the words of the first three verses in the immortal poem as having been quoted, and not forget to omit small items such as curfews, ploughmen, and sheep-folds, which do not exist largely in Alaska; then, I say, you will have an exact reproduction of my own feelings at the time, and also the actual state of affairs.   By this I mean that the solemn stillness was there in its most approved style, and the only thing to break it was the occasional hooting of the large eagle-owls, and the more regular, but less poetic, snoring of my natives in the tent near by my seat.

It is surprising how few noises one hears in the woods on the Kenai Peninsula.   Poison and traps have wrought havoc with the wolves and such like noisy denizens of the forest by night.   Occasionally the clashing of horns echoes through the trees, coming from the scene of some deadly strife between two lords of the forest; and now and again is heard the swish of wings overhead, accompanied by the familiar call of wild geese and ducks, as they travel down from the Arctic regions, making their way to the warmer coasts of California as winter approaches.   However, although this kind of thing is very charming, it was not exactly what I had travelled some 9000 miles to hear, and my temper was getting a little short when we had worked hard until September 20 and only seen one moose with a decent head. Small bulls and cows we could see, but the big bulls seemed to be scarce.   The country in which we then were was really the headquarters and favourite hunting-ground of the celebrated Andrew Berg, who is undoubtedly the best moose-hunter in that part of Alaska.   He and his brother had built several small cabins and huts, for use when hunting there, in different parts of the forest.   Pitka was of opinion that Berg had pretty well thinned out the big heads in that district during the past few seasons.   I felt certain that there were plenty left, and that as long as the cows remained there, so long would the big bulls come in search of them.

On the morning of September 20 I took both the natives, Pitka and Ivan, and made tracks for a high hill some six or seven miles from camp which I had observed some days before, and from the summit of which a good view of the surrounding ground could be obtained. My plan was to vary the monotony of wandering aimlessly through the dense brush and trees, by spending a few hours watching from the top of the hill. Pitka, who was now thoroughly disgusted, and swore he would never come hunting another season in that district, was ready to adopt any new method. Arrived on the hill, one hour's waiting produced no result, except the filling and lighting of my pipe at the end of the time, as I was unable to sit still without smoking any longer. Once again "my Lady Nicotine" served me a good turn. As the smoke went drifting lazily down wind in the soft breeze that was blowing, and I kept looking in the direction it followed, my eyes were greeted with the sight of a fine bull moose as he sprang up from a spot where he had been lying. He started running at a great pace through the short brush. His head was up and his great horns lay back along his flanks. Pitka was apparently looking straight at him, and I said to him, "What can you see?" He replied, "Me no can see nothing; me think all big moose dead." I then pointed out the moose in front of us. He was running in a complete circle round the hill on which we sat, and about 1000 yards away. On seeing him, both Pitka and Ivan said, "Big horns—come—run quick." They both dashed off in a direction at right angles to the direction in which the moose ran. I saw that the idea was to try to intercept him if he continued following the same course, but had little hopes of our doing so, as we could not

travel half as fast through the bushes as the moose, and we
had about an equal distance to go if I was to get within shot
as he passed us.   However, fortune favoured us, for the
moose entered a small patch of stunted spruce firs, and as it
was some time before he appeared again we got to within 400
yards of the trees in the interval.   Our surprise was great to
see, a moment later, two bull moose walk out of the cover of
these trees.   The leading bull had evidently been startled by
the other one, and had joined him in his flight.   They came
leisurely out at a walk, and seemed to be following a trail
which ran along the near side of a ridge running at right
angles to our line of advance.   If they followed this ridge it
would bring them to within 100 yards of us, and in that case I
stood a good chance of bagging the two.   When they had
come about 50 yards towards us both bulls stopped, evidently
listening.   The leader was a splendid animal with a
tremendous spread of horns, beside which the second one
seemed to have but a small head.   Between us and the
moose stood hundreds of dead fir-trees, killed by the fire
which had swept over that spot.   The bare poles were so
thick together that it was only possible to get glimpses of
parts of the moose as they walked.   When they stopped, the
whole body of the leader was covered from my view by the
tree-stems.   In spite of this, and also the fact that if they
remained quiet the moose would probably come nearer, both
natives started saying, in loud and excited tones, "Shoot
quick. Hurry up."   I was furious, and cursed them *sotto
voce*, but they would not be denied.   Meanwhile, seeing
that the moose had now really heard us, and that when they
did move it would be any way but in the right direction,
I hastily shoved up the 300-yards sight, and remained standing, keeping my eyes fixed on an open space in the trees

THE FRUIT OF A LONG SHOT.

My best Moose.

about two yards ahead of the leading bull, into which he must walk if he came two steps forward. Alas! he did exactly what I was afraid of—that is to say, turned short to the left and walked away covered by the trees, only presenting his hind-quarters to me as he moved over the brow and out of sight in a few yards.

Immediately the other bull prepared to follow him, but now, being desperate and catching sight of some part of his body between two trees, I fired. He immediately stopped and looked round, the bullet evidently having hit some of the innumerable tree-stems near him. This was fatal to the beast, as he stood for a second showing part of his side and shoulder. Taking as steady an aim as I could standing, I fired again, and much to my surprise down went the bull like a log. The distance was, as near as I could pace it afterwards, about 330 yards, and considering how little of the beast I could see, I was pleased with my performance, for I do not class myself very high as a rifle-shot. Both the natives were very disgusted, and kept saying, " You no shoot quick, now you kill 'um little horns. That no good, we lose 'um big horns." Pitka added, " Me never see moose such big horns, same as one we lose 'um." Then I turned on them, and told them in the most forcible and emphatic manner that, if they had only remained quiet, we should probably have bagged both moose. They almost refused to come and see the moose I had killed, saying, " Little head no good." However I went across, and as I got to about ten yards from the moose, he suddenly stood up and looked at me. He was pretty sick, and I soon gave the poor brute a bullet in the chest which finished him. The first bullet had passed in just behind his shoulder, and had only missed the heart by about two inches. I soon saw I had got a really good head, and one which I have not seen beaten as regards its perfect symmetry, with long points running all the way up the horn on each side. Again the number of points was only 23, but the head measured very little under 68 inches from tip to tip, and had very fine palmations on each horn. What the size of the other bull's head was I have never dared to conjecture, but it is certain that this really fine head looked quite small beside the bigger one as the two bulls stood close together. While waiting for the natives to come up, my first sensation on viewing the dead beast was one of pride at having slain so good a trophy. This was shortly followed by a feeling of remorse as I stood silently regarding the fallen monarch, a mere pigmy myself in comparison with his size, holding in my hand the small but deadly weapon, an invention of modern gunsmith's craft, from which a few seconds before a small lead missile had stilled for ever the heart beating inside the huge frame now lying an inert mass at my feet. Shortly it would become, for the greater part, the food of bears, foxes, and ravens, or other roving marauders, all of which he while living had held in sovereign contempt, as king in his own domain. Alas, poor beast, that you should thus end your days, in order that your head and horns may be conveyed thousands of miles to adorn walls in the home of a wandering British sportsman! Far better is this, however, could you but know it, than that the horns on which you prided yourself, and relied on for defence against your own species and others, should be left to lie and rot on the ground, had you fallen (as it is more than likely that you would) by the hand of some native, hunting for meat. Rest assured that long after you are forgotten in your own land, these trophies may be for many years the admired and treasured possession of your slayer, and of those who come after him.

As the afternoon was drawing on, we set hastily to work, skinning off the scalp with the head and horns. Then began the job of packing them home, a distance of some eight miles at least, and most of it through very dense brush. It was fortunate that both natives had come up, so that they could relieve each other in turns with the pack. Even then our pace was very slow. To make matters worse, it came on to stream with rain about 5 o'clock; under the clouded heaven it grew almost dark by 7 P.M. It was about this time that, after going for something like two hours, Pitka, who professed to know the way back to camp, and was then leading, suddenly stopped. On reaching him I saw in front and below us at no great distance the gleam of Kussiloff Lake. This was a charming prospect, as I at once saw that we had been walking the whole time almost with our backs turned to our camp. When I asked Pitka where he now was, he replied cheerfully, " Me lose 'um camp all right. No can find 'um now to-night." Both natives at once gave up the job as hopeless, and were in favour of sitting down then and there to spend the night; but I was horribly hungry, and would not hear of chucking up the sponge so soon. Telling them to follow me, I laid a course as well as I could without my compass, and with but a vague idea of where the sun had set. How many miles away we were, I knew not, but I knew the general line of the camp, and after three hours' steady walking, at 10 P.M. I struck the tents, having gone in a dead straight line to them. This good steering made a very favourable impression on my men, and Pitka afterwards confided to me, " Me think you native all right, no white man find 'um camp same way in dark. You bet, you never lose 'um camp."

It was a case of a late supper that night, but it tasted

none the worse for that, since it was our first meal since about 6 A.M.

Next day I moved camp again to a fresh bit of country, and sent word to Glyn telling him to join me if he was having no luck. Of course, as is always the case, my two natives came across three large bull moose, all close to them and standing in the open looking at them with their packs. I had taken a different line of country, thinking that the men crashing through the brush with their loads would make it impossible that we should see a moose if we went together. I only set eyes on one small bull during the day.

The following day Glyn arrived in camp with his natives and tents, having left Little at the old camp. The latter was fairly busy now with a number of skins on hand which required a certain amount of attention. Glyn went straight out in front of the camp, and was lucky enough to come on a very fine moose soon after starting. He returned with the skull and horns in the evening. It was a grand head, very massive, with 28 points, and a spread of 70 inches. Glyn had well deserved his luck, as he had been three weeks in the moose country, and this was the first decent bull he had seen.

We heard that two American sportsmen had engaged the brothers Berg and were then hunting somewhere near us. On September 25 I met one of the party, who informed me that his name was Mr. Forbes, and that he had been lucky enough to kill a moose two days before which had a head measuring 74 inches. I congratulated him, and told him he had probably got the record head of 1903 from Kenai. This afterwards turned out to be the case so far as regarded the heads killed by sportsmen.

Mr. Forbes informed us that he and his friend Mr.

Hasard were camped about three miles from us, and that
Hanbury was camped at no great distance again from them.
We all seemed to have got huddled up in a corner, and, as
Hanbury remarked when looking down from a high mountain
in the sheep country on several camps about a month before,
the Kenai Peninsula was getting too much like a Scotch
deer forest.

I decided to move my camp shortly and to cross to the
other side of the lake.   Little persuaded me to try Nicolai
Creek, where Colonel Cane had been the previous season.
In a weak moment I decided to do this, although from
his account Colonel Cane had not seen very many moose
during the whole time he spent there.   Two days before
leaving my old camp, whilst Pitka and I were taking
our daily prowl through the forest, I saw, as we were
crossing an open glade, three objects moving in the grass
about 200 yards away.   Pitka was as usual looking on the
ground, and when I pointed out the objects he said, " Me
think that cow moose lie down."   I said, " You fool, they are
three black bears feeding on berries."   Pitka said, " Yes, old
woman bear, two little ones.   Go quick, you catch 'um."
Leaving him where he was, I started crawling on my hands
and knees up to the bears, which were so busy grubbing up
the blue-berries that I got within 50 yards of them without
being seen.   Then, thinking I could not possibly miss the
old one, I stood up, and taking steady aim at her shoulder,
fired.   She fell like a log, but a second afterwards, as I was
very leisurely reloading, jumped up and dashed towards the
thick brush a few yards away.   I was so astonished that I
fired hurriedly at her again, and think that I hit her in the
hind-quarters.   At any rate the shot did not stop her, but
the two cubs, starting off after their mother, suffered from

THE NATIVES PITKA AND IVAN WITH LARGE BULL MOOSE.

my wrath, and of course, as I did not particularly want them, I managed to make a good right and left, hitting both of them through the heart.

We fully expected to find the old bear at no great distance in the brush, but although we spent three hours trying to track her, or find any traces of blood, we never saw a sign of anything. That is the great disadvantage of the small-bores like the Mannlicher—hardly any blood comes from the wound, whereas, if it had been a larger bullet, we must have found a considerable blood-trail, as the beast must have been very badly hit. I was much annoyed at losing this bear, and swore that every black bear in the country was bewitched, and that I would not shoot at another. However, we had got the two cubs, and a very pretty pair they were, but I almost regretted afterwards that I had killed them. They were far too big to attempt to capture alive, or we should have done so.

The last day we remained in the old camp I happened to meet Glyn while returning to the tents. We walked back together, telling Pitka to lead the way, and to keep his eyes open, as one never knows how and when you may come upon a moose in the forest. Soon we reached a large open clearing several hundred yards long. It was a marshy bit of ground covered with tundra. As we were crossing this, a cow moose, followed by a calf, dashed into the open and crossed the clearing about 100 yards in front of us. Pitka, as usual having his eyes glued to the ground, never saw the moose until Glyn stepped up and seized him by the arm. It was obvious that the cow was being chased by a bull, and she must have travelled some distance, as the calf was terribly beaten. Glyn whispered to me, saying he would stay back with Pitka while I went on to try to intercept a bull if he was following the cow. I ran forward about 100 yards, and sat down on the open tundra about 10 yards from the cow's tracks.

A second afterwards I saw two forms moving in the brush whence the cow had first appeared. Knowing they must be two bulls, I was reckoning on one of them at least being a good one. They came into the open at about 150 yards, and I well remember how anxiously I looked at the head of each one as it appeared. But alas for vain hopes, the leader was a young bull with a head not exceeding 45 inches' spread, and the second a miserable little two-year-old bull. Still, the situation was not without interest to the spectators, and, as on a previous occasion, I would have given something to have had my camera on the spot.

As soon as the leading bull appeared in the open, he looked carefully around for a few seconds and seeing no sign of the cow, put his nose to the ground, and ran the trail by scent exactly like a dog. It was a most interesting thing to watch. He ran the line fairly fast, going at a trot, until he came opposite to me. Not once was he at fault on the scent. I was sitting to the windward of the cow's tracks, and, although on the bare tundra, as I remained absolutely motionless neither of the bulls saw me. When at no more than 10 yards from my position the leader winded me, and throwing up his head for a moment and looking towards me, made a noble picture. Another second, and he bounded away down wind for about 20 yards, followed by the small bull. There they both stopped for a moment and looked back, but were soon off again and vanished from our sight into the dense forest.

On the same day I met Mr. Hasard, the other American sportsman who was hunting with the Bergs not far from our camp. He said that they had temporarily lost the services of Andrew Berg, since the Deputy U.S. Marshal of that district had discovered an illicit whisky still at Berg's cabin and had arrested the owner and taken him to Kenai. The younger Berg, by name Emile, seemed to me a particularly smart-looking fellow, and Mr. Hasard said that the way in which he found moose and took the sportsman up to them was extraordinary. They had seen a number of good bulls, but not one exceeding 70 inches according to Berg's estimate, except the 74-inch head which Mr. Forbes had bagged a few days previously. Emile Berg admitted to me that he was only a novice when compared with his brother Andrew as a hunter, but Mr. Hasard said that he had seen him call up a bull moose quite close to them, in a similar manner to that in which his brother calls them. My natives, and other people who have hunted formerly with Andrew Berg, declare that they have repeatedly seen him call up bull moose by imitating the challenge call of another bull, and that they have even had to take refuge behind trees to avoid being charged by a bull called up in this way.[1] Both the brothers Berg have the reputation also of being able to judge the size of any head on sight to within an inch or two of its actual measurements. This is a great advantage, especially to a novice who has never seen a moose before. Mr. Hasard modestly remarked that as he had never previously killed anything larger than a rabbit, the first moose they encountered looked to him as big as an elephant, and that he should certainly have shot it, if Berg had not told him it was only a small head, and had promised ere long to show him one of over 70 inches' spread. Berg carried out his part of the bargain, and when I next

[1] In Alaska the hunters do not attempt to use the cow's call, as is the case with the Canadians, who prefer this call to that of the bull.

met Mr. Hasard at Kenai he had secured a grand head of 71 inches.

I know there are many people who scoff at the idea, but I maintain that to any in need of a hunter when after moose, the services of such men as these two brothers are invaluable at any reasonable price. " The proof of the pudding is in the eating," and every season sportsmen who have employed Berg have come out with the record heads of the year obtained on the Kenai Peninsula. If further proof than this is required in support of my argument, I know not what it can be.

Leaving Glyn in possession of my old camp, I set out towards the lake, meaning to join Little at our base camp, then to cross the lake and strike a trail leading to Nicolai Creek. We little expected what stirring events were to happen ere we all three met again. I found Little just returning to camp with a fine lot of willow-ptarmigan, having been out with the gun since daylight to collect some good specimens of these splendid birds, which we wanted for the British Museum. We both set to work skinning these and a few other birds, such as hawks and owls, which he had on hand.

That evening we camped on the lake shore at the mouth of a small creek which was full of dead and dying salmon. The smell of these dead fish and the consequent pollution of the water were awful, but we had to make the best of the water for cooking purposes.

Next morning we were favoured with a calm day for crossing the lake, and a row of six or seven miles took us to the other side. Here there was an old and uninhabited cabin, where we left our base supplies and started off on a five hours' pack along the trail to Nicolai Creek. We reached the site of Colonel Cane's old camp in the evening, and found many traces of his previous occupation of the place. Amongst other things was an old tin containing several novels and old magazines, which I found very acceptable to while away an hour or two in the evenings. The books were in good order, and during our travels in Alaska we made several similar deposits, which may at some future day be found similarly useful to any one following in our tracks.

I was not favourably impressed with the look of this new country. The trees were too thick, and there were few open places, and nothing like the same amount of good feeding for moose as on the ground we had left. Pitka, who knew the place well, said that the moose did not frequent the ground round Nicolai Creek much before November, but at that season the first snows would drive them down from the higher ground, and they would collect in large numbers all along the valley through which the creek ran. This accounted for the great number of shed antlers lying on the ground, which on first sight led one to believe that moose were very numerous in that district.

Little stated that on the occasion of their former visit to this camp the spruce-grouse were very plentiful, and consequently if we carried the small .22 rifle we should not want for fresh meat. We therefore travelled very light as regarded our meat supply. But to our intense disgust, after a whole day spent in search of the spruce-grouse, Pitka and Little only managed to bag a brace of grouse and one rabbit. This was not much to make a meal of for two natives and ourselves. The second day produced no grouse, nor could I see a single moose, and the state of our food supply was getting a serious question. On the third day Little took his rifle and went out in one direction with Pitka, and I alone on another route. Pitka returned with nine grouse, Little having seen

BULL MOOSE IN KENAI FOREST.

no moose ; and I brought back a contribution for the pot in
the shape of one large porcupine, which I was fortunate enough
to find in a low tree so that I could knock it down with a stick.
During that afternoon I walked almost on top of a small bull
moose lying in a patch of stunted spruce-trees. On seeing
me he jumped up and stood looking at me as I remained
perfectly still. The wind being directly towards me, he was
unable to smell danger, and evidently regarded me as some
strange animal, since he remained for more than a minute
staring at me in the open. Then turning he leisurely walked
away, stopping every now and again to look back over his
shoulder. This bull had the finest bell I ever saw, and when
standing with his head raised, the tag at the end of the
bell reached well down to the level of his knees. He
carried a small but very graceful head with about 7 points
on each antler.

On October 1, as I was prowling about alone in the
dense forest, I suddenly heard two bulls fighting in some
thick alders quite close at hand. The crash of their horns
as they rushed together was terrific, and I could distinctly
hear their hard breathing and blowing as I pushed my way
towards the spot where they stood. I expected every
moment to get a view of them, 'but unfortunately one bull
seemed to be driving the other before him, and they kept
moving on in front as I pushed forward. Here and there I
came on places where the moss and turf were rooted up and
the bush beaten down, but in spite of all my efforts, the
moose moved too fast for me to get a sight of them. They
were evidently following a cow, as I could hear the soft call
of the cow at intervals between the crash of horns. She was
evidently moving fast, and had it not been for her presence, I
should inevitably have overtaken the bulls, since they certainly

never winded or heard me.   Two more blank days thoroughly disgusted me with that country, and as fresh tracks were few and far between, we decided to return to the lake and cross over again to a place near where Hanbury had been hunting. I heard from some natives that he had gone back to Kenai with at least one head over 70 inches, and that he had found plenty of moose near his camp.   We had still a fortnight before us, and from signs and sounds in the forest, the big bulls were now running and fighting freely, so that there was a good chance of picking up a really good head or two in a few days.   We retraced our steps to the lake, somewhat mournfully, having wasted a week at Nicolai Creek, during which time, although Little and I were both out every day, and covered miles of ground, we only saw one small bull.

On the evening of October 3 we reached the empty cabin, and took up our quarters there for the night.

Next morning the wind began to blow hard, and in consequence we delayed starting at daylight, as we had intended to do.   Had it not been for this circumstance, we should have avoided a very unpleasant surprise.

CHAPTER XII

THE HALLS OF JUSTICE

THIS day was Little's birthday, and I remember remarking
to him that it was unfortunate I had no small souvenir to
give him in remembrance of the occasion. It was, however,
destined to be a memorable birthday for him.

About noon Pitka came to report that two dories were
sailing across the lake and evidently heading for our camp.
Taking our glasses to a high bit of ground, we soon made
out one dory heavily laden with tents and horns to be Glyn's
boat. The other one was unknown to us. Then arose the
question as to what had made Glyn abandon his original
scheme of remaining in his old camp until we called for him
as arranged.

As soon as the boats drew near enough, we saw Glyn's
natives in one boat, and he himself in the other one with a
man who was unknown to Little and myself. On nearing
the shore, Glyn, who was sitting in the stern of the boat and
slightly behind the stranger, went through some extraordinary
antics which were quite unintelligible to me, but clearly
represented a man hauling in a rope. Little, however, being
more versed in certain expressions than myself, said, " By
Jove, he is 'pulled' for something." Pitka said, " That
d—d man, he Marshal allright."

The stranger, on stepping ashore, walked up to me and held out his hand, saying, " You are Captain Radclyffe, I believe." I shook hands and said " Yes." He added, " I arrest you." As far as I remember my exact words were,

A TOUGH-LOOKING GROUP.
The Author, R. F. Glyn, C. Little, and Natives, Kenai Forest, September 1903.

" The devil you do, and pray what for ? " His reply was, " For killing game unlawfully out of season." I demanded a specific charge, but he said that that would be made in due course when he took me before a judge at Kenai, which he proposed to do forthwith. He also arrested Little on the same charge.

Before describing what followed, it is necessary to digress slightly from the subject in order to make matters clear.

When we visited Washington in the spring, Glyn and myself were given full permits allowing us to take out of Alaska the full number of trophies allowed by law.

In addition to my ordinary permit, I was given a special permit allowing me to kill two extra specimens of each kind of big game for scientific purposes, as I had promised Professor Ray Lankester, Director of the Natural History Museum in London, that I would, if possible, obtain some good specimens of Alaskan game for the Museum. This special permit distinctly stated that the specimens for scientific purposes might be killed *at any time of year*.

Furthermore, when in Seattle, knowing that I was likely to have a rough trip along the Bering Sea shores, where papers might get lost or damaged, I had a type-written copy made of each permit, so that if occasion arose I could leave the originals behind in safe custody at Kodiak, and carry the copies in case I might meet any officials on my travels who might want something more than my word to prove that I actually possessed a permit. It so happened that I left all my papers at Kodiak, and thus had nothing more than my word to inform the District Commissioner on the Bering Sea coast that I held such permits. Fortunately this man was a gentleman—Mr. Barstow, to whom I have already referred, and being such he took my word as equal to my bond.

The original permits were of course signed by the Minister of Agriculture at Washington, Mr. James Wilson. Naturally the copies bore no such signature, nor the stamp of the Government Offices at Washington ; in other words, they in no way resembled the originals, so that no one could possibly have mistaken them for such. I admit that the girl who did the type-writing had omitted to put the word copy on each document, nor had I noticed this fact, never having had occasion to look at the papers afterwards.

All these papers were left in a small bag at Glyn's base camp, together with a number of private letters. I had also written a letter to Mr. Hanbury the day I left that camp, and, as previously arranged, I had placed it in a split stick which was stuck in the ground inside our store tent, where Hanbury said he would look for a note any time he might be passing the camp.

I guessed that by some means the Marshal had heard that I had killed a sheep before September 1. But I could, according to my special permit, have killed two sheep in August, and therefore was in a position to prove I had in no way exceeded my powers, if only he would have made any specific charge.

Glyn then came to me and said that the Marshal had gone to our tent, where he had seized all my papers and private effects, and that on seeing the type-written copies of permits, although they were together with the originals, he stated that I was in possession of dangerous documents, as these were forgeries and I might use them to evade the law.

He had also taken my letter addressed to Hanbury, and opened and read it. In addition to this, Hanbury, who was then at Kenai, had met this man, and hearing that he was coming up to Kussiloff Lake and was likely to see me, had given him a letter to deliver to me. He accepted the trust, but curiosity to see what Hanbury had written to me, induced him to open and read this letter. He calmly informed me that " he anticipated the letter to be one which might be intended to warn me against him, and thus to frustrate the ends of justice."

On being informed of these matters by Glyn, and the Marshal having admitted the facts, and also that he possessed no search warrant to cover his actions, I was furious, and if he only knew it, as he stood on the extreme edge of the lake calmly telling me of his despicable actions, that man was nearer being knocked into the lake with a straight punch from the shoulder than he ever will be again without the event actually happening.

He had the audacity to tell me after all this, that the duty of arresting gentlemen for breaking the game laws was repugnant to him. This finished me, and how to keep my hands off him I did not know, except by walking away, which I quickly did. I knew that he had a six-shooter in his pocket, which he would have been only too pleased to let off at one of us if an excuse had been given him. Had this happened I do not think that he would ever have seen Kenai again, for the survivors of our party would pretty soon have " filled him up with lead." We had always a Mannlicher or two within reach of our hands, whether by day or night. When my ire had somewhat abated, and I had begun to realise the comic side of the whole episode, it afforded me no small amusement to see the minute care with which this brave Marshal (who had apprehended a gang of English desperadoes) at once made an inspection of the interior of our cabin, and said that he was afraid he should have to take possession of all our guns, rifles, etc. This gave me the impression that he thought we should " shoot on sight " if the slightest provocation was offered. I thought at the time that he must have had previous experience as a Deputy Marshal in some particularly bloodthirsty mining camps of America, but when we subsequently discovered that he had been a travelling tout in some "dry" or "wet goods" line of business, before starting life as a limb of the law in Cook's Inlet, I knew at once that he was only suffering from an attack of nerves.

I remember quite well that as soon as I had grasped the full extent of the indignities under which we suffered, I remarked, "Well, sir, I give you fair warning that if you persist in taking me out of this country now, and spoiling the end of my shooting trip on a trumped-up charge like this, after your action is over I shall bring a counter-charge against you for wrongful arrest, libel, and defamation of character, and shall claim heavy damages." He replied by saying that if I got any damages out of him over the job he would "stand drinks all round." I was ignorant at the time of the fact that there is practically no redress in America for libel or defamation of character in its worst form, but a study of the columns in the society papers will soon convince the reader of this fact. I believe, indeed, one instance is known of a certain English peer who did actually recover damages for libel against an American paper; but *en passant* it may be stated that his legal expenses amounted to considerably more than the damages awarded him, if reports of the case are correct.

I also remember telling Little that Glyn had brought him a nice birthday present in the shape of this visitor.

After due consideration, I concluded that the only thing to be done was to submit to the indignity of going down to Kenai as a prisoner. My sole consolation was the knowledge that I should make the Marshal the laughing-stock of the whole district, when I once got him before the court.

About Glyn's case we did not feel so confident, as he

certainly had killed one or two sheep before September 1 ; but as he and Little were badly in want of meat at that time, we considered that the words of the game laws, "travellers and explorers when in need of meat," would acquit him on that charge.

Also he had killed three moose, but as Little, who was with him, had a permit for an extra moose, we considered Glyn to be entitled to shoot another one in addition to those allowed by his own permit, so long as our total number of heads did not exceed the lot allowed by our combined permits. This may have been a somewhat broad interpretation of the Act, but we knew of instances where it had been so read before, and nothing had been said against it then.

It was quite obvious to me that this episode meant a premature ending to our trip, and rendered it impossible for me to return to the sheep country for a few days to get my complement of sheep, or to remain and get another big moose, as I was entitled to do. It may well be imagined that my temper was pretty sore, when I considered the troubles and expense of travelling some 9000 miles into the country, and many hundreds of miles after arrival there, only to be taken right out of the heart of the good game country just at the best time of the whole season, and charged with an offence I had not committed.

The next twenty-four hours were not the most pleasant ones in our lives. We crossed part of the lake in our three dories during the afternoon, but it came on to blow so violently towards evening that we were almost swamped, and had to beach the dories in a heavy surf, and camp on shore for the night.

Our party now occupied a very subordinate position, as the Marshal took control of everything, ordering his and our own natives about in the most lordly manner.   Judging from the looks of all these men, and some odd remarks I heard, there was no love lost between them and the Marshal.

October 5 was occupied in reaching the end of the lake, and afterwards drifting down the river.   The latter was a very different job from the arduous task of towing up it, and four or five hours only were needed to cover the distance which had taken us two days to get over on the way up. During the evening we arrived at Kussiloff Cannery, and were greeted with some expressions of surprise by Mr. Morgan and his wife.   Mr. Morgan had been left in charge of the cannery throughout the long and dreary winter months.

Mr. Wetherbee and his staff had long ago left for warmer climes, and the deserted wharf and empty houses presented a very different appearance from what they did when we last saw them alive with bustling Chinamen and men of other nationalities, packing and loading the summer's catch of salmon on board the steam tugs.

We were entertained at supper by Mr. and Mrs. Morgan, and afterwards were allotted quarters in a big bunk-house, where Glyn, Little, and I were told off into upper rooms under close supervision of the Marshal, who occupied a room below us.   In other rooms below us were also a number of miners on their way down from a mine at Kussiloff Lake, all of whom we had met previously.

One of these miners was a most estimable old gentleman who appeared to take the rights and wrongs of the American nation under his personal charge and responsibility. I happened to be an unintentional eavesdropper at a conversation which was carried on between him and the Marshal in

R

the room below mine, after we had retired to bed. The floor-boards being thin, every word was audible to us above, and it appeared that the worthy upholder of his country's rights considered that since we had killed one or two sheep before September 1, we must be what he called " game hogs" of the worst type, and that as we had apparently come there with the expressed intention of breaking the game laws, we ought to be prosecuted to the full extent of the law.

This kindly disposed person took the trouble to approach me next morning and say that " we had his entire sympathy in our troubles." I could not resist saying that as I had overheard his conversation with the Marshal during the night, I thought his present statement might be taken *cum grano salis.*

Early next morning we started to walk along the beach to Kenai, a distance of some twelve miles, our warder saying he would follow close behind. However, as we got away with a slight start and were all in pretty hard condition, we soon walked clean away from him, as he was no match for us at that game. Here an amusing incident happened. Half-way between Kussiloff and Kenai lies a native settlement, and on reaching this the Marshal evidently imagined we were trying to give him the slip. He hastened to the settlement and commandeered a bidarki with two natives to take up the pursuit by water. I saw the whole affair from about a mile and a half ahead of him. I told Little and Glyn to step out, and we fairly " foot slogged it" along the shore. A river lay between us and Kenai, but we were fortunate enough to find an old boat hauled up on our bank. Launching this, we pulled across the river, and reached the village of Kenai about five minutes ahead of our custodian, who came puffing up after us evidently furious at having been left

GROUP OF ENGLISH SPORTSMEN IN ALASKA DURING 1903.

D. T. Hanbury, R. F. Glyn, C. Little, P. B. Vander Byl, Lord Elphinstone, Capt. Radclyffe.

behind. However, he could say nothing except that we were all very fine walkers, and in this we were able to agree with him.

The first man we met was Hanbury, and Glyn soon gave him details of the case. Hearing that Lord Elphinstone and Mr. P. B. Vander Byl were also in the village, having just returned from hunting together near Kenai Lake, I walked across to their house and detailed to them our latest adventures. They had done very well on their trip, getting a complement of sheep and moose, and also two or three black bears, in about five weeks' hunting.

They rejoiced rather at the prospect of our forthcoming trial as something to relieve the monotony of life at Kenai whilst waiting for the steamer to take them out of Cook's Inlet.

Our next visit was to the house of Mr. G. Mearns, who is the local magnate of Kenai, and a thorough American gentleman in every sense of the word. He holds the position of local postmaster, and is also a notary public. He manages a big store at Kenai belonging to Mr. Wetherbee, and is altogether the man to make friends with on arrival in that village. He kindly gave us the use of an empty cabin, in which Glyn, Hanbury, Little, and myself took up our headquarters.

We soon learnt that the local Judge or Deputy Commissioner from Sunrise was also in Kenai, waiting to try our party of malefactors. Everything, as it appeared, had been arranged between him and the Marshal before our arrest. Thinking to gain some enlightenment on the knotty points of American law, we strolled across to interview the Judge, only to find that he was hopelessly mixed on the subject of the game laws. He admitted that this would be somewhat in the nature of a test case, as hitherto no cases had been tried in the country under the new laws. I next proceeded to question him regarding my own case, and he requested time to look through my papers before saying anything in the matter. To this I agreed, and on returning in the afternoon he said that he wished to dismiss the case against me, as there was nothing in it to go before a court. I was so riled at the treatment I had received from the hands of the Marshal, and at the reports which had been freely circulated in the village regarding our supposed indiscriminate slaughtering of game, that I demanded as my due that my case should be taken within twenty-four hours, adding that although I was informed that it was a case in which I was entitled to a jury, that he, acting as Judge alone, would suffice for me. I added, however, that in the event of receiving any unfavourable decision in his court, I should take the case through every court in the country, until I could finally reach the Supreme Court at Washington, where I knew the charge would not hold water.

Finally the Judge decided to hear my case on the following day.

The court was held at the Russian school-house, and nearly every seat was occupied soon after the doors opened, every white man in the village putting in an appearance. The place happened then to be very full, owing to a number of miners, fishermen, and others waiting to catch the last steamer going out of Cook's Inlet before winter set in. This pleased me considerably, the more particularly as I found the sympathy of the majority was on the side of sportsmen who come annually to the country and spend money freely whilst there. The party of five Englishmen besides myself occupied prominent seats. The solemnity with which the opening formalities of the court were invested was very impressive, and when finally Glyn's case came up for trial, and he elected to have a jury, the swearing and seating of these worthy men would have put to shame the most solemn conclave of the learned Ephori of ancient Sparta.

In my case the evidence was so simple that the Marshal, who acted as prosecutor, merely called Pitka and asked if he saw me kill a sheep during August. He replied that he did see me do so, and when cross-questioned by me he admitted having skinned the beast whole and taking the bones, etc., for scientific purposes. This closed the evidence for the prosecution.

I then handed to the court my special permit giving me permission to kill two sheep at any time of year for scientific purposes, and stated that I had only killed one of these out of the open season.

Thereupon the prosecutor arose, and in an impassioned address said that he would like to know what authority Mr. Wilson, the Secretary of Agriculture, had to give extra liberty to any one to kill game out of season, and why I should have a permit different from those of others; and furthermore what was to prevent my taking out these trophies for scientific purposes, and when once safely out of America, taking them to my own house and hanging them up, instead of presenting them to a museum.

Up to that point I had been so much amused by the whole case that I was in a fairly good humour, and might have been inclined to let him down easily, but that finished me. Getting on my feet, as he sat down, I started what perhaps will ever remain my best oratorical effort. I showed, in answer to his questions, how the Minister of Agriculture, according to the words of the game laws, had always the right to issue special permits for scientific purposes, and produced letters from the authorities of the British Museum asking me to collect specimens for them. As regarded what prevented me from doing the dirty tricks the prosecutor had hinted at, I said that there was one thing which would prevent my ever committing them, and although it was no uncommon thing, still it was something which this man had clearly shown himself utterly unable to appreciate or understand, and that was simply the word of honour of an English gentleman. I believe that he thought I was going to throw myself on the mercy of the court. But, continuing my address, I detailed how this man had seized my private papers, how he had opened a letter lying in my tent addressed to a friend, how he had accepted a post of trust to bring a letter from Hanbury to me, and had then opened and read that letter, which he still had in his possession, and how finally he had the audacity to tell me that he found the duty of arresting gentlemen for breaking the game laws repugnant to him.

I concluded with these words : " It appears to me that a man who can stoop to such measures to obtain evidence, and adopt means which I verily believe the lowest street car ' spotter ' in New York, or detective on the track of a criminal in my own country, would hesitate to employ, can find nothing on God's earth which would be repugnant to his nature. And furthermore, if he could produce anything in the shape of evidence to show that I have in the slightest degree infringed the laws of this country, or abused the courtesy extended to me by the authorities at Washington, then it is not before such a court as this that I ought to be standing, but rather before a court *de lunatico inquirendo*, for I should fear that my sanity must be very much in danger."

He rose once more to thank me sarcastically for the "dressing down" he had received, and I begged him not to mention it. The look on his face, and that on the faces of the audience in court, told the whole tale, and he must have realised that for once he had "cut off a bigger lump than he could chew."

Needless to remark, the verdict was "Not guilty," and I afterwards received the congratulations of nearly every American in the house, who begged me not to consider this as a typical instance of how English sportsmen were treated in the States. I appreciated their kindness, but alas, it did not help to repair the ruination of the latter part of my shooting trip, as it was now too late to return to the moose country.

The afternoon was occupied in the hearing of the cases against Glyn and Little.

The former admitted having killed two sheep out of season, and also one moose above the number allowed by his own permit. In a very able speech for the defence, he pleaded the need of meat in the one case and the rights of travellers and explorers to kill it, and in the other case he claimed that as Little had not got his second moose, he was entitled to shoot one for him, and that even if he had broken the law in the letter he had not done so in its spirit, as we had come out with considerably less trophies than we were entitled to under our combined permits.

In this case the prosecutor, suffering from his recent soreness, made a most bitter and violent attack upon the defendant; and so vindictive was it that one good-natured miner said to me afterwards, "I guess that was a persecution, and not a prosecution."

In Glyn's case the Judge ruled that a sportsman could

under no circumstances be considered a traveller or explorer (a finding with which I do not agree), and in the second case that one man could not kill game for another. In this he was probably correct. Suffice it that he fined Glyn $150 and costs, but did not confiscate his trophies, as he might have done ; and for this Glyn was duly grateful.

Little's case was more extraordinary still, as the prosecutor called two natives to prove that he had killed a sheep before September 1. The first native swore that he saw Little shoot a sheep before September 1. The second one swore he saw him kill this same sheep after September 1. Little justly claimed that one evidence was as good as the other, and that therefore the case was " Not proven."

The Judge, however, inclined to the first evidence, and fined Little $100, at which there was a good deal of surprise in court.

Here I may add, that seeing how far-reaching in effect these cases would be, and having determined under any circumstances to bring the whole thing correctly to the notice of the officials at Washington, I engaged the services of a shorthand writer to take down the evidence. This copy of the proceedings was duly attested by the Judge, and delivered by me to the authorities at Washington, who have since displayed considerable interest in the matter, and were most courteous to me when I visited them on my return journey through Washington.

If no other result arises from my efforts in the case, I think it is safe to predict that visitors to the Cook's Inlet country in future will not be subjected to such indignities as the writer suffered.

The whole affair afforded the residents of Kenai an unusual excitement, and, emboldened by getting two convictions, we heard that the energetic Marshal was soon off on the warpath again, after more marauders, in the shape of two other parties of sportsmen who were hunting in the Kachemak Bay country, near the mouth of Cook's Inlet.

The most amusing part of the whole thing was that natives, miners, and others had been killing moose and sheep in season and out of season indiscriminately, right under the noses of the custodians of the law for months past, and that no notice was taken of the facts by them. It cannot for a moment be supposed that persons who are always in constant communication with, or in immediate proximity to, some local store, can be in such urgent need of fresh meat as a party of sportsmen who push as far as possible into a country isolated from civilisation ; and yet the very man who was most bitter against what he called the " game hogs of sports-men," admitted to me that every week some of the men from his mining camp went out and brought in plenty of mountain sheep for food in camp. This camp was situated on a lake where fresh salmon were abundant, and regular communica-tion kept up with the local stores. This is a very different position from that of a sportsman perched in a camp many thousand feet high, and dependent on one or two natives to pack his supplies from a store many miles distant. Truly, " 'tis a mad world " in which men reason thus !

CHAPTER XIII

ON THE HOMEWARD TRAIL

WHEN the excitement caused by the recent great trials had subsided, and the great town of Kenai had once more assumed its normal state, the question arose as to how the time should be spent whilst waiting for the steamer *Bertha*, which was due at Saldovia on October 21. As it still wanted a fortnight to that date, I was sorely tempted to try a short trip up the Kenai River in the hopes of getting one more good moose. My natives were loath to undertake the task, saying that the period was too short to allow of our reaching a decent bit of country, and then spending any time in it, since all our time would be occupied in getting up and down the river. It was with a sore heart that I finally abandoned the idea, particularly as it had now begun to snow slightly, and, with sharp frosts every night, the natives declared it to be just the time to " catch 'um big-horn moose," if we had only been left in peace in the forest. The only amusement remaining was to walk along some of the marshes near the river on the chance of getting a few geese, ducks, or snipe with the gun. Although the two first-named kinds were very numerous, and kept passaging south by day and night in great flocks, only a few of these flocks came low enough to give the chance of a shot at them. Occasionally

251

numbers would pitch in the river or marshes, but their
temporary halt was generally of short duration, and the geese
in particular, owing to their habit of posting look-out
sentinels, were almost impossible to approach within gunshot. However, by means of much walking, a certain
number of wild-fowl were added to the *menu* in our abode.

One evening we were treated to an exhibition of moose-
hunting as carried out by the natives when after meat.
Pitka came running into our hut saying that there was a
bull moose feeding on a large open marsh on the opposite
side of the river in front of our house. Looking out with
the telescope, we soon distinguished a small bull feeding in
the open some way from the timber, and distant about three-
quarters of a mile. Other eyes besides ours had marked the
quarry, and even had the beast been a big one, none of our
party could have stood a chance of getting a shot at him.
For instantly the village presented the appearance of a
place attacked by an enemy. Apparently every able-bodied
man who possessed a rifle had turned out. Rushing in a mob
to the river, some fifteen or more men jumped into boats
and bidarkis and soon crossed to the other bank. Then,
starting in single file, and led by the first man who jumped
ashore, they made a wide detour, travelling at a quick run.
Soon they reached the shelter of the trees and disappeared
from our sight. The light was waning fast, but the luckless
moose was still visible with the glasses, and remained feeding
in the same spot. As time went on we knew that he was
doomed, since his pursuers must now be close on him, and
between him and the friendly shelter of the forest. Ere
long from the edge of the wood about half-a-dozen jets of
flame flashed in the dusk, followed by the reports of the
Winchesters. Galloping forward a few yards, the bull

NATIVES REPAIRING A BIDARKI, BEAR RIVER, JULY 1903.

staggered and fell. Rising once more, he was met with a furious fusilade which terminated the hunt. Shortly afterwards the gang of men returned bearing portions of the meat, which they offered for sale, together with the head and horns. The horns were very poor, and apparently less than 40 inches in span. This beast had the most remarkably long bell that I had seen. It exceeded 15 inches in length.

For a wonder most of the meat from this moose was brought in by the natives, but merely on account of the fact that it was killed so near the settlement. If a beast is killed any distance from home the natives are generally content to pack home the haunches and leave the remainder of the carcass to rot, hoping soon to get another animal nearer home. Stories which I have been told on this subject by the natives themselves warrant me in making this statement.

A round of festivities now commenced in the native quarters, for the men employed by the sportsmen no sooner receive their pay than they proceed to spend it as fast as possible. After making vast purchases from the local store of all kinds of supplies, and many useless articles, they then distribute things freely to all their friends, and finally end up by giving a big dance. Pitka was no exception to the rule, and one evening came to us and said, " To-night everybody dance. You come too." We went, and spent an hour at the ball. No striking beauty was to be seen amongst the ladies, and the music was supplied by natives playing guitars. They all had a good idea of dancing, and the whole performance was carried out on strictly European lines, and in a most orderly manner.

After spending a quiet week at Kenai, on the morning of October 13 the steamer *Tyonook* was reported off the mouth of the river, and an opportunity was presented for getting down to Saldovia.   Hearing that the Marshal had already gone there, and that the Judge was going down on this steamer on the chance of apprehending some more "game hogs," I decided to go and see the fun.   Mr. Vander Byl and Lord Elphinstone also accompanied us, and we bade farewell to Kenai, leaving Glyn, Hanbury, and Little to follow us to Saldovia a week later, when the *Tyonook* made her last trip up and down Cook's Inlet before winter set in.   We found the *Tyonook* fairly full with a number of miners and others coming down from the head of the Inlet.   Whilst on board we heard an item of news which illustrated forcibly the stupidity of the Kenai natives, and the consequences which may result from their dangerous habit of firing blindly at anything which they can see or hear moving in the brush.

At the headquarters of a mining camp on Kussiloff Lake there were two valuable cart-horses which had been conveyed up from Seattle at considerable trouble and expense to their owners.   These horses were allowed to roam loose around the settlement by day and night.   Soon after our departure from the lake, a party of natives came there to hunt moose for meat.   They camped on arrival close to the mining settlement.   During the night, being aroused by the noise of some big animal near their tent, they turned out with their rifles.   Seeing two large beasts a few yards away, they at once opened fire, and on going to the spot found they had shot one horse dead, and so severely wounded the other that it was not expected to recover when we last heard news of it.   The staff of this mining company were on board the *Tyonook*, and their feelings and language on receiving the news can be better imagined than described.

With half a gale blowing dead astern, the *Tyonook* made

the run from Kenai to Saldovia in nine hours, which, according to the statement of her worthy skipper, Captain Shaw, was her record run.

We found the settlement already crowded with people waiting for the *Bertha*, and almost every available cabin occupied. In addition some prospectors had pitched tents and were living in them. Fortunately our friend Mr. Cleghorn, the postmaster, had kindly lent us a cabin in which we stored our bear skins before leaving Saldovia in August. This was still unoccupied, and here Elphinstone, Vander Byl, and I took up our quarters, finding a hut with a small stove far preferable to a tent at night, as a sharp foretaste of winter had already set in. A good lot of snow was now falling, and the temperature at nights was down to zero. One enterprising man and his wife had started a small restaurant in a big tent, where it was possible to obtain very decent meals, and this place was duly patronised by our party and several others who found a relief from the daily routine of doing their own cooking.

Rumours of stirring events filled the air at Saldovia. We heard that Mr. Sexton, the Marshal, had arrived a few days previously to us, and had hurried off up Kachemak Bay and into the forest on the track of an American hunter, and of a German gentleman, both of whom were reported to be doing all kinds of dreadful deeds amongst the game. Concerning the German we were given a graphic description of his arrival at Saldovia, and reports of his apparent unbounded wealth, and of his lavish expenditure in pursuit of sport. Articles dealing with his trip to Alaska had already found their way into the New York journals, and were even then to be seen in Saldovia. The story as told, which was highly embellished, but the main facts of which were true, was briefly as follows.

It appeared that this German gentleman, whose name was Mr. P. Niedieck, had set out from Seattle on board the steamer

THE AUTHOR AND LORD ELPHINSTONE IN NATIVE PARKI DRESS.

Nome City. He had determined to hunt in Cook's Inlet, and was informed that Saldovia was the place of disembarkation, and that, local guides or hunters being scarce there, he would

s

probably have some difficulty in obtaining a guide so late in
the season, more particularly as Lord Elphinstone and Mr.
Vander Byl had left Seattle two days previously on the
ss. *Excelsior*, which was due to arrive at Saldovia before
the *Nome City*.   Mr. Niedieck discovered that the *Excelsior*
was bound to call at many small places along the coast, and
that she might be delayed some time at Valdez.   The
Nome City was also scheduled to call at Valdez, but it was
possible that by avoiding this port and running direct to
Saldovia she might just beat the *Excelsior*.   This was clearly
a matter where the almighty dollar might be useful.   So,
approaching the captain on the subject and explaining the
case, Mr. Niedieck suggested the possibility of the *Nome City*
running direct to Saldovia without stopping at Valdez.   The
skipper stated that it was out of the question, since he carried
passengers and cargo for Valdez.   Mr. Niedieck (to use the
words of the American Press), " knowing that money talks,
merely said, ' How much ? '   The captain retired to consider
the question, and returning, said it could be arranged for
$1000.   Placing the money on the table, Mr. Niedieck said,
' Go ahead.' "   A full description of his triumphal landing at
Saldovia was then given, and the account of how the ship's
crew struggled to unload his cases of champagne, and other
luxuries, was well dished up for the American taste.   He had
at least the satisfaction of beating the *Excelsior* by several
hours, but the amusing part of the whole thing was (and this
the American Press missed) that Lord Elphinstone and Mr.
Vander Byl were only getting off the *Excelsior* at Saldovia,
and then going on to Kenai, where they had already arranged
to get guides and natives.

   When eventually I did meet Mr. Niedieck and we became
great friends, this episode led to so much unlimited chaff that

he vowed never again to bribe an American ship, since it made him too conspicuous. The title of the lengthy article in the New York Press was headed, " Great Race to Alaska : a German Baron against an English Lord for $1000."

Soon after our arrival the Marshal returned to Saldovia, having failed to find either of the parties he sought, and having suffered a severe buffeting from the sea, which was then very rough, as he had only a small sailing-sloop in which to make his trip.

It was not long before matters became interesting. On the morning of the second day after our arrival, news flew round the settlement to the effect that two dories were approaching the shore, and it was obvious that they contained a sportsman's outfit, as moose-horns could be seen in the boats. The visitors and inhabitants formed an expectant audience, standing at a short distance from the landing-place. Here was an opportunity for the zealous Marshal, who at once advanced, full of importance, and after briefly questioning a native in one of the boats, and hearing that three moose had been killed, he informed Mr. Niedieck, who then stepped ashore, that he was arrested for breaking the game laws. The latter appeared in no degree concerned at the enormity of his crime, and strolling across to him I tendered him my sympathy as a fellow-sufferer at the hands of his captor. He remarked that probably all that was required was to make him pay $200, which he was quite ready to do and so save the bother of any trial. However, it would have been a pity to disappoint the residents of Saldovia by avoiding what they regarded as an afternoon's amusement. The trial was eventually held at the schoolhouse, which was filled to its utmost extent. It was a trial attended by all the solemnity of those previously described at Kenai. The prosecution

proved that three moose had been killed by the party, and
that the defendant had fired at all of them.   The defence
showed that Mr. Niedieck had killed two of them, and that
although he did fire at a small bull early in September, when
in need of meat, he had not killed it, but that the beast was
finally shot by his hunter.   The case was soon over, and the
verdict was " Guilty."   The sentence was " Fined $200,"
that is to say, the full limit of the fine.   Mr. Niedieck was

Photo by P. Niedieck.

Mr. P. Niedieck with his largest Moose.

even grateful to the Judge for not confiscating his trophies,
as he had power to do in the case of any person convicted of
breaking the game laws.   After the trial I accepted an invita-
tion to dine with the defendant, and we compared notes over
an excellent bottle of champagne and a fine cigar, both
luxuries which I had not seen for many months.   Niedieck
had got two good moose-heads of 69 and 64 inches respectively, but he had utterly failed to get any sheep, finding no
good heads in the places where he had hunted for them.
Nevertheless, being a good sportsman, who had killed game

in all the best countries on earth, he was satisfied with his two big moose-heads, although taken individually, as compared with the expense of his trip to Alaska, each head represented a fairly expensive trophy.

After Niedieck's trial a dull period intervened, and it was not till six days later that the monotony was broken by the arrival of the *Tyonook*, bringing down the final crowd of people leaving Cook's Inlet for the winter. Hanbury, Glyn, and Little were obliged to pitch a tent near our cabin, as no available corner could by this time be found in any hut. Their experiences were not very pleasant during the remainder of their stay at Saldovia, as it snowed and blew hard most nights, and the tent had an unpleasant habit of falling on its occupants in the middle of the small hours. It was generally quite easy to tell when this had happened without looking out of the door of our cabin, since a chorus of muffled remarks would arise, and the tones of well-known voices would give vent to the feelings of their owners, as regarded the snow, wind, the country of Alaska, and the nature of that tent in particular.

There was still a prospect of a little more excitement before we left Saldovia, and this was the arrival of the American hunter who was daily expected, and whose doings in the way of slaughtering game were said to far exceed anything done by any of the other offenders. The Marshal set out once more on an attempt to find this man's camp in the moose country. But he was again driven back by the severity of the gale still raging.

About noon, however, on the 23rd, the long-expected hunter was seen making his way towards Saldovia in a dory. The Marshal, who had been for days breathing vengeance against this man, had been publicly stating that if they could only catch him, the Judge had decided to give him the full penalty of the law. This appeared rather strange to the inhabitants of Saldovia, who remarked that it sounded like shooting a man before he was proved guilty.

The new arrival, little suspecting what a surprise awaited him, on landing was at once informed by the Marshal that he was arrested on the usual charge of breaking the game laws. Some cases containing specimens, which he had previously sent to Saldovia, had already been seized by the Marshal.

The trial was fixed for that afternoon, and once again the schoolhouse was crowded. This was a trial by jury, and the defendant, who was no fool, soon discovered that the jury which had been empanelled consisted chiefly of men who came from the same district as the Judge and Marshal. He at once objected to all these men on the grounds of their friendship with the judge and prosecutor. Finally a fresh jury was sworn and the trial proceeded.

The Marshal, acting as prosecutor, declared that he had seized cases containing sixteen sheep, and that as the defendant had only permits to kill twelve sheep for himself and an American Museum, he had violated the game laws. The defendant declared that he had got only twelve sheep. On this, the jury adjourned to examine the specimens, which they made out to be fourteen in number. Here was a problem which they had to face. In a subsequent conversation with a member of the jury, he said to me, " We guessed the defendant was doing a bit of tall swearing, but when we found the prosecutor was also overshooting the mark, we decided to give the defendant the benefit of the doubt." Therefore, although things looked as bad as possible for him, the verdict was given : " Not guilty." One of the most amusing things I ever heard was the way in which the defendant thanked the jury for acquitting an innocent man. The rage of the Marshal and disgust of the Judge on hearing the verdict were comical, and the latter informed the jury on dismissing them that it was the last time any of them should serve on a jury in that district so long as he remained in office.

The general opinion of the public, which was freely expressed, was that things looked bad when this case was dismissed, in which the defendant was an American, after the heavy fines which had been inflicted on sportsmen who were visitors from distant countries, all of whom had committed only small breaches of the game laws, and had distributed large sums of money, to the considerable benefit of the natives and local storekeepers.

The Judge, who was exceedingly annoyed at the turn of events, on discovering that I was a magistrate in my own country, much to my amusement came to interview me on some nice points of law, as he seemed to think that an English magistrate must be well versed in all such matters. He particularly wanted to know if it was not possible to re-try the case in any way, with a fresh jury, or by any other means. I replied saying that so far as I knew, both in England and America, a man once acquitted by a jury was free from any further prosecution under the same charge. And, moreover, there appeared no possibility in this case of being able to exercise the privileges of Scots law in a case where the verdict was " Not proven."

Two more days of snow and sleet ended our stay at Saldovia, and on the 25th the welcome sound of a steamer's whistle, as she rounded the point outside the bay, announced the arrival of the *Bertha*. Indeed, there were few people who did not rejoice to see her, since she was some days overdue, and owing to the great number of strangers in the settlement, supplies were getting alarmingly short at the local stores, and a few more days would have seen the end of all eatable provisions in the place. There was every prospect of the ship being crowded, and we congratulated ourselves on having written a month earlier to bespeak cabins when the ship last called at Saldovia.

The moose and sheep heads, as they were placed in the hold, made an imposing array, for in addition to the five Englishmen, there were one German and four American hunters, who all travelled down on the *Bertha*. The collection of moose-horns was particularly fine. The record head killed by any sportsman in 1903 was a fine one of 74 inches killed by Mr. Forbes, an American.

Our expectations of a crowded ship were fully realised, and on stepping aboard we were welcomed by Captain Knudson, who assured us that every berth on the ship was occupied, and many passengers would be sleeping in the saloon, and other odd places where a spare corner could be found. There were many faces amongst the passengers familiar to our party, since these people had made the trip up on the *Bertha* in April; and as she is by far the most comfortable boat on that route, and her officers from the captain downwards are exceedingly kind and courteous, her list of passengers in the spring and fall of the year is always a large one. She is by no means remarkable for her pace, although, as Colonel Cane facetiously remarks in his book, "under exceptionally favourable circumstances, she has been known to have attained the terrific speed of eight knots an hour."

Personally I have seen her doing better pace than this, according to the log, but I have also seen the time when she has lost considerable ground, after battling against a head wind such as blows in a way peculiar to Alaska, and the skipper has had reluctantly to give it up, and run under the friendly shelter of some island or point on the mainland. She has at least the qualification of being a really good sea-boat, and the strength of her timbers is enormous. Originally she was, I believe, built for a whaler, but has since

CASTLE CAPE ROCKS, NEAR CHIGNIK, ALASKA PENINSULA.

been cut in half and an additional 40 feet added to her length. Speaking of the stoutness of the old ship, during the voyage down to Seattle, an American who had made many trips on board her said to me, " Yes, sir, I guess this old craft is a tough one ; she is the only boat on this coast that can do what she has done without going to the bottom. She has run slap into a rock, going at full speed, and didn't give a d—n for that rock, and you bet I should not be scared

if she just did it now with all her sails set and steam up."
If ever there was a coast to tempt the skippers on to rocks,
the western coast of Alaska is the place best suited for it.
Even the most recent charts, as supplied to me by the
Washington Geographical Survey Department, are hopelessly inaccurate as regards many of the bays along the coast.
The waters abound with swarms of dangerous rocks, sharp
pointed and jagged, the best-adapted things for sending a
ship to the bottom that I have ever seen, only excepting a
Whitehead torpedo. The rise and fall of the tide being
enormous, many of these rocks which are safe at high tide
stand many feet out of water when the tide is out, and as a
skipper never knows when he may have to run into some
bay for shelter, unless he or his pilot is well acquainted with
that particular spot, he is always taking chances of suddenly
finding some rock not yet shown on the chart. Until a
person has actually sailed many hundreds of miles in a small
vessel along these shores as we did, it is impossible to
imagine the dangers encountered, and how utterly dependent
you are on the nerve, caution, and knowledge of the man
who handles the craft. In winter, during fogs and snow-
storms, when passing through many hundreds of miles of
narrows, with rocks close on either side, the captain's only
means of ascertaining his whereabouts is to keep the whistle
blowing, and judge by the echo how near he is to land on
one side or the other. The exposure to the elements which
the man on the bridge has to face in cold weather is no
child's play, and although dressed in heavy furs, the task of
ships' officers and pilots in the cold weather on the Alaskan
shores is not a job to be envied. Hence the hardy
Scandinavians are found in great numbers as officers and
men on board most of the coasting steamers.

After leaving Saldovia the *Bertha* sailed for Kodiak, and arrived there on the afternoon of the next day. Here we landed a few passengers who intended to winter on the island, and we were welcomed by a number of old friends standing on the wharf to watch the steamer's arrival. On going ashore we went to the house of our friend Mr. Goss, who soon regaled us with all the items of local news, in spite of the fact that he himself had only just arrived with us on board of the *Bertha*, after making a trip to the head of Cook's Inlet. We found that some enterprising American had turned down a large number of cattle on the island since we last visited Kodiak, with a view to supplying the meat market along the coast. Such of the beasts as we saw looked in good condition, and during the summer months they can roam for miles in good grass which grows higher than their backs. There appears no reason why the cattle-farming industry should not be a success at Kodiak, if enough hay is made in summer to last them through the winter. It would hardly be possible for cattle to remain self-supported throughout the winter, although a large number of sheep have done so, since they were turned out on the island some two years before. The mortality was, however, considerable amongst them in severe weather, but this might have been avoided if shelters had been erected and good hay provided for them during the winter months. The severity of winter on Kodiak Island does not approach that which is experienced on many farms in Norway, where both cattle and sheep thrive under the careful attention of the thrifty Scandinavian farmers. Moreover, the quantity of grass which springs up in Alaska when once the snow has melted far exceeds anything of the kind that I have ever seen in Norway.

There is no doubt that if cattle and sheep farming can

be made a success on Kodiak Island there will be an ever-increasing demand for the meat, especially if the projected railway is constructed which is intended to run from Valdez into the Yukon Valley. The mining centres in Alaska are daily increasing in size and numbers, and at such places price is no particular object provided that such luxuries as fresh beef and mutton are to be had by paying for them.

It appears to the ordinary visitor that the soil and climate of Kodiak and Cook's Inlet should be capable of growing good crops of corn and other farm produce. But the U.S. Government has started an experimental farm at Kenai, which is managed by a Norwegian named Mr. Nielsen. He informed us that although cereals would grow and apparently mature, the seed was not fertile, and would not produce another crop if sown again.

Hearing that Mr. Goss had a young cub of the Kodiak brown bear (*Ursus middendorffi*) which was intended for the Zoological Park at Washington, we went to inspect it in the stable where it was kept. The poor brute looked very miserable. It was in poor coat, and did not appear to me as if it would live long. It had been captured by our old native hunter Nicolai after he returned with us to Kodiak, and it was no mean performance to kill the old she-bear and capture the cub single-handed as he did. The latter job he effected by throwing his coat over the cub. So far there is no specimen of a true Kodiak bear in the Park at Washington, although there is a magnificent specimen of the Alaska brown bear captured on the mainland near Cape Douglas, which is misnamed by the officials of the Zoological Park a Kodiak bear. It is in reality a specimen of either *Ursus kidderi* or *Ursus dalli gyas*, and is referred to elsewhere in these pages.

Whilst at Kodiak we inspected the skins of all the bears

killed on the island during the season of 1903 which the natives had brought into the Alaska Commercial Company's store, and were then awaiting shipment down to San Francisco. There were a matter of some sixty skins, but although many of them had been stretched on pegs we were pleased to find on measuring the largest ones that not one skin reached the same measurements as those of our largest bear.

Here also we again met our friend Mr. Folstad, and saw once more his schooner, the *Alice*, in which we had made our adventurous trip in the spring. Folstad was full of enthusiasm over the prospects of some coal and oil lands which we had discovered during our travels on the Alaska Peninsula. He had staked large quantities of ground, and had hopes that some day we might all reap a fortune from the lucky strike. Whether or no these hopes will ever be realised I cannot say, but there is no doubt that the whole country is teeming with mineral wealth, and many valuable strikes are now lying idle in Alaska owing to lack of capital to develop them.

It was not without regret that we finally bade farewell to Kodiak, for here began and ended our first experience of wild Alaska. Since we first landed there, we had travelled many hundreds of miles by land and water. We had sailed in waters which are at times a terror to hardy mariners and natives whose lives are spent along those inhospitable shores. We had traversed miles of barren, desolate lands, and miles of endless primeval forests, following rivers, crossing lakes, and climbing mountains, places where the hand of man has yet left few traces, where wild nature may still be seen untarnished by the march of civilisation, and where still abound some of the grandest specimens of big game yet remaining

on the face of the earth.   Under such circumstances, the
discomforts of wet and cold, bad cooking, or hardships, any
of which, even taken separately, would cause us grievous
vexation at home, are here but trivial matters, and are taken
cheerfully as they come, all in the day's march.   Fortunate
indeed is the man who, if his inclinations lead him to do so,
can turn his back on the life of cities and, having escaped
from his friends and creditors, shake the dust from his feet,
and with rifle and blankets strike out for such a land as this.

COAST SCENERY, QUEEN CHARLOTTE ISLANDS.

Leaving Kodiak on the evening of the 26th, we reached
Valdez early on the morning of the 28th.   During this run
the sea was anything but calm, and the number of empty
seats at meals in the saloon spoke eloquently for the feelings
of many of the passengers.

The Judge and Marshal from Cook's Inlet were amongst
our fellow-passengers, and although I had no particular dis-
like to the Judge, who probably only did what he considered
his duty in the recent trials, it was not surprising that I did
not force my company on the Marshal.   My first move on

reaching Valdez was to pay an early visit to the leading
attorney in the town to discover if it was possible to get any
redress at law for the outrageous treatment I had received,
and the ruination of the end of my shooting trip. The
learned man said he would consider the matter, and I
furnished him with all particulars, and also a copy of the trial
and proceedings in my own case, promising to return a little
later for his opinion. It appeared that at the same time my
friend the Marshal had paid a visit to his commanding
officer, who was at Valdez, and was the Head Marshal for
that district of Alaska. No doubt the latter had received a
very highly coloured account of the case from his subordinate,
but he was rather foolish to act as he subsequently did. It
so happened that he had occasion to go into the office of my
attorney shortly after my call, and told him that he had
heard all about me, and that he knew I was shooting in
Alaska with forged permits, and that the documents I carried
were not genuine ones. The amusing part of it was that
the attorney was at that very moment holding my permits,
signed by the Minister at Washington, in his hand, and he
remarked that he thought the Marshal was going a little too
far, as he also knew something about the case in point.

On my return to his office he said that the state of the
case was as follows. It appears that the Head Marshal of
a district, such as this man was, had to put up a bond of
security before being appointed. This bond was a fairly
large sum, and so far as I could understand it was put up as
a guarantee of good behaviour on the part of the Marshal
whilst in the execution of his duty. The Head Marshal of a
district appoints the Deputy-Marshals under him, such as
our friend of Cook's Inlet. These Deputies do not put up a
bond, and generally have little or nothing beyond the salary

of their post.   Therefore, as the attorney remarked, it was
not much use claiming damages from a Deputy-Marshal, as
one could not get blood from a stone.   But since, as he said,
quaintly checking off the points of the present case, the Head
Marshal was going round making libellous statements concerning me, his advice to me was "not to go shooting at a
squirrel when I had a chance at an elephant," but to have
a go at the Head Marshal himself.   Had it not been for the
fact that this would have entailed losing the *Bertha*, and a
probably protracted stay at Valdez, I should have taken his
advice, but finally decided, as a salve to my injured feelings, to
take all the papers and documents to Washington, and there
lay them before the Minister of Justice and other officials,
trusting that they would make things lively for these over-
zealous Marshals in Alaska.   This I did, and at Washington
received the sympathy and interest of the officials in my case,
and from letters since received, I have reason to believe that
certain men in Alaska found that in this case they had, as I
said before, "cut off a bigger lump than they could chew."

The chief topics of interest for the day in Valdez appeared
to be the shooting of a man on the previous evening in a
saloon, and the arrival of some prospectors from the Sushitna
River, where they had made a wonderful strike of gold in a
gravel creek, some of the lucky finders getting out as much
as $100 per man in the day.   We saw a lot of fine samples
of the gold, and numbers of the inhabitants of Valdez were
even then talking of, and preparing for, a wild rush over the
trails into the Sushitna country in the coming spring.   The
long-talked-of railway from Valdez into the Tanana and
Yukon districts had not yet been commenced, although
rumour stated, when we were last there in the spring, that
a lot of work would be done on it during that summer.   If

this railway ever becomes an accomplished fact, then the future prosperity of Valdez will be assured, since a very large trade will be thrown open with the mining centres along the valley of the Yukon.

As we were standing on the wharf bidding final adieus to a number of the residents at Valdez, an amusing incident happened. I was talking to a friend, when suddenly Mr. Sexton, the Marshal, walked up to me in front of a crowd of spectators and fellow-passengers, most of whom knew our story. Holding out his hand he said, " Well, captain, I have come to shake hands, and wish you good-bye." As I had my hands in my pockets, I did not trouble to remove them, and said to him, " Well, sir, you may do one of those things, but the other you never will do." He feigned immense surprise, and said, " Do you mean to say that you bear me ill-will for doing my duty?" " Certainly not," I rejoined, " but I do blame you for the way in which you exceeded it in my case." Once more he said, " Won't you shake hands with me as one citizen with another?" and I replied, " No, sir, because you never treated me as one citizen should another, much less as you should have treated an English gentleman." This settled him, and he turned away, saying that if he had only known that, he would like to have the case tried over again, so as to prosecute me in a different manner. This was rather good, for, as I told him, he knew perfectly well that he had no shadow of a case against me, and that if he wanted to hear more of the case his wish might soon be gratified, as I intended to carry the matter a little further than the petty courts of Alaska. It was rather gratifying to hear the remarks of the bystanders, who were almost entirely Americans, and one of them remarked to the audience, as the Marshal turned his back and walked away, " I guess he's got it in the neck,"

T

and then, slightly elevating the thumb of his left hand in my direction, added, " You bet your life he's all right anyhow, and no darned Marshal ain't going to scare him."

Before leaving Valdez there was a further inspection of all our permits to export trophies, evidently in the hope that some legal flaw might be discovered at the last moment. Here also a certain number of trophies belonging to the American who had escaped lightly at Saldovia were confiscated by the authorities, as they were intended for a museum, and had no label on the cases stating that they were being exported for scientific purposes, which should be done, according to the regulations of the Act.

Leaving Valdez at noon, and facing the open sea once more, we reached Kayak early the next morning. Here a certain number of passengers got on board, and gave glowing descriptions of the new oil and coal strikes along the coast. According to one man, who was returning disgusted, any one seeking a claim might roam many miles north or south of Kayak without finding a bit of ground which was not already staked. He compared it with the state of affairs during the first great rushes into the Yukon, and said that a man who had travelled scores of miles there without finding a bit of vacant ground had finally returned to the local store. Here there was a tall flag-pole erected, and this being about the only thing unclaimed which he could see, the heart-broken prospector went to the pole and fixed the following notice on it : " J. Smith, his claim is 20 feet straight up and down this blasted pole."

Another day's sailing saw us at Yakutat. Here there are more oil and coal strikes, and, like Kayak, the place was being considerably boomed. A number of natives soon surrounded the ship, coming out in open canoes resembling what is called the " dug-out," or the Siwash canoe, seen on the coasts of British Columbia. These natives brought on board a number of curios in the way of fancy-worked skins and baskets. The latter were far inferior to the really fine work which is done by the natives in the Aleutian Isles, and to the far west of the Alaska Peninsula. This basket-work is done in very fine grass, and looks somewhat similar to the plaiting of the best Panama grass. I have seen many of these made in former years by the Aleut natives, which are

VIEW IN THE FJORDS NEAR WRANGELL NARROWS, S.W. ALASKA.

so cleverly woven that they will hold water, and although very common a few years ago, such numbers have been bought up by the curio-collectors that to-day in New York some of these genuine old baskets will fetch as much as $30 and $40 each, and until quite recently they were purchased from the natives for a few cents.

On the following day after leaving Yakutat we entered the narrows in Icy Straits, and our troubles on the open sea were at an end. The evening before entering the Straits we had a rare tossing in a rough sea, and in the storm we passed a small steamer called the *Discovery*. She was apparently having a bad time of it, and I have since heard that she has never been seen since that day. The next port of call was Juneau. Arriving there in the evening, we went ashore, and here again all our permits and trophies were subjected to a close scrutiny. Some kind friend had telegraphed to the chief officer of the customs at Sitka warning him that my permits should be carefully examined, and saying that they thought I was exporting too many trophies. A friend of ours saw a wire from the customs officer at Juneau reporting this fact, and warned me about it. But as I had not even got my full number of trophies, thanks to the actions of my friend Mr. Sexton, I felt safe enough, and had no trouble with the authorities at Juneau. Here again the American who escaped at Kenai was once more closely cross-questioned, and I heard that the remainder of his trophies were confiscated, but on what grounds this was done I never could make out.

From Juneau onwards to Seattle the scenery was the same magnificent succession of fjords, islands, mountains, and forests which we had already seen in the spring. The weather was now, however, anything but suitable for sight-seeing, since rain, snow, and gales of wind were the prevailing order of things. In fact, whilst attempting to cross Queen Charlotte Sound we encountered such a terrific gale that the *Bertha* was obliged to run under the shelter of an island, and we remained at anchor there all night on November 3.

Three more days of ploughing the waters saw us safely arrived at Seattle, and we finally bade farewell to the good ship *Bertha* and her officers. Little did we envy the latter their task of braving the elements every month, both summer and winter, along the treacherous though picturesque coast of Alaska. There indeed the sun often shines, and the face of nature looks innocent and harmless for a while to sailors, but they are never certain that at any moment the treacherous gales of wind, known locally as " woollies," may not come rushing down like a tornado from the glaciers and mountain-tops, soon to lash the sea up into a perfect inferno.   The passengers of the *Bertha* parted with many tokens of mutual

COAST SCENERY IN SPRING ON THE FRAZER REACH.

regret, and with recollections of a pleasant voyage down, owing to the host of good company that had been gathered on board.

Seattle was, as usual, full of life and bustle.   Every one there seems bent on making money, and many of them are doing it fast.   During our short stay we met a number of amusing characters, many of them full of anecdotes.   One of these men regaled me with a funny dog story, and as it

was new to me I give it as it was told. "Yes, sir, we see
some queer cusses right here in Seattle. A little time back
a man came down here from Alaska. He didn't have nothing
'cepting just a Malamut sleigh-dog along with him. He'd
come from somewhere way back in the Yukon, and was just
about dead broke, and you bet he looked real wild and woolly.
Feelin' as how he kinder wanted a drink, he walks into a
saloon and orders one. Now, sir, this man was a ventrilo-
quist, and pretty smart at the job too. The bar-keeper was
sorter fond of dorgs, and seeing this one, says to the man,
'Say, that is a niceish dorg you've got there.' The man says,
'I guess that's so.' The barman said, 'If you want to sell
him I will give you $25 for him.' 'No,' says the man, 'I
can't sell that dorg; he is all I've got in the world, and he
can talk.' 'How's that?' says the barman. The man he
takes a ham sandwich and eats it, then he takes another and
says to his dorg, 'Would you like a ham sandwich?' The
dorg looks up and says, 'Yes, please.' The barman he looks
scared at that, and leans over the counter to look at the dorg,
saying, 'I guess I'll give $50 for that dorg.' 'No,' says the
man, 'I can't sell him.' Just then the dorg looks at the sandwich plate and says, 'Give me another.' By that time the
barman was just dead stuck on gettin' that dorg. 'Say, now,
I'll give $75 for that dorg.' 'Wal, now, that's a pile of
money,' says the man, 'and I guess that would pay my way
down to 'Frisco.' 'It would so, and more too,' says the
barman. 'Make it $100,' says the man, 'and the dorg goes.'
'All right,' says the barman, '$100 goes, and what shall I do
with the dorg?' 'Why, come right along and take him now,'
says the man. Wal, sir, the barman he puts a rope round
the dorg's neck and starts a-leadin' of him away. The dorg
he kinder hangs back, and looks at his master, and then

says, ' Did you sell me ? ' The barman looks at the dorg
pretty queer like. The man said, ' Yes, old dorg, I sold
you.' The dorg says, ' Did you sell me because I talked ? '
The man says, ' Yes, old dorg.' The dorg says, ' I shall
never speak again,' "—and, the narrator added, " By Gad, sir,
the blasted thing never did."

The inhabitants of the Pacific coast have many quaint
sayings to express their feelings. Many of them will not
bear repetition, but some of their similes, when taken from
their own surroundings, are decidedly droll. One day a
prospector showed me an illustrated paper in which was the
portrait of a lady of some celebrity in American society.
Pointing to the picture he said, " Why, look here, I always
heard she was a beauty. I guess she is a homely-looking
cuss ; she's got a face like a gum-boot and a mouth like a
stab in the dark." It may be childishness, but I could not
help laughing at many of their quaint sayings and fine
original lies.

On the evening of our arrival in Seattle a great dinner
was given at the Lincoln Hotel by Major Kenney (late of
the U.S. Army) in honour of the returned sportsmen. We
all received invitations and turned up in force, no less
than six Englishmen, namely, Hanbury, Elphinstone, and
Vander Byl with our own party, two German sportsmen, and
Mr. Sam Hill, the son-in-law of James Hill the railway king.
After a great dinner, Mr. Hill announced that he had something special to show us, in the shape of two champion
wrestlers whom he had brought over from Japan after great
trouble and expense. Accordingly we adjourned to the Uni-
versity Club, where we received a royal welcome from a big
crowd of members assembled there. Moving into a large
room at the back of the club, we found it cleared for action,

with thick carpets on the ground, and seats arranged for the audience. Mr. Hill had hoped to secure some American wrestlers to meet his men, but it appeared that a few nights before the only good men in Seattle had received such a shaking up at the hands of the Japs, that they were not "looking for any more trouble." Therefore, to open the proceedings, the two wrestlers gave an exhibition of their art, and very clever it was. They had devices of every kind to repel attacks from various assailants, and by means of an interpreter they explained how they could render each fall of their opponent fatal by breaking an arm or a leg.

Failing to find a customer for his men, Mr. Hill urged me to go into the ring. My knowledge of wrestling is small, and knowing that I could make no show against the Japs at this game, I refused to try. But on the urgent appeals from the spectators to give them some kind of a show, I consented to enter the ring if I might be allowed to wear a pair of boxing gloves and try to keep the wrestler off by using them. This led to a tremendous amount of preliminary talking, carried on between the wrestlers and myself through the interpreter. Never having seen gloves used, they seemed to think they might be some kind of infernal machine, and were not content till I put them on and experimented lightly with them on their faces and bodies. I, on the other hand, feared lest they might lose their tempers if hit, and then closing with me should throw me in such a manner as to break a limb, as they had demonstrated that they could do with ease. However, the preliminaries were arranged to our mutual satisfaction, and we started at it, but not before I had stripped nude to the waist, as I observed that if once these men got a hold on a man's shirt or any other garment, they threw him in a moment. I must confess that I have never been "up against" such a slippery customer as the little Jap who was pitted against me. To land him fairly on the head or body was impossible. He avoided punishment by every form of antic known to man or beast, falling backwards or forwards, and once even passing between my legs in a scrimmage, almost throwing me as he did so, and recovering his feet behind me in time to avoid a vicious back-handed swing. I tried everything, from straight punches to wild forms of windmill fighting, but he was too good for me, and once he had come to close quarters a certain fall for me was the result. Altogether it must have been rather a comical exhibition for the spectators, and judging by the laughter and applause, I fancy that the show amused them. After taking three or four good tosses, I had had enough of it, having due regard to the fact that I had only an hour or so before just got through a particularly long and good dinner. After this, nothing would satisfy the members of the club except an adjournment to the smoking room, where every member in the room insisted on the guests taking a drink with each of them. As the club was pretty full, the early hours of the morning were well advanced before we escaped from all this hospitality. Fortunately we were a pretty hard-headed lot, and I noticed that as the English contingent marched back to their respective quarters, not a man wavered in the ranks, although all had been subjected to a pretty severe ordeal.

Next morning early I crossed in the ss. *Clallam* to Victoria, where I spent the day, visiting the Union Club and bidding good-bye to several friends there. Here also I parted with Glyn, who had decided to push on as far south as Mexico, where he had determined to hunt the *Ovis nelsoni*, another form of the big-horn sheep inhabiting the desolate hills in the interior of that country.   He has since returned, after having covered some 650 miles of ground, and getting three good rams.   His best head measured 16 inches round the butt, and 36 inches round the curve of the horns.   It is clear from this that *Ovis nelsoni* carries finer horns than *Ovis dalli* of Alaska.

I returned the same evening to Seattle again, on board the *Clallam*. A large travelling theatrical company had occupied nearly every berth on board.   They had just experienced a severe "train wreck," and many of the members had been severely injured.   Several of the unfortunate actresses had to be carried on board, being unable to move on account of their injuries.   However, the sound ones managed to make things fairly lively in the saloon throughout the night, and as my cabin opened into the saloon, I spent a second night without getting much sleep, owing to the noise they made.   This boat, the *Clallam*, has since been lost, as she sank on January 9, 1904, with all on board, making a total loss of sixty lives.

I spent the next day at Seattle, and that evening Hanbury gave a big dinner at the Washington, a fine new hotel.   The English sportsmen again rolled up in force, and afterwards we adjourned to witness a performance of *Florodora* at the theatre, which was given by those of the theatrical company who escaped injury in the railway accident.

On the following morning I bade adieu to Seattle.   Mr. Sam Hill, who was travelling accompanied by his champion wrestlers to St. Paul, kindly offered Elphinstone, Vander Byl, and myself seats in his private car to St. Paul, an offer which, needless to say, we all three accepted.

Travelling *via* St. Paul and Chicago, I reached Washington

THE AUTHOR AND MR. R. F. GLYN.

on November 13. Here I remained three days, most of which I spent in the company of the officials at the head-quarters of the Biological Survey Office, who displayed great interest in the results of our trip, and in the treatment we had received at the hands of the custodians of the law in Alaska. Accompanied by Mr. Osgood and Dr. T. S. Palmer, I again paid visits to the Smithsonian Institute and the National Zoological Park, at the latter of which we were taken in charge by one of the officials, who was exceedingly kind in showing us all over the fine Zoo, and even stirring up with a long pole all the various bears so as to parade them outside their dens for my edification. I was much impressed with the magnificent accommodation and ample space provided for the various animals and birds in the park, which far excels anything in our own Zoo, where the space is somewhat limited. The monkey house was a marvel of cleanliness, and its inhabitants looked splendid in health and coat. I was informed that tuberculosis or consumption was practically unknown amongst the monkeys, which the official in charge of them attributed to a special diet he gave them of fruits and cooked meat. Milk is strictly prohibited by him as a diet in the monkey house.

On the termination of a very pleasant visit to Washington, I set out for New York, and on arrival there found that the guardians of the game laws still considered that I looked a suspicious character. I was much amused when, on stepping out of the train, a keen-eyed official in plain clothes, who had noticed my rifles being taken from the car, and also that I was carrying a small dressing-bag, stepped up to me, and pointing to the bag said, " Have you got any game in that bag, sir?" I replied that as I had only been shooting a few bears and moose in Alaska, I had not taken the trouble to bring any of them back in my bag. Judging by his look of surprise, he was hardly expecting this kind of a repartee from one who was obviously a thick-headed Britisher, but it had the effect of getting my kit through the station without any inspection.

On arrival at the Waldorf Hotel I met Mr. Niedieck and also Elphinstone and Vander Byl. After dinner we paid a visit to the great New York Horse Show, then in full swing at Madison Square. The place was crowded with an immense throng of smartly dressed men and women up till a late hour at night, and the whole exhibition, from the horses to the general arrangements for the convenience of the competitors and spectators, was magnificent.

As the *Kaiser Wilhelm II.*, the finest ship of the Nord-deutscher-Lloyd Line, was leaving New York early next morning, and she is the most luxurious and fastest liner in the world, I decided to journey home on board this boat. The fact that the *Oceanic* was leaving one day later induced Elphinstone, Vander Byl, and other Englishmen more patriotic than myself, to travel by the English line. In consequence, an examination of the list of passengers on board the *Kaiser Wilhelm* revealed the fact that the Duke of Roxburghe and myself were the only two Englishmen amongst the lot. The former was returning home after his recent marriage in New York, and previous to that event he had just completed a very successful shooting trip in Wyoming, where he informed me he had been fortunate enough to secure a very fine wapiti and also a good head of the Rocky Mountain big-horn sheep, which are now getting hard to procure in that country.

Time does not drag heavily on board the great Atlantic liners of to-day, and on such a one as the *Kaiser Wilhelm II.*,

which only occupies a little over five days in the run from
New York to Plymouth, and is fitted with every luxury and
comfort that man's heart can desire, the life on board is
similar to that in a small town.

Sufficient time is afforded on such a voyage to contemplate
leisurely the return once more to the old life at home in the
old country, to compare it with that through which we have
journeyed for many months since last leaving it, to live once
more in imagination through some of the stirring scenes
witnessed in a far-off land, when with rifle in hand we have
found ourselves face to face with some of the wildest and
grandest beasts on earth, when indeed for the nonce we have
felt the strange thrill and sensation of a quickening pulse,
now, alas, so rare and hard to rouse in the body of the average
man of the twentieth century, save only if he be a sportsman
and indulging in his favourite pastime. And after all, when
the trip is done, and the familiar shores of Albion are once
more in sight, the only sensation is that of real pleasure
on approaching what, "in spite of all its faults," is still the
greatest country on earth, and the one which holds the first
place in the heart of every true Englishman.

Full well we know that a few months, or even weeks,
spent in the tight little island, with its cramped life, its daily
decreasing possibilities of getting far from the madding
crowd, and the ever-increasing artificiality of the sports of
our ancestors, will soon reawaken in our hearts the longing
for distant climes. For, as my friend Major Cumberland
aptly describes it, "there is a disease (the Germans call it
Wanderlust) which no time can cure," and when once this
has taken hold of an individual, he knows no peace until he is
on the move once more. Alas, the sportsman is not able to
retain his pristine youth and strength beyond that of his

fellow-mortals, but whilst engaged in his favourite pastime his spirit is ever young.   To such men Kingsley's immortal lines will ever recur :—

> When all the world is young, lad,
>   And all the trees are green ;
> And every goose a swan, lad,
>   And every lass a queen ;
> Then hey for boot and horse, lad,
>   And round the world away ;
> Young blood must have its course, lad,
>   And every dog his day.
>
> When all the world is old, lad,
>   And all the trees are brown ;
> And all the sport is stale, lad,
>   And all the wheels run down ;
> Creep home and take your place there,
>   The spent and maimed among :
> God grant you find one face there,
>   You loved when all was young.

Good men and true will generally go like a good horse until they drop in harness.   Although the following episode was related by one who was not an eye-witness of the scene, and therefore it is impossible to vouch for the accuracy of the details, it is so characteristic of the man about whom the story is told, that I quote it as related to me.   Not long since a friend of the author's, under whose command the latter formerly had the honour to serve, passed away in such a manner.   He was a gallant and distinguished officer, who finally attained a high rank in the British Army.   His kindly nature and great love of sport endeared him to all who served under him.   A good rider, a fine shot, and one of the best of fishermen, he finally retired into private life, hoping that one sport at least might last him to the end.   One day, whilst fishing with an old friend, and towards the evening hour, he sat down by the river-bank, placing the rod by his side. Calling his companion, he said calmly, "Old friend, we have had a good day's sport. I have had a good innings, but my day is done, I am going to die." He never spoke again, and died shortly afterwards, just as he would have wished it, "game to the last."

The extraordinary way in which the ubiquitous English sportsmen go rushing off to the uttermost parts of the earth in quest of some kind of sport, is a constant source of amazement to most foreigners, and to many of their own countrymen, who cannot appreciate the love of a roving life.

But it is a remarkable fact that there are many amongst us who have tried all forms of sport, and to whom, whilst actually engaged in any particular one of them, whether it be a fast fifty minutes with a pack of hounds, the first rush of a clean-run salmon and the reel screaming, the stalking of some much-coveted specimen of big game, or the tearing down of rocketers as they come high and fast overhead, the general verdict at the time has always been, "this is the best sport on earth."

Such, indeed, I believe are the sentiments with which every genuine sportsman should be imbued if he wishes to get the most enjoyment out of life, and when the inevitable day comes, on which the whips, rods, guns, and rifles are hung on the wall for ever, when the armchair by the fireside, the pipe and old diaries have become the solace of an aged sportsman, and nothing remains save to live the old life over again in yarns with the feet under the mahogany, such a man can then point to the trophies on the wall and say to those who come after him, "That meant life, go you and live it."

INDEX

Afognak Island, 16, 87
Age of sheep, determination of, 69
Alaska : area, 1 ; early explorers, 2 ;
 Russian expeditions, 2 ; history, 2, 75 ;
 principal industries, 3 ; salmon fisheries,
 4 ; fur trade, 7 ; variety of races and
 languages, 8 ; religion, 8 ; climate, 11,
 188 ; Game Laws, 27 ; small game,
 73 ; purchased by United States, 75 ;
 English and American sportsmen in, 76 ;
 mountain scenery, 84, 276 ; winds of,
 96, 112, 137, 265, 277 ; dangers of
 coast, 266
Alces gigas, 58
Aleutian natives, 103 ; strength of, 110 ;
 dexterity in cleaning skins, 110
Alice, schooner, 71, 86, 102, 115
Allen, Dr. J. A., 72
Ammunition, conveyance of, 78
Andrew, Russian Finn, 150
Aniakchak Bay, 17, 87, 104 ; abundance
 of small game at, 118
Antlers, shedding of, 59
Arrest of party by U.S. Marshal, 235

Barabara, native hut, 9
Barren Lands of Alaska, 20, 65
Barstow, Mr. D., U.S. Commissioner, 127,
 131, 236 ; conveys party in his yacht,
 129
Basket-work, native, 275
Bear River, 89, 132 ; immense numbers of
 salmon in, 134, 141 ; bears killed at,
 136, 139
Bears : where found, 13, 15, 95 ; gestation of,
 51 ; number of cubs, 52 ; after hiber-
 nation, 52 ; favourite food, 102, 120
Bears, black : distribution of, 49 ; misadventures with, 214, 226
 blue : distribution of, 50 ; description by
 Prof. Dall, 51

Bears, brown : confusion in naming, 45 ;
 distinct forms of, 45 ; distribution, 46 ;
 measurements and weights, 47, 100, 115;
 in National Zoological Park, Washing-
 ton, 48, 268 ; skulls of, 53 ; killed at
 Aniakchak Bay, 100, 107, 114 ; mis-
 adventures with, 122, 130, 138 ;
 catching salmon, 134 ; killed at Bear
 River, 135, 139 ; narrow escape from,
 146
Berg, Andrew, offers cabin, 176 ; reputation
 as a hunter, 216, 228
 Emile, 228
Bering Sea, 17, 125
Bertha, steamer, 71, 82 ; at Kodiak, 86 ; at
 Saldovia, 263 ; sea-going qualities, 265 ;
 goodbye to, 276
Bidarki, native canoe, 87, 152, 155
Birthday, a memorable, 235
Blacktail deer, 66
Blake, Mr., 15, 76
Bristol Bay, 17
Bonham, Mr., Denver, Colorado, 182, 190
Books, deposits of, 230
Boots, 23, 79, 92

Calling up moose, 228
Camp equipment, 24, 78
Candle-fish, 120
Cane, Colonel, 14, 20, 72, 76, 224
Canneries, salmon, 6, 167, 173
Cape Douglas, 49
Caribou : classification, 64 ; species and
 distribution, 65 ; protection of, 66 ;
 record head, 80 ; at Bear River, 90,
 102 ; slaughter of, 157
Cattle-farming, Kodiak, 267
Chignik, 167
Chinitna Bay, 14
Clallam, steamer, 282
Climate of Alaska, 11, 188

THE END

Printed by R. & R. CLARK, LIMITED, *Edinburgh.*

ROWLAND WARD'S

BOOKS FOR SPORTSMEN

THE DEER OF ALL LANDS. By R. LYDEKKER. Illustrated by Twenty-four Hand-coloured Plates and a number of Photographic Reproductions of Living Deer. Price £5 : 5s. net.

WILD OXEN, SHEEP, AND GOATS OF ALL LANDS. By R. LYDEKKER. Companion volume to *Deer of all Lands*. Illustrated by Twenty-seven Hand-coloured Plates and other Illustrations. Price £5 : 5s. net.

THE GREAT AND SMALL GAME OF INDIA, BURMA, AND TIBET. By R. LYDEKKER. With Nine Hand-coloured Plates and other Illustrations. Price £4 : 4s. net.

THE GREAT AND SMALL GAME OF EUROPE, WESTERN AND NORTHERN ASIA, AND AMERICA. By R. LYDEKKER. With Eight Hand-coloured Plates and other Illustrations. Price £4 : 4s. net.

THE GREAT AND SMALL GAME OF AFRICA. By Various Contributors. With Fifteen Hand-coloured Plates of Heads and Fifty-seven other Illustrations. Price £5 : 5s. net.

SPORT IN SOMALILAND. By COUNT JOSEPH POTOCKI. With a Coloured Frontispiece, Fifty-eight Coloured Illustrations, Eighteen Page Photogravures, Seven Text Figures, and Map. *[Out of print.*

TRAVEL AND ADVENTURE IN SOUTH-EAST AFRICA. By F. C. SELOUS. With numerous Illustrations and Map. Price 25s. net.

SUNSHINE AND STORM IN RHODESIA. By F. C. SELOUS. Fully Illustrated. With Map. Price 10s. 6d. net.

RECORDS OF BIG GAME. With the Distribution, Characteristics, Dimensions, Weights, and Horn and Tusk Measurements of the Different Species. Fourth Edition. By ROWLAND WARD, F.Z.S. With 253 Illustrations. Price 30s. net.

ELEPHANT HUNTING IN EAST EQUATORIAL AFRICA. By A. H. NEUMANN. With Illustrations and Map. Price 21s. net.

SEVENTEEN TRIPS THROUGH SOMALILAND AND A VISIT TO ABYSSINIA. With Supplementary Preface on the "Mad Mullah" Risings. By Major H. G. C. SWAYNE, R.E. Third Edition. With Illustrations and Maps. Price 7s. 6d. net.

SPORT IN THE HIGHLANDS OF KASHMIR. Being a Narrative of an Eight Months' Trip in Baltistan and Ladak. By H. Z. DARRAH. With Illustrations and Map. Price 21s. net.

HUNTING TRIPS IN THE CAUCASUS. By E. DEMIDOFF (Prince San Donato). With Ninety-six Illustrations and Map. Price 21s. net.

AFTER WILD SHEEP IN THE ALTAI AND MONGOLIA. By E. DEMIDOFF (Prince San Donato). With Eighty-two Illustrations, Map, and Coloured Frontispiece. Price 21s. net.

A SHOOTING TRIP TO KAMCHATKA. By E. DEMIDOFF (Prince San Donato), Author of *Hunting Trips in the Caucasus, After Wild Sheep in the Altai and Mongolia.* With 113 Illustrations, Five Photogravures, and Two Maps. Price 21s. net.

THROUGH THE HIGHLANDS OF SIBERIA. By Major H. G. C. SWAYNE, R.E., F.R.G.S., F.Z.S., Author of *Seventeen Trips through Somaliland.* With Sixty Illustrations and Map. Price 12s. 6d. net.

SPORT IN EAST CENTRAL AFRICA. Being an Account of Hunting Trips in Districts of East Central Africa. By F. V. KIRBY, F.Z.S. With Illustrations. Price 8s. 6d. net.

THE ENGLISH ANGLER IN FLORIDA. With some Descriptive Notes of the Game, Animals, and Birds. By ROWLAND WARD, F.Z.S. With numerous Illustrations. Price 7s. 6d. net.

THE SPORTSMAN'S HANDBOOK TO PRACTICAL COL-LECTING, PRESERVING, AND ARTISTIC SETTING UP OF TROPHIES AND SPECIMENS. With a Synoptical Guide to the Hunting Grounds of the World. By ROWLAND WARD, F.Z.S. Price 3s. 6d. net.

A SPORTING TRIP THROUGH ABYSSINIA. With a Description of the Game, from Elephant to Ibex, and Notes on the Manners and Customs of the Natives. By P. H. POWELL-COTTON, F.Z.S., F.R.G.S. With Ninety-two Illustrations and Map. Price 21s. net.

NATURE PORTRAITS: STUDIES WITH PEN AND CAMERA OF OUR WILD BIRDS, ANIMALS, FISH, AND INSECTS. Text by the Editor of *Country Life in America.* With Fifteen Large Plates, and many Illustrations by the best Nature Photographers. Price 21s. net.

AMERICAN ANIMALS: A POPULAR GUIDE TO THE MAMMALS OF NORTH AMERICA, NORTH OF MEXICO, WITH INTIMATE BIOGRAPHIES OF THE MORE FAMILIAR SPECIES. By WITMER STONE and WILLIAM EVERETT CRAM. With numerous Illustrations. Price 12s. 6d. net.

CAMERA SHOTS AT BIG GAME. By A. G. WALLIHAN. With an Introduction by THEODORE ROOSEVELT. Price 30s. net.

LONDON:

ROWLAND WARD, LIMITED,
"The Jungle," 166 Piccadilly.